A Message to Mankind

In a series of encyclical letters
beginning at the close of the
nineteenth century, the popes have
spoken to all men in an attempt
to challenge injustice and
to offer a vision of a world where
each member of society receives
his God-given rights.

*In this Mentor-Omega volume
editor Anne Fremantle has distilled
from the famous social
encyclicals—including those of
beloved Pope John—the essence of
Catholic social teaching,
a set of doctrines that offers the
tranquillity of order in a world
of change and crisis.*

MENTOR-OMEGA Books
of Related Interest

The
Social
Teachings
of
the
Church

edited by
ANNE FREMANTLE

A Mentor-Omega Book

Published by THE NEW AMERICAN LIBRARY
of CANADA LIMITED

From twenty centuries of literature and scholarship, Mentor-Omega Books present a treasury of Catholic thought for the modern reader.

FIRST PRINTING, DECEMBER, 1963

MENTOR TRADEMARK REG. U.S. PAT. OFF. AND FOREIGN COUNTRIES
REGISTERED TRADEMARK—MARCA REGISTRADA
HECHO EN WINNIPEG, CANADA

MENTOR-OMEGA BOOKS are published in Canada by The New American Library of Canada Limited Toronto, Ontario

PRINTED IN CANADA

COVER PRINTED IN U.S.A.

Nihil Obstat
> Daniel V. Flynn, J.C.D.
> Censor Liborum

Imprimatur
> ✠ Francis Cardinal Spellman
> Archbishop of New York

Contents

Preface

The Church is "the Lord among us," that is, it is Christ socially contemporary with me and you and all our associates. The Church is "catholic" or universal, and thus includes the total visibility of the Lord in every time and place, in every society, in every age.

All men, immersed in time and place, whatever their historical setting (which includes all societies), are called to the Church. Every human social system, therefore—whether tribe, town, nation, epoch, or culture—has the right to pursue a claim to its own Church. And though the Church thus found is then a true, integral, living part of that society at a given time in its history, this Church is *the* Church incarnate there and then.

All cultures have a place in the Church and the Church has a place in all cultures. Accordingly, the Church is one as residence of all cultures, and many as resident in them. We can as truly speak about the one Church of the Apostles as we can discuss the many differences between the Church of France and the Church of Ruanda-Urundi, or between the Church of the Middle Ages and the Church of today. "Vertically" the Church is catholic because it has descended through centuries of history since its origin; "horizontally" the Church is Catholic because it is one despite a variety in its cultural manifestations today.

Every Christian holds the faith that comes to him from its source almost two thousand years ago. He makes this faith present by living it in such a way as to affect those social structures that make his life human. He is contemporary with Christ through identification with the traditions of the past; Christ is contemporary with him and his time through his Christian life by which traditions become socially present, lived reality.

ix

The Christian finds the guarantees of his faith in the definitions of the teaching authorities of the Church regarding revealed truth, just as he finds the concrete guide for his personal translation of these truths into communitary institutions—especially during the last century—in the social encyclicals of the popes.

These encyclicals have one thing in common: they outline the principles governing modern man's responsibility for the structures or institutions of a social world in the process of continuous man-made and planned change. They relate the gospel to the social consequences of man's planned conquest of the powers of nature.

They are neither cookbooks nor collections of laws: they do not tell man how to affect society through technology nor do they lay down technical and detailed norms of behavior. They simply outline the theoretical framework within which modern man—that is, man in a man-made world—is responsible as a Christian for the consequences increased technology is having on the humaneness of human society.

Every Christian—and even more, every group of Christians committed to a common social goal—will have to contribute to give concrete form to his own society under the impulse of these teachings. Dogmas are here to be understood and believed; social encyclicals are mostly to be lived and applied. Their purpose is to create among Christians a community sense of responsibility to make the Lord (and therefore the Church) socially contemporary to a present dominated by technology and in continuous change.

The New American Library has recognized that the social encyclicals can become the common property of society only through such personal assimilation and rebroadcast of them as is represented in this popular presentation of papal thought.

IVAN D. ILLICH

Introduction

God meets man in and through the Church. She is their meeting-place, in time and in space, and to bring men to Himself through her God uses many means, of which the Church's teaching is the first. She is, as Pope John XXIII's famous encyclical (letter) tells us, Mother and Teacher, *Mater et Magistra*. By what authority does she teach?

Not by her own. The Church's authority, whether in theology or ethics, is only relative. The Church's authority comes only from the fact that the divine truth possesses her: she is sacred, the Bride of the Lord. She speaks only "by His authority" and must continually strive to be worthy of the trust placed upon her. But whatever she says, in the realm of natural law, she says to all men, not just to Catholics. For example, when she says, "Thou shalt not kill," she claims the authority to do so from the author of life itself. The infallibility of the Pope pertains only to statements made, *ex cathedra,* that is, "from the Chair [of Peter]" on faith or morals. Yet infallibillity is personal to the Pope, "as identified with him as his black eyes."

Obviously, the Church's social teaching falls into the domain of morals. And the Church's claim to a social doctrine emanates from her authority to legislate morals. Whence comes this authority?

For Catholics, the Church is an organized, visible fellowship, the mystical body of Christ. The Church was instituted by Jesus Christ, and came into organized being after his death, on the feast of Pentecost, when the Holy Spirit "confirmed" the apostles by appearing in tongues of flame above their heads. Because the Church is a visible society, it has a social structure. "Because it is divine in institution and dynamism, the Holy Spirit dwells in it, keeping it alive, keeping it true, making it grow" (Gustav Weigel, S.J.). Be-

cause the Church is universal—the word "catholic" has no
other meaning—it must be concerned with every human
being and with every human activity. To be a Catholic means
that one must, as Father de Foucauld put it, "see Jesus
Christ in everyone and treat him accordingly." Or, as the
Church's Founder put it (Matt. 25:35 *et seq.*), "For I was
hungry, and you gave me to eat; I was thirsty, and you gave
me to drink." Asked when, where, He replied that it was
"to one of these my least brethren" that unwittingly the
Christian had given—or refused to give. It might be argued
that such giving is charity. But it cannot ever be charity in
the light of the doctrine of the mystical body. For if the
Church *is* the mystical body, as Catholics are bound to believe, then each and every other human being is "another
Christ" (*alter Christus*), and what we owe Christ—and ourselves—is not charity, it is justice.

The Church not only believes that its doctrine is revealed,
it also believes that its doctrine is always reasonable and, as
such, acceptable to any thinking man, religious or not. The
Church always explains, always gives reasons for its positions; this is as true of the Church's position on social questions as on any other.

Thus it is in the name of *man* that the Church affirms its
social doctrine, speaking for all men, not only for Christians.
As Pope Pius XII declared in 1954, the Church's province
comprises not only strictly religious matters, but the whole
range of natural law—its principles, its interpretation, and
its application. Natural law is another name for the moral
order, and it is intimately related to the *magisterium,* the
teaching function of the Church.

The Church insists not only that human reason can know
the existence of a moral law, but, as Pius XII put it, that it
"can express correctly (*rite exprimendam*) this law written
by the Creator in the heart of man" (*Humani generis*). Natural law is both an object of knowledge as well as the expression of the moral obligation written into man's very
nature. By the unaided light of its own reason, the human
mind can know man's inherent obligations, as well as the
ultimate source of this natural law—that is to say, God.

It might be asked whether, in appealing to natural law,
the Church was not laying herself open to the charge of
invading the domain of philosophy and of weakening her
own case—for does not "sane reason" always form a private
and individual judgment? The answer is, of course, that there

are two sources for the social doctrine of the church:
divine revelation and natural law. But these sources themselves have the same divine source. Moreover, the social
doctrine of the Church as expressed in this encyclical is
principally concerned with the moral aspects of social and
economic problems. And the Church is perfectly aware that
however essential her solutions are to social problems, to
put them into practice she needs the help of all men and
of all nations. Thus the natural law is one of the two sources
from which the Church derives her social teaching. It is in
virtue of this intimate relationship between natural law and
the *magisterium* that the Church intervenes in economic and
social matters. This intervention is based on a twofold
authority: the Church's tradition, which throughout history
has been a civilizing one, and the Church's doctrine of the
universal kingship of Christ, which is central both to the
Church's anthropology and to her apologetics.

Historically, the Church has constantly intervened in order
to ameliorate social and economic conditions. The Epistles
in the Christian Bible are filled with minute directions as
to how slaves should be treated and how kings; how servants
should "submit to their masters with all fear"; how the hungry must be fed, for "faith without works is dead." St.
James, for example, writes sternly: "Behold, the hire of the
labourers who have reaped down your fields, which you have
kept back by fraud, crieth." From the beginning, the church
cared for human beings even before they were born and extended its care to their bodies and souls even after they were
separated in death. Tertullian, writing around A.D. 200 noted
that

for us, to whom homicide has been once for all forbidden,
it is not permitted to break up even what has been conceived
in the womb while the blood is still being drawn from the
mother's body to make a new creature. Prevention of birth
is premature murder, and it makes no difference whether it
is a life already born that one snatches away, or a life that
is coming to birth that one destroys. The future man is a
man already, the whole fruit is present in the seed.

So too, the early Christians were minutely directed as to
how to dispose of their own and their friends' bodies;
prayers for the dead, begun under Judaism at the time of
the Maccabees, were also part of early Christian life.

After the apostolic age, the Church Fathers continued to

be concerned for all mankind. The social teachings of St. Basil are of especial importance; St. Augustine loudly proclaimed that "charity is no substitute for justice withheld." Indeed justice, one of the four cardinal virtues—the others are temperance, fortitude, and prudence—stands next to faith, hope, and charity in importance.

The gradual abolition of slavery in Roman days; the imposition on all of the Truce of God and the Peace of God after the conversion of the barbarians in Europe; the foundation of religious orders devoted to the sick and to the alleviation of the miseries of prisoners and of the wounded in wars; the attention to education and to such special horrors as leprosy; the ban on female infanticide; the protection of women—these are but a few of the areas where the Church has acted, and always with total authority.

"The Church, a universal society of the faithful of all languages and of all peoples, has her own social doctrine, profoundly elaborated since the first centuries and up to the present time, and studied in its development and perfectionment from all angles and under every aspect." So Pope Pius XII defined the Church's historical claim to social theory.

As for the doctrine of the kingship of Christ, Leo XIII declared that it embraced all men, without exception, even those who were not of the Christian faith. In fact, he added, "to be strictly accurate, the empire of Jesus Christ is the totality of the human race."

Indeed, it is of faith for every Catholic that Christ, as king, is the sovereign legislator, the originator and custodian of the moral law. Thus the Church, without arrogating to herself any temporal powers, without seeking to usurp any civil authority, brings to all social problems the teaching and the efficacious example of Jesus Christ. Indeed, as Leo XIII noted, "without the Church, it is impossible to find an effective solution to the problem of working class conditions" (*acta apostolicae sedis* 23 [1890-91], p. 647).

Thus it is from two separate sources that the social teachings of the Church are derived: natural law and Revelation. As Pius XI said, natural law is written by the Creator's hand in the human heart, and what He wrote sane reason can read there whenever not blinded by sin or passion (*Mit brennender Sorge*). It is moral law that, by the sole light of reason, enables man to know his moral obligations and the ultimate basis of the moral order to which he, and all men, are bound. The universal kingship of Christ is the ultimate authority that all men must acknowledge.

The distinction between the "social teaching" of the Church and the general body of Christian philosophy and doctrine dates from the great encyclical of Leo XIII, *Rerum Novarum*, issued in 1891. This is the first encyclical published in this collection, as it is the first papal pronouncement specifically concerned with social problems.

In 1931 Pius XI used the phrase "social philosophy" when commenting on this encyclical, and he went on later to say that in his own encyclical (*Quadragesimo Anno*) he would clarify certain details of this Catholic social and economic theory. Then Pius XII, in a letter dated 1 November 1945, wrote to the German Cardinal Faulhaber that it is the "principles of spiritual life which, because they are the norms of the essential liberty and dignity of man, constitute the foundation and base of society." It was he, too, who first used the expressions "social doctrine of the Church" and "Catholic social doctrine." In 1953 he stated: "It is not possible to separate social reforms and the religious and moral life of individuals and of society, for one cannot separate this world from the other, nor break man, who is one living whole, into two" (Allocution of 14 May 1953). Thus Pius XII envisaged the Church as the true guardian of the liberty and equality of man.

Natural law presupposes certain fundamental characteristics of human nature and of society, as evidenced by their appearance in every historical situation. Three of these, the family, private property, and the State, are often mentioned as the foundations of the "natural order." "Why," asked Pius XII in his Christmas message of 1950, "is the spirit of solidarity which should unite men not the support of the natural social order in its three essential forms: family, property, State?" Pius was also opposed to all who would make a clean sweep of these essential forms in order to provide man with so-called security. He wrote in his Christmas message of 1955:

> There is no reason why security should not be established by making use of the results of technical advances and industrial production. But the temptation to make order and security depend on a purely quantitative basis, which does not take nature into account, as do those who confide man's entire destiny to today's immense industrial potential, must be resisted.

Pope Pius went on to excoriate those who think to base
security wholly on an ever-increasing general productivity
and on a continually increased national economic productivity. In such a system, overly artificial, the security of individual life is dangerously separated from the energies
destined necessarily for the organiaty of the communiy.
These are inherent in human nature as it truly is, and these
alone make possible human solidarity. In a certain manner,
although with adaptations made necessary by changing
times, the family and private property must always remain
among the foundations of the free association of persons.
For Pius XII went on to emphasize that

> there is a natural order, even if its forms change with his-
> torical and social developments; but the essential outlines
> are, and always have been, the same: the family and the
> right to private property as the bases of personal security,
> then local institutions and professional groups, and finally
> the State.

It is in the name of natural law, too, that the same pope
denounced any "social situation," that is to say, any society,
where an enormous mass of very poor people live confronted with a small privileged group. He declared that such
a "situation" was "contrary to nature" (speech to the Spanish
workers, 11 March 1951). Earlier, Pope Pius had spelled
out the fact that, under certain conditions, in certain situations, the good of the whole was paramount, and there were
occasions when the State had a right to expropriate private
property. In a radio message to the world on 1 September
1943 he said:

> The social and economic policy of the future, the di-
> rective activity of the State, of the communities and pro-
> fessional institutions, cannot attain their lasting aim, which
> is the real fecundity of social life and the normal yield of the
> national economy, if not by respecting and safeguarding the
> vital function of private property in its personal and social
> value. When the distribution of property is an obstacle to
> this end—and this is not necessarily always originated by
> the extensiveness of private property—the State may, in
> the common interest, intervene to regulate its use, or even,
> if it is impossible to arrive at another solution, decree ex-
> propriation, giving a fair and equitable indemnity. For the
> same purpose, the small and medium-sized properties in
> agriculture, in the arts and trades, in commerce and in-

dustry, must be guaranteed and promoted; co-operative unions must assure to them the advantages of a large concern; where the large business concern today manifests itself to be more productive, the possibility must be offered to temper the labor agreement with a company-sharing contract.

Nor let it be said that technical progress is opposed to such a regime and pushes in its irresistible current all activity toward gigantic concerns and organizations, before which a social system founded on the private property of the single individual must perforce collapse. No; technical progress does not determine, as a fatal and necessary fact, economic life. Too often it has bowed docilely before the demands of egotistical calculations avid to increase capital indefinitely; why, then should it not also bend to the need of maintaining and assuring the private property of all, the cornerstone of the social order? Even technical progress, as a social fact, must not prevail over the general good, but must instead be regulated by and subordinated to it.

The authority of the Church's social teaching as enunciated in the papal encyclicals has been defined by Monsignor Joseph Fenton writing in the *American Ecclesiastical Review*. He pointed out that:

It is quite probable that some of the teachings set forth on the authority of the various papal encyclicals are infallible statements of the Holy Father. It is absolutely certain that all the teachings contained in these documents and dependent on their authority, merit at least an internal religious assent from every Catholic.

Father Thomas Pegues, writing in the *Revue Thomiste XII*, noted further that:

The authority of the encyclicals is in a sense sovereign. It is the teaching of the supreme pastor and teacher of the Church. Hence the faithful have a strict obligation to receive this teaching with infinite respect. A man must not be content simply not to contradict it openly . . . an internal mental assent is demanded. It should be received as the teaching of the sovereign authority of the Church.

Thus the cumulative teaching of the so-called "social encyclicals," excerpts of which are printed in this collection, can be taken to be, *in toto,* a complete documentation of Catholic social doctrine. The latest, and greatest, of the "social encyclicals," *Mater et Magistra,* was issued just seventy years after the first, *Rerum Novarum.* Those seventy years have seen perhaps more social changes in the world than the preceding seven hundred. The Church has met these social changes with a regard for the development of her doctrine to meet current necessities and a reiteration of the position she has taken from her foundation. This position is based on the two authorities: reason, as exemplified by natural law, and revelation, as manifest in the universal kingship of Christ.

The principal papal pronouncements containing the social teachings of the Church are assembled here, together with one or two statements by members of the hierarchy, which are included to show how the Church speaks not only *urbi et orbi*—to the City and the World—but also locally, in Australia and France, in America and Africa, always with one and the same voice.

Chapter 1

✠

Leo XIII (1878-1903)

GIOACCHINO Vincenzo Pecci, born on March 2, 1810, in the Papal States, studied first with the Jesuits, then at the Collegio Romano, and finally at the Sapienza, where he took his doctorate in canon law. Ordained at twenty-seven, he served as head of the police in Benevento, and then as Governor of Perugia. Later papal nuncio to Brussels, he became Bishop of Perugia in 1846. Thirteen days after the death of Pius IX, Cardinal Pecci was elected pope, taking the name of Leo XIII. He is one of the greatest of all the popes, and his eighty-six encyclicals constitute a collection of statements on various modern problems that is the most important single contribution to Catholic doctrine since the Middle Ages. All good everywhere belongs absolutely to the Church, but hers is the job of distinguishing it from error, and also of assimilating it, so that she can nourish the weakest of her children with it without fear of their taking harm.

"Never was science so arrogant as when Leo XIII began to recommend to Catholics the study of sound philosophy. . . . Scientists everywhere were proclaiming the victory of science over religion, when Leo declared that there could be no question of victory where there was no conflict," wrote Father John Wynne, S.J.* The real value to the Church of the new awareness of labor problems is distilled in the greatest of all Leo's encyclicals, *Rerum novarum;* the true nature

---

* *The Great Encyclical Letters of Leo XIII.* New York: Benziger, 1903, p. 4.

and the real limits of human liberty are set forth in *Libertae praestantissimum;* Christian citizenship is discussed in *Sapientiae Christiane,* the Christian constitution of states in *Immortale Dei,* and Christian democracy in *Graves de Communi.*

"Liberalism having come to stay, Catholics must be shown how to live in a Liberal world, and yet live by their Catholic principles; they must learn, not only how they could survive in such a world, but how to be active loyal citizens of the liberal states." * Leo XIII had to cope with a violently anticlerical France; with the *Kulturkampf* of Bismarck in Germany; with a hostile Italy digesting the temporal lands and powers it had taken from the Church. The Italian revolutionaries almost succeeded in throwing Pius IX's body into the Tiber, when it was being removed to the cemetery of San Lorenzo, and the Italian government actually tried to confiscate Catholic alms, but the pope was undeterred, working twelve hours a day seven days a week in the Vatican. His death in 1903 ended a notably productive twenty-five years as pope.

RERUM NOVARUM
The Condition of Labor †

March 15, 1891

1. It is not surprising that the spirit of revolutionary change, which has long been predominant in the nations of the world, should have passed beyond politics and made its influence felt in the cognate field of practical economy. The elements of a conflict are unmistakable: the growth of industry, and the surprising discoveries of science; the changed relations of masters and workmen; the enormous fortunes of individuals and the poverty of the masses; the increased self-reliance and the closer mutual combination

---

* Rev. Philip Hughes, *A Popular History of the Church* (New York: Doubleday Image Books, 1954).

† Official translation. The Vatican Polyglot Press.

of the working population; and, finally, a general moral deterioration. The momentous seriousness of the present state of things just now fills every mind with painful apprehension; wise men discuss it; practical men propose schemes; popular meetings, legislatures, and sovereign princes, all are occupied with it—and there is nothing which has a deeper hold on public attention.

Therefore, Venerable Brethren, as on former occasions, when it seemed opportune to refute false teaching, We have addressed you in the interests of the Church and of the commonwealth, and have issued Letters on Political Power, on Human Liberty, on the Christian Constitution of the State, and on similar subjects, so now We have thought it useful to speak on

The Condition of Labor

It is a matter on which we have touched once or twice already. But in this Letter the responsibility of the Apostolic office urges Us to treat the question expressly and at length, in order that there may be no mistake as to the principles which truth and justice dictate for its settlement. The discussion is not easy, nor is it free from danger. It is not easy to define the relative rights and the mutual duties of the wealthy and of the poor, of capital and of labor. And the danger lies in this, that crafty agitators constantly make use of these disputes to pervert men's judgments and to stir up the people to sedition.

2. But all agree, and there can be no question whatever, that some remedy must be found, and quickly found, for the misery and wretchedness which press so heavily at this moment on the large majority of the very poor. The ancient workmen's Guilds were destroyed in the last century, and no other organization took their place. Public institutions and the laws have repudiated the ancient religion. Hence by degrees it has come to pass that Working Men have been given over, isolated and defenseless, to the callousness of employers and the greed of unrestrained competition. The evil has been increased by rapacious Usury, which, although more than once condemned by the Church, is nevertheless, under a different form but with the same guilt, still practiced by avaricious and grasping men. And to this must be added the

custom of working by contract, and the concentration of so
many branches of trade in the hands of a few individuals,
so that a small number of very rich men have been able to
lay upon the masses of the poor a yoke little better than
slavery itself.

3. To remedy these evils the *Socialists,* working on the
poor man's envy of the rich, endeavor to destroy private
property, and maintain that individual possessions should become the common property of all, to be administered by the
State or by municipal bodies. They hold that, by thus transferring property from private persons to the communiy, the
present evil state of things will be set to rights, because
each citizen will then have his equal share of whatever
there is to enjoy. But their proposals are so clearly futile for
all practical purposes, that if they were carried out the
working man himself would be among the first to suffer.
Moreover they are emphatically unjust, because they would
rob the lawful possessor, bring the State into a sphere that is
not its own, and cause complete confusion in the community.

Private Ownership

4. It is surely undeniable that, when a man engages in
remunerative labor, the very reason and motive of his work
is to obtain property, and to hold it as his own private possession. If one man hires out to another his strength or his
industry, he does this for the purpose of receiving in return
what is necessary for food and living; he thereby expressly
proposes to acquire a full and real right, not only to the
remuneration, but also to the disposal of that remuneration
as he pleases. Thus, if he lives sparingly, saves money, and
invests his savings, for greater security, in land, the land in
such a case is only his wages in another form; and, consequently, a working man's little estate thus purchased should
be as completely at his own disposal as the wages he receives
for his labor. But it is precisely in this power of disposal
that ownership consists, whether the property be land or
movable goods. The *Socialists,* therefore, in endeavoring to
transfer the possessions of individuals to the community,
strike at the interests of every wage earner, for they deprive
him of the liberty of disposing of his wages, and thus of all

hope and possibility of increasing his stock and of bettering his condition in life.

5. What is of still greater importance, however, is that the remedy they propose is manifestly against justice. For every man has by nature the right to possess property as his own. This is one of the *chief points of distinction* between man and the animal creation. For the brute has no power of self-direction, but is governed by two chief instincts, which keep his powers alert, move him to use his strength, and determine him to action without the power of choice. These instincts are self-preservation and the propagation of the species. Both can attain their purpose by means of things which are close at hand; beyond their surroundings the brute creation cannot go, for they are moved to action by sensibility alone, and by the things which sense perceives. But with man it is different indeed. He possesses, on the one hand, the full perfection of animal nature, and therefore he enjoys, at least, as much as the rest of the animal race, the fruition of the things of the body. But animality, however perfect, is far from being the whole of humanity, and is indeed humanity's humble handmaid, made to serve and obey. It is the mind, or the reason, which is the chief thing in us who are human beings; it is this which makes a human being human, and distinguishes him essentially and completely from the brute. And on this account—viz., that man alone among animals possesses reason—it must be within his right to have things not merely for temporary and momentary use, as other living beings have them, but in stable and permanent possession; he must have not only things which perish in the using, but also those which, though used, remain for use in the future.

The Power of Reason

6. This becomes still more clearly evident if we consider man's nature a little more deeply. For man, comprehending by the power of his reason things innumerable, and joining the future with the present—being, moreover, the master of his own acts—governs himself by the foresight of his counsel, under the eternal law and the power of God, Whose Providence governs all things. Wherefore it is in his power to exercise his choice not only on things which regard his present welfare, but also on those which will be for his ad-

vantage in time to come. Hence man not only can possess
the fruits of the earth, but also the earth itself; for of the
products of the earth he can make provision for the future.
Man's needs do not die out, but recur; satisfied to-day, they
demand new supplies to-morrow. Nature, therefore, owes to
man a storehouse that shall never fail, the daily supply of
his daily wants. And this he finds only in the inexhaustible
fertility of the earth.

Nor must we, at this stage, have recourse to the State. Man
is older than the State and he holds the right of providing
for the life of his body prior to the formation of any State.

7. And to say that God has given the earth to the use and
enjoyment of the universal human race is not to deny that
there can be private property. For God has granted the earth
to mankind in general; not in the sense that all without
distinction can deal with it as they please, but rather that no
part of it has been assigned to any one in particular, and that
the limits of private possession have been left to be fixed by
man's own industry and the laws of individual peoples. Moreover, the earth, though divided among private owners, ceases
not thereby to minister to the needs of all; for there is no
one who does not live on what the land brings forth. Those
who do not possess the soil, contribute their labor; so that it
may be truly said that all human subsistence is derived
either from labor on one's own land, or from some laborious industry which is paid either in the produce of the land
itself or in that which is exchanged for what the land brings
forth.

The Law of Nature

Here, again, we have another proof that private ownership
is according to nature's law. For that which is required for
the preservation of life and for life's well-being, is produced
in great abundance by the earth, but not until man has
brought it into cultivation and lavished upon it his care and
skill. Now, when man thus spends the industry of his mind
and the strength of his body in procuring the fruits by nature, by that act he makes his own that portion of nature's
field which he cultivates—that portion on which he leaves,
as it were, the impress of his own personality; and it cannot

but be just that he should possess that portion as his own, and should have a right to keep it without molestation.

8. These arguments are so strong and convincing that it seems surprising that certain obsolete opinions should now be revived in opposition to what is here laid down. We are told that it is right for private persons to have the use of the soil and the fruits of their land, but that it is unjust for anyone to possess as owner either the land on which he has built or the estate which he has cultivated. But those who assert this do not perceive that they are robbing man of what his own labor had produced. For the soil which is tilled and cultivated with toil and skill utterly changes its condition; it was wild before, it is now fruitful; it was barren, and now it brings forth in abundance. That which has thus altered and improved it becomes so truly part of itself as to be in a great measure indistinguishable, inseparable from it. Is it just that the fruit of a man's sweat and labor shoud be enjoyed by another? As effects follow their cause, so it is just and right that the results of labor should belong to him who has labored.

With reason, therefore, the common opinions of mankind, little affected by the few dissentients who have maintained the opposite view, has found in the study of nature, and in the law of nature herself, the foundations of the division of property, and has consecrated by the practice of all ages the principle of private ownership, as being pre-eminently in conformity with human nature, and as conducing in the most unmistakable manner to the peace and tranquillity of human life. The same principle is confirmed and enforced by the civil laws—laws which, as long as they are just, derive their binding force from the law of nature. The authority of the Divine Law adds its sanction, forbidding us in the gravest terms even to covet that which is another's: "Thou shalt not covet thy neighbor's wife; nor his house, nor his field, nor his man-servant, nor his maid-servant, nor his ox, nor his ass, nor anything which is his." [1]

A Family Right

9. The rights here spoken of belonging to each individual man, are seen in a much stronger light if they are considered in relation to man's social and domestic obligations.

[1] Deut. v. 21

In choosing a state of life, it is indisputable that all are at full liberty either to follow the counsel of Jesus Christ as to virginity, or to enter into the bonds of marriage. No human law can abolish the natural and primitive right of marriage, or in any way limit the chief and principal purpose of marriage, ordained by God's authority from the beginning. "Increase and multiply." [2] Thus we have the family; the "society" of a man's own household; a society limited indeed in numbers, but a true "society," anterior to every kind of State or nation, with rights and duties of its own, totally independent of the commonwealth.

That right of property, therefore, which has been proved to belong naturally to individual persons must also belong to a man in his capacity of head of a family; nay, such a person must possess this right so much the more clearly in proportion as his position multiplies his duties.

10. For it is a most sacred law of nature that a father must provide food and all necessaries for those whom he has begotten; and, similarly nature dictates that a man's children, who carry on, as it were, and coninue his own personality, should be provided by him with all that is needful to enable them honorably to keep themselves from want and misery in the uncertainties of this mortal life. Now, in no other way can a father effect this except by the ownership of profitable property, which he can transmit to his children by inheritance. A family, no less than a State, is, as we have said, a true society, governed by a power within itself, that is to say, by the father. Wherefore, provided the limits be not transgressed which are prescribed by the very purposes for which it exists, the family has, at least, equal rights with the State in the choice and pursuit of those things which are needful to its preservation and its just liberty.

We say, at least equal rights; for since the domestic household is anterior both in idea and in fact to the gathering of men into a commonwealth, the former must necessarily have rights and duties which are prior to those of the latter, and which rest more immediately on nature. If the citizens of a State—that is to say, the families—on entering into association and fellowship, experienced at the hands of the State hindrance instead of help, and found

[2] Gen. i. 28.

their rights attacked instead of being protected, such association were rather to be repudiated than sought after.

Socialism Rejected

11. The idea, then, that the civil government should, at its own discretion, penetrate and pervade the family and the household, is a great and pernicious mistake. True, if a family finds itself in great difficulty, utterly friendless, and without prospect of help, it is right that extreme necessity be met by public aid; for each family is a part of the commonwealth. In like manner, if within the walls of the household there occur grave disturbance of mutual rights, the public power must interfere to force each party to give the other what is due; for this is not to rob citizens of their rights, but justly and properly to safeguard and strengthen them. But the rulers of the State must go no further: nature bids them stop here. Paternal authority can neither be abolished by the State nor absorbed; for it has the same source as human life itself; "the child belongs to the father," and is, as it were, the continuation of the father's personality; and, to speak with strictness, the child takes its place in civil society not in its own right, but in its quality as a member of the family in which it is begotten. And it is for the very reason that "the child belongs to the father," that, as St. Thomas of Aquin says, "before it attains the use of free-will, it is in the power and care of its parents." [3] The Socialists, therefore, in setting aside the parent and introducing the providence of the State, act *against natural justice*, and threaten the very existence of family life.

12. And such interference is not only unjust, but is quite certain to harass and disturb all classes of citizens, and to subject them to odious and intolerable slavery. It would open the door to envy, to evil speaking, and to quarrelling; the sources of wealth would themselves run dry, for no one would have any interest in exerting his talents or his industry; and that ideal equality of which so much is said would, in reality, be the leveling down of all to the same condition of misery and dishonor.

[3] St. Thomas, *Summa Theologica*, 2a 2æ Q. x. art. 12.

Thus it is clear *that the main tenet of Socialism, the community of goods, must be utterly rejected;* for it would injure those whom it is intended to benefit, it would be contrary to the natural rights of mankind, and it would introduce confusion, and disorder into the commonwealth. Our first and most fundamental principle, therefore, when we undertake to alleviate the condition of the masses, must be the inviolability of private property. This laid down, We go on to show where we must find the remedy that We seek.

The Church is Necessary

13. We approach the subject with confidence, and in the exercise of the rights which belong to Us. For no practical solution of this question will ever be found without the assistance of Religion and the Church. It is We who are the chief guardian of Religion, and the chief dispenser of what belongs to the Church, and we must not by silence neglect the duty which lies upon Us. Doubtless this most serious question demands the attention and the efforts of others besides Ourselves—of the rulers of States, of employers of labor, of the wealthy, and of the working population themselves for whom We plead. But We affirm without hesitation that all the striving of men will be vain if they leave out the Church. It is the Church that proclaims from the Gospel those teachings by which the conflict can be brought to an end, or at least made far less bitter; the Church uses its efforts not only to enlighten the mind, but to direct by its precepts the life and conduct of men; the Church improves and ameliorates the condition of the working man by numerous useful organizations; does its best to enlist the services of all ranks in discussing and endeavoring to meet, in the most practical way, the claims of the working classes; and acts on the decided view that for these purposes recourse should be had, in due measure and degree, to the help of the law and of State authority.

14. Let it be laid down, in the first place, that humanity must remain as it is. It is impossible to reduce human society to a level. The *Socialists* may do their utmost, but all striving against nature is vain. There naturally exists among mankind innumerable differences of the most im-

portant kind; people differ in capability, in diligence, in health, and in strength; and unequal fortune is a necessary result of inequality in condition. Such inequality is far from being disadvantageous either to individuals or to the community; social and public life can only go on by the help of various kinds of capacity and the playing of many parts, and each man, as a rule, chooses the part which peculiarly suits his case. As regards bodily labor, even had man never fallen from the state of innocence, he would not have been wholly unoccupied; but that which would then have been his free choice, his delight, became afterwards compulsory, and the painful expiation of his sin. "Cursed be the earth in thy work; in thy labor thou shalt eat of it all the days of thy life." [4] In like manner, the other pains and hardships of life will have no end or cessation on this earth; for the consequences of sin are bitter and hard to bear, and they must be with man as long as life lasts. To suffer and to endure, therefore, is the lot of humanity; let men try as they may, no strength and no artifice will ever succeed in banishing from human life the ills and troubles which beset it. If any there are who pretend differently—who hold out to a hard-pressed people freedom from pain and trouble, undisturbed repose, and constant enjoyment—they cheat the people and impose upon them, and their lying promises will only make the evil worse than before. There is nothing more useful than to look at the world as it really is—and at the same time look elsewhere for a remedy to its troubles.

Employer and Employee

15. The great mistake that is made in the matter now under consideration, is to possess oneself of the idea that class is naturally hostile to class; that rich and poor are intended by nature to live at war with one another. So irrational and so false is this view, that the exact contrary is the truth. Just as the symmetry of the human body is the result of the disposition of the members of the body, so in a State it is ordained by nature that these two classes should exist in harmony and agreement, and should, as it

[4] Gen. iii. 17.

were, fit into one another, so as to maintain the equilibrium of the body politic. Each requires the other; capital cannot do without labor, nor labor without capital. Mutual agreement results in pleasantness and good order; perpetual conflict necessarily produces confusion and outrage. Now, in preventing such strife as this, and in making it impossible, the efficacy of Christianity is marvelous and manifold.

16. First of all, there is nothing more powerful than Religion (of which the Church is the interpreter and guardian) in drawing rich and poor together, by reminding each class of its duties to the other, and especially of the duties of justice. Thus Religion teaches the laboring man and the workman to carry out honestly and well all equitable agreements freely made, never to injure capital, nor to outrage the person of an employer; never to employ violence in representing his own cause, nor to engage in riot and disorder; and to have nothing to do with men of evil principles, who work upon the people with artful promises, and raise foolish hopes which usually end in disaster and in repentance when too late. Religion teaches the rich man and the employer that their work people are not their slaves; that they must respect in every man his dignity as a man and as a Christian; that labor is nothing to be ashamed of, if we listen to right reason and to Christian philosophy, but is an honorable employment, enabling a man to sustain his life in an upright and creditable way; and that it is shameful and inhuman to treat men like chattels to make money by, or to look upon them merely as so much muscle or physical power. Thus, again, Religion teaches that, as among the workmen's concerns are Religion herself, and things spiritual and mental, the employer is bound to see that he has time for the duties of piety; that he be not exposed to corrupting influences and dangerous occasions; and that he not be led away to neglect his home and family or to squander his wages. Then, again, the employer must never tax his work-people beyond their strength, nor employ them in work unsuited to their sex or age.

17. His great and principal obligation is to give to every one that which is just. Doubtless before we can decide whether wages are adequate many things have to be considered; but rich men and masters should remember this —that to exercise pressure for the sake of gain, upon the indigent and destitute, and to make one's profit out of the need of another, is condemned by all laws, human and

divine. To defraud any one of wages that are his due is a crime which cries to the avenging anger of Heaven. "Behold, the hire of the laborers . . . which by fraud has been kept back by you, crieth; and the cry of them hath entered the ears of the Lord of Sabaoth." [5] Finally, the rich must religiously refrain from cutting down the workman's earnings, either by force, fraud, or by usurious dealing; and with the more reason because the poor man is weak and unprotected, and because his slender means should be sacred in proportion to their scantiness.

Were these precepts carefully obeyed and followed would not strife die out and cease?

The Great Truth

18. But the Church, with Jesus Christ for its Master and Guide, aims higher still. It lays down precepts yet more perfect, and tries to bind class to class in friendliness and good understanding. The things of this earth cannot be understood or valued rightly without taking into consideration the life to come, the life that will last forever. Exclude the idea of futurity, and the very notion of what is good and right would perish; nay, the whole system of the universe would become a dark and unfathomable mystery. The great truth which we learn from nature herself is also the grand Christian dogma on which Religion rests as on its base—that when we have done with this present life then we shall really begin to live. God has not created us for the perishable and transitory things of earth, but for things heavenly and everlasting; He has given us this world as a place of exile, and not as our true country. Money and the other things which men call good and desirable —we may have them in abundance or we may want them altogether; as far as eternal happiness is concerned, it is no matter; the only thing that is important is to use them aright. Jesus Christ, when He redeemed us with plentiful redemption, took not away the pains and sorrows which in such large proportion make up the texture of our mortal life; He transformed them into motives of virtue and occasions of merit; and no man can hope for eternal reward

5 St. James v. 4.

unless he follow in the blood-stained footprints of his
Savior. "If we suffer with Him, we shall also reign with
Him." [6] His labors and His sufferings accepted by His
own free will, have marvelously sweetened all suffering and
all labor. And not only by His example, but by His grace
and by the hope of everlasting recompense, He has made
pain and grief more easy to endure; "for that which is at
present momentary and light of our tribulation, worketh
for us above measure exceedingly an eternal weight of
glory." [7]

The Right Use of Money

Therefore, those whom fortune favors are warned that
freedom from sorrow and abundance of earthly riches, are
no guarantee of that beatitude that shall never end, but
rather the contrary; [8] that the rich should tremble at the
threatenings of Jesus Christ—threatenings so strange in the
mouth of our Lord; [9] and that a most strict account must
be given to the Supreme Judge for all that we possess.

19. The chief and most excellent rule for the right use
of money is one which the heathen philosophers indicated,
but which the Church has traced out clearly, and has not
only made known to men's minds, but has impressed upon
their lives. It rests on the principle that it is one thing
to have a right to the possession of money, and another
to have a right to use money as one pleases. Private ownership, as we have seen, is the natural right of man; and
to exercise that right, especially as members of society, is
not only lawful but absolutely necessary. "It is lawful," says
St. Thomas of Aquin, "for a man to hold private property;
and it is also necessary for the carrying on of human
life." [10] But if the question be asked, How must one's possessions be used? the Church replies without hesitation in
the words of the same holy Doctor: "Man should not consider his outward possessions as his own, but as common

---

[6] II. Tim. ii. 2.

[7] II. Cor. iv. 17.

[8] St. Matt. xix. 23, 24.

[9] St. Luke vi. 24, 25

[10] 2a 2æ O. lxvi. art. 2.

to all, so as to share them without difficulty when others
are in need. Whence the Apostle saith, Command the rich
of this world . . . to give with ease, to communicate." [11]
True, no one is commanded to distribute to others that
which is required for his own necessities and those of his
household; nor even to give away what is reasonably required to keep up becomingly his condition in life; "for
no one ought to live unbecomingly." [12] But when necessity has been supplied, and one's position fairly considered,
it is a duty to give to the indigent out of that which is
over. "That which remaineth give alms." [13] It is a duty,
not of justice (except in extreme cases), but of Christian
charity—a duty which is not enforced by human law.
But the laws and judgment of men must give place to the
laws and judgment of Christ, the true God; Who in many
ways urges on His followers the practice of almsgiving—
"It is more blessed to give than to receive;" [14] and Who
will count a kindness done or refused to the poor as done
or refused to Himself—"As long as you did it to one of
My least brethren, you did it to Me." [15] Thus to sum up
what has been said:—Whoever has received from the Divine
bounty a large share of blessings, whether they be external
and corporal, or gifts of the mind, has received them for
the purpose of using them for perfecting his own nature,
and, at the same time, that he may employ them, as the
minister of God's Providence, for the benefit of others.
"He that hath a talent," said St. Gregory the Great, "let
him see that he hideth not; he that hath abundance, let
him arouse himself to mercy and generosity; he that hath
art and skill, let him do his best to share the use and
utility thereof with his neighbor." [16]

The Dignity of Labor

20. As for those who do not possess the gifts of fortune,
they are taught by the Church that, in God's sight poverty

---

11 *Ibid.*, Q. ixv, art. 2.
12 2a 2æ Q. xxxii. art. 6.
18 St. Luke xi. 41.
14 Acts xx. 35.
15 St. Matt. xxv. 40.
16 St. Gregory the Great. Hom. ix. *in Evangel.* n. 7.

is no disgrace, and that there is nothing to be ashamed of in seeking one's bread by labor. This is strengthened by what we see in Christ Himself, "Who whereas He was rich, for our sakes became poor;" [17] and Who, being the Son of God, and God Himself chose to seem and to be considered the son of a carpenter—nay, did not disdain to spend a great part of His life as a carpenter Himself. "Is not this the carpenter, the son of Mary?" [18] From the contemplation of this Divine example, it is easy to understand that the true dignity and excellence of man lies in his moral qualities, that is, in virtue; that virtue is the common inheritance of all, equally within the reach of high and low, rich and poor; and that virtue, and virtue alone, wherever found, will be followed by the rewards of everlasting happiness. Nay, God Himself seems to incline more to those who suffer evil; for Jesus Christ calls the poor blessed; [19] He lovingly invites those in labor and grief to come to Him for solace; [20] and He displays the tenderest charity to the lowly and oppressed. These reflections cannot fail to keep down the pride of those who are well off, and to cheer the spirit of the afflicted; to incline the former to generosity, and the latter to tranquil resignation. Thus the separation which pride would make tends to disappear, nor will it be difficult to make rich and poor join hands in friendly concord.

21. But, if Christian precepts prevail, the two classes will not only be united in the bonds of friendship, but also those of brotherly love. For they will understand and feel that all men are the children of the common father, that is, of God; that all have the same end, which is God Himself, Who alone can make either men or angels absolutely and perfectly happy; that all and each are redeemed by Jesus Christ, and raised to the dignity of children of God, and are thus united in brotherly ties both with each other and with Jesus Christ, "the first born among many brethren;" that the blessings of nature and the gifts of grace belong in common to the whole human race, and that to all, except to those who are unworthy, is promised the in-

---

[17] II. Cor. viii. 9.

[18] St. Mark vi. 3.

[19] St. Matt. v. 3: "Blessed are the poor in spirit."

[20] *Ibid.*, xi. 28: "Come to Me all you that labor and are burdened, and I will refresh you."

heritance of the kingdom of Heaven. "If sons, heirs also; heirs indeed of God, and co-heirs of Christ." [21]

Such is the scheme of duties and of rights which is put forth to the world by the Gospel. Would it not seem that strife must quickly cease were society penetrated with ideas like these?

The Church Applies the Remedy

22. But the Church, not content with pointing out the remedy, also applies it. For the Church does its utmost to teach and to train men, and to educate them; and by means of its Bishops and clergy, it diffuses its salutary teachings far and wide. It strives to influence the mind and heart so that all may willingly yield themselves to be formed and guided by the commandments of God. It is precisely in this fundamental and principal matter, on which everything depends, that the Church has a power peculiar to itself. The agencies which it employs are given it for the very purpose of reaching the hearts of men by Jesus Christ Himself, and derive their efficiency from God. They alone can touch the innermost heart and conscience, and bring men to act from a motive of duty, to resist their passions and appetites, to love God and their fellow-men with love that is unique and supreme, and courageously to break down every barrier which stands in the way of a virtuous life.

On this subject We need only recall for one moment the examples written down in history. Of these things there cannot be the shadow of doubt; for instance, that civil society was renovated in every part by the teachings of Christianity; that in the strength of that renewal the human race was lifted up to better things—nay, that it was brought back from death to life, and to so excellent a life that nothing more perfect had been known before or will come to pass in the ages that are yet to be. Of this beneficent transformation, Jesus Christ was at once the first cause and the final purpose; as from Him all came, so to Him all was to be referred. For when, by the light of the Gospel message, the human race came to know the grand mystery

[21] Rom. viii. 17.

of the Incarnation of the Word and the redemption of man,
the life of Jesus Christ, God and Man, penetrated every
race and nation, and impregnated them with His faith, His
precepts, and His laws. And, if Society is to be cured now,
in no other way can it be cured but by a return to the
Christian life and Christian institutions. When a society is
perishing, the true advice to give to those who would restore it is, to recall it to the principles from which it
sprung; for the purpose and perfection of an association is
to aim at and to attain that for which it was formed; and
its operation should be put in motion and inspired by the
end and object which originally gave it its being. So that
to fall away from its primal constitution is disease; to go
back to it is recovery. And this may be asserted with the
upmost truth both of the State in general and of that body
of its citizens—by far the greatest number—who sustain
life by labor.

The Church and the Poor

23. Neither must it be supposed that the solicitude of the
Church is so occupied with the spiritual concerns of its
children as to neglect their interests temporal and earthly.
Its desire is that the poor, for example, should rise above
poverty and wretchedness, and should better their condition
in life; and for this it strives. By the very fact that it
calls men to virtue and forms them to its practice, it promotes this in no slight degree. Christian morality, when it is
adequately and completely practiced, conduces of itself to
temporal prosperity, for it merits the blessing of that God
Who is the source of all blessings; it powerfully restrains
the lust of possession and the lust of pleasure—twin plagues,
which too often make a man without self-restraint miserable in the midst of abundance; [22] it makes men supply by
economy for the want of means, teaching them to be content with frugal living, and keeping them out of the reach
of those vices which eat up not merely small incomes, but
large fortunes, and dissipate many a goodly inheritance.

24. Moreover, the Church intervenes directly in the interest of the poor, by setting on foot and keeping up many

---

[22] "The root of all evils is cupidity." I Tim. vi. 10.

things which it sees to be efficacious in the relief of poverty. Here, again, it has always succeeded so well that it has even extorted the praise of its enemies. Such was the ardor of brotherly love among the earliest Christians that numbers of those who were better off deprived themselves of their possessions in order to relieve their brethren; whence "neither was there any one needy among them." [23] To the order of Deacons, instituted for that very purpose, was committed by the Apostles the charge of the daily distributions; and the Apostle Paul, though burdened with the solicitude of all the churches, hesitated not to undertake laborious journeys in order to carry the alms of the faithful to the poorer Christians. Tertullian calls these contributions, given voluntarily by Christians in their assemblies, "deposits of piety," because, to cite his words, they were employed "in feeding the needy, in burying them, in the support of boys and girls destitute of means and deprived of their parents, in the care of the aged, and in the relief of the shipwrecked." [24]

Thus by degrees came into existence the patrimony which the Church has guarded with jealous care as the inheritance of the poor. Nay, to spare them the shame of begging, the common Mother of the rich and poor has exerted herself to gather together funds for the support of the needy. The Church has stirred up everywhere the heroism of charity, and has established Congregations of Religious and many other useful institutions for help and mercy, so that there might be hardly any kind of suffering which was not visited and relieved. At the present day there are many who, like the heathen of old, blame and condemn the Church for this beautiful charity. They would substitute in its place a system of State-organized relief. But no human methods will ever supply for the devotion and self-sacrifice of Christian charity. Charity, as a virtue, belongs to the Church; for it is no virtue unless it is drawn from the Sacred Heart of Jesus Christ; and he who turns his back on the Church cannot be near to Christ.

[23] Acts iv. 34.
[24] *Apologia Secunda*, xxxix.

The State and Poverty

25. It cannot, however, be doubted that to attain the purpose of which We treat, not only the Church, but all human means must conspire. All who are concerned in the matter must be of one mind and must act together. It is in this, as in the Providence which governs the world; results do not happen save where all the causes coöperate.

Let us now, therefore, inquire what part the State should play in the work of remedy and relief.

By the State We here understand, not the particular form of government which prevails in this or that nation, but the State as rightly understood; that is to say, any government conformable in its institutions to right reason and natural law, and to those dictates of the Divine wisdom which We have expounded in the Encyclical on *The Christian Constitution of the State*.

26. The first duty, therefore, of the rulers of the State should be to make sure that the laws and institutions, the general character and administration of the commonwealth, shall be such as to produce of themselves public well-being and private prosperity. This is the proper office of wise statesmanship and the work of the heads of the State. Now a State chiefly prospers and flourishes by morality, well-regulated family life, by respect for religion and justice, by the moderation and equal distribution of public burdens, by the progress of the arts and of trade, by the abundant yield of the land—by everything which makes the citizens better and happier. Here, then, it is in the power of a ruler to benefit every order of the State, and amongst the rest to promote in the highest degree the interests of the poor; and this by virtue of his office, and without being exposed to any suspicion of undue interference—for it is the province of the commonwealth to consult for the common good. And the more that is done for the working population by the general laws of the country, the less need will there be to seek for particular means to relieve them.

27. There is another and a deeper consideration which must not be lost sight of.

Justice Towards All

To the State the interests of all are equal whether high or low. The poor are members of the national community equally with the rich; they are real component parts, living parts, which make up, through the family, the living body; and it need hardly be said that they are by far the majority. It would be irrational to neglect one portion of the citizens and to favor another; and therefore the public administration must duly and solicitously provide for the welfare and the comfort of the working people, or else that law of justice will be violated which ordains that each shall have his due. To cite the wise words of St. Thomas of Aquin: "As the part and the whole are in a certain sense identical, the part may in some sense claim what belongs to the whole." [25] Among the many and grave duties of rulers who would do their best for their people, the first and chief is to act with strict justice—with that justice which is called in the Schools *distributive*—towards each and every class.

But although all citizens, without exception, can and ought to contribute to that common good in which individuals share so profitably to themselves, yet it is not to be supposed that all can contribute in the same way and to the same extent. No matter what changes may be made in forms of government, there will always be differences and inequalities of condition in the State. Society cannot exist or be conceived without them. Some there must be who dedicate themselves to the work of the commonwealth, who make the laws, who administer justice, whose advice and authority govern the nation in times of peace, and defend it in war. Such men clearly occupy the foremost place in the State, and should be held in the foremost estimation, for their work touches most nearly and effectively the general interests of the community. Those who labor at a trade or calling do not promote the general welfare in such a fashion as this; but they do in the most important way benefit the nation, though less directly. We have insisted that, since it is the end of Society to make men better, the chief

[25] 2a 2æ Q. lxi. art. 1 and 2.

good that Society can be possessed of is virtue. Nevertheless, in all well-constituted States it is a by no means unimportant matter to provide those bodily and external commodities, "the use of which is necessary to virtuous action." [26] And in the provision of material well-being, the labor of the poor—the exercise of their skill and the employment of their strength in the culture of the land and the workshops of trade—is most efficacious and altogether indispensable. Indeed, their coöperation in this respect is so important that it may be truly said that it is only by the labor of the working man that States grow rich. Justice, therefore, demands that the interests of the poorer population be carefully watched over by the Administration, so that they who contribute so largely to the advantage of the community may themselves share in the benefits they create—that being housed, clothed, and enabled to support life, they may find their existence less hard and more endurable. It follows that whatever shall appear to be conducive to the well-being of those who work, should receive favorable consideration. Let it not be feared that solicitude of this kind will injure any interest; on the contrary, it will be to the advantage of all; for it cannot but be good for the commonwealth to secure from misery those on whom it so largely depends.

The First Law of Government

28. We have said that the State must not absorb the individual or the family; both should be allowed free and untrammelled action as far as is consistent with the common good and the interests of others. Nevertheless, rulers should anxiously safeguard the community and all its parts; the community, because the conservation of the community is so emphatically the business of the supreme power, that the safety of the commonwealth is not only the first law, but is a Government's whole reason of existence; and the parts, because both philosophy and the Gospel agree in laying down that the object of the administration of the State should be not the advantage of the ruler, but the benefit of those over whom he rules. The gift of authority

[26] St. Thomas of Aquin. *De Regimine Principum*, I, cap. 15.

is from God, and is, as it were, a participation of the highest of all sovereignties; and it should be exercised as the power of God is exercised—with a fatherly solicitude which not only guides the whole but reaches to details as well.

Whenever the general interest of any particular class suffers, or is threatened with, evils which can in no other way be met, the public authority must step in to meet them.

29. Now, among the interests of the public, as of private individuals, are these: that peace and good order should be maintained; that family life should be carried on in accordance with God's laws and those of nature; that Religion should be reverenced and obeyed; that a high standard of morality should prevail in public and private life; that the sanctity of justice should be respected, and that no one should injure another with impunity; that the members of the commonwealth should grow up to man's estate strong and robust, and capable, if need be, of guarding and defending their country. If by a strike, or other combination of workmen, there should be imminent danger of disturbance to the public peace; or if circumstances were such that among the laboring population the ties of family life were relaxed; if Religion were found to suffer through the workmen not having time and opportunity to practice it; if in workshops and factories there were danger to morals through the mixing of the sexes or from any occasion of evil; or if employers laid burdens upon the workmen which were unjust, or degraded them with conditions that were repugnant to their dignity as human beings; finally, if health were endangered by excessive labor, or by work unsuited to sex or age—in these cases there can be no question that, within certain limits, it would be right to call in the help and authority of the law. The limits must be determined by the nature of the occasion which calls for the law's interference—the principle being this, that the law must not undertake more, nor go further, than is required for the remedy of the evil or the removal of the danger.

The Right of Protection

Rights must be religiously respected wherever they are found; and it is the duty of the public authority to prevent and punish injury, and to protect each one in the possession of his own. Still, when there is question of protecting the rights of individuals, the poor and helpless have a claim to special consideration. The richer population have many ways of protecting themselves, and stand less in need of help from the State; those who are badly off have no resources of their own to fall back upon, and must chiefly rely upon the assistance of the State. And it is for this reason that wage-earners, who are, undoubtedly, among the weak and necessitous, should be specially cared for and protected by the commonwealth.

30. Here, however, it will be advisable to advert expressly to one or two of the more important details.

It must be borne in mind that the chief thing to be secured is the safeguarding, by legal enactment and policy, of private property. Most of all it is essential in these times of covetous greed, to keep the multitude within the line of duty; for if all may justly strive to better their condition, yet neither justice nor the common good allows anyone to seize that which belongs to another, or, under the pretext of futile and ridiculous equality, to lay hands on other people's fortunes. It is most true that by far the larger part of the people who work prefer to improve themselves by honest labor rather than by doing wrong to others. But there are not a few who are imbued with bad principles and are anxious for revolutionary change, and whose great purpose it is to stir up tumult and bring about a policy of violence. The authority of the State should intervene to put restraint upon these disturbers, to save the workmen from their seditious arts, and to protect lawful owners from spoliation.

The Workman's Rights

31. When work-people have recourse to a strike, it is frequently because the hours of labor are too long, or the work too hard, or because they consider their wages insufficient. The grave inconvenience of this not uncommon occurrence should be obviated by public remedial measures; for such paralysis of labor not only affects the masters and their work-people, but is extremely injurious to trade, and to the general interests of the public; moreover, on

such occasions, violence and disorder are generally not far off, and thus it frequently happens that the public peace is threatened. The laws should be beforehand, and prevent these troubles from arising; they should lend their influence and authority to the removal in good time of the causes which lead to conflicts between masters and those whom they employ.

32. But if the owners of property must be made secure, the workman, too, has property and possessions in which he must be protected; and, first of all, there are his spiritual and mental interests. Life on earth, however good and desirable in itself, is not the final purpose for which man is created; it is only the way and the means to that attainment of truth, and that practice of goodness in which the full life of the soul consists. It is the soul which is made after the image and likeness of God; it is in the soul that sovereignty resides, in virtue of which man is commanded to rule the creatures below him, and to use all the earth and ocean for his profit and advantage. "Fill the earth and subdue it; and rule over the fishes of the sea and the fowls of the air, and all living creatures which move upon the earth." [27] In this respect all men are equal; there is no difference between rich and poor, master and servant, ruler and ruled, "for the same is Lord over all." [28] No man may outrage with impunity that human dignity which God Himself treats with reverence, nor stand in the way of that higher life which is the preparation for the eternal life of Heaven. Nay, more; a man has here no power over himself. To consent to any treatment which is calculated to defeat the end and purpose of his being is beyond his right; he cannot give up his soul to servitude; for it is not man's own rights which are here in question, but the rights of God, most sacred and inviolable.

From this follows the obligation of the cessation of work and labor on Sundays and certain festivals. This rest from labor is not to be understood as mere idleness; much less must it be an occasion of spending money and a vicious excess, as many would desire it to be; but it should be rest from labor consecrated by Religion. Repose united with religious observance disposes man to forget for a while the business of this daily life, and to turn his thoughts to

[27] Gen. i. 28.
[28] Rom. x. 12.

heavenly things and to the worship which he so strictly owes to the Eternal Deity. It is this, above all, which is the reason and motive for the Sunday rest; a rest sanctioned by God's great law of the ancient covenant, "Remember thou keep holy the Sabbath day," [29] and taught to the world by His own mysterious "rest" after the creation of man, "He rested on the seventh day from all His work which He had done." [30]

Hours of Labor

33. If we turn now to things exterior and corporal, the first concern of all is to save the poor workers from the cruelty of grasping speculators, who use human beings as mere instruments for making money. It is neither justice nor humanity so to grind men down with excessive labor as to stupefy their minds and wear out their bodies. Man's powers, like his general nature, are limited, and beyond these limits he cannot go. His strength is developed and increased by use and exercise, but only on condition of due intermission and proper rest. Daily labor, therefore, must be so regulated that it may not be protracted during longer hours than strength admits. How many and how long the intervals of rest should be, will depend upon the nature of the work, on circumstances of time and place, and on the health and strength of the workman. Those who labor in mines and quarries, and in work within the bowels of the earth, should have shorter hours in proportion, as their labor is more severe and more trying to health. Then, again, the season of the year must be taken in account; for not unfrequently a kind of labor is easy at one time which at another is intolerable or very difficult. Finally, work which is suitable for a strong man cannot reasonably be required from a woman or a child.

Child Labor

And, in regard to children, great care should be taken not to place them in workshops and factories until their

29 Exod. xx. 3.
30 Gen. ii. 2.

bodies and minds are sufficiently mature. For just as rough weather destroys the buds of spring, so too early an experience of life's hard work blights the young promise of a child's powers, and makes any real education impossible. Women, again, are not suited to certain trades; for a woman is by nature fitted for home-work, and it is that which is best adapted at once to preserve her modesty, and to promote the good bringing up of children and the well-being of the family. As a general principle, it may be laid down, that a workman ought to have leisure and rest in proportion to the wear and tear of his strength; for the waste of strength must be repaired by the cessation of work.

In all agreements between masters and work-people, there is always the condition, expressed or understood, that there be allowed proper rest for soul and body. To agree in any other sense would be against what is right and just; for it can never be right or just to require on the one side, or to promise on the other, the giving up of those duties which a man owes to his God and to himself.

Just Wages

34. We now approach a subject of very great importance and one on which, if extremes are to be avoided, right ideas are absolutely necessary. Wages, we are told, are fixed by free consent; and, therefore, the employer when he pays what was agreed upon, has done his part, and is not called upon for anything further. The only way, it is said, in which injustice could happen, would be if the master refused to pay the whole of the wages, or the workman would not complete the work undertaken; when this happens the State should intervene, to see that each obtains his own, but not under any other circumstances.

This mode of reasoning is by no means convincing to a fair-minded man, for there are important considerations which it leaves out of view altogether. To labor is to exert one's self for the sake of procuring what is necessary for the purposes of life, and most of all for self-preservation. "In the sweat of thy brow thou shalt eat bread." [31] Therefore, a man's labor has two notes or characters. First of

---

[31] Gen. iii. 1.

all, it is *personal;* for the exertion of individual power belongs to the individual who puts it forth, employing this power for that personal profit for which it was given. Secondly, a man's labor is *necessary;* for without the results of labor a man cannot live; and self-conservation is a law of nature, which it is wrong to disobey. Now, if we were to consider labor merely so far as it is *personal,* doubtless it would be within the workman's right to accept any rate of wages whatever; for in the same way as he is free to work or not, so he is free to accept a small remuneration or even none at all. But this is a mere abstract supposition; the labor of the working man is not only his personal attribute, but it is *necessary;* and this makes all the difference. The preservation of life is the bounden duty of each and all, and to fail therein is a crime. It follows that each one has a right to procure what is required in order to live; and the poor can procure it in no other way than by work and wages.

Let it be granted, then, that, as a rule, workman and employer should make free agreements, and in particular should freely agree as to wages; nevertheless, there is a dictate of nature more imperious and more ancient than any bargain between man and man, that the remuneration must be enough to support the wage-earner in reasonable and frugal comfort. If through necessity or fear of a worse evil, the workman accepts harder conditions because an employer or contractor will give him no better, he is the victim of force and injustice. In these and similar questions, however—such as, for example, the hours of labor in different trades, the sanitary precautions to be observed in factories and workshops, etc.—in order to supercede undue interference on the part of the State, especially as circumstances, times, and localities differ so widely, it is advisable that recourse be had to Societies or Boards such as We shall mention presently, or to some other method of safeguarding the interests of wage-earners; the State to be asked for approval and protection.

Benefits of Property Ownership

35. If a workman's wages be sufficient to enable him to maintain himself, his wife, and his children in reasonable

comfort, he will not find it difficult, if he is a sensible man, to study economy; and he will not fail, by cutting down expenses, to put by a little property: nature and reason would urge him to do this. We have seen that this great labor question cannot be solved except by assuming as a principle that private ownership must be held sacred and inviolable. The law, therefore, should favor ownership, and its policy should be to induce as many people as possible to become owners.

Many excellent results will follow from this; and first of all, property will certainly become more equitably divided. For the effect of civil change and revolution has been to divide society into two widely different castes. On the one side there is the party which holds the power because it holds the wealth; which has in its grasp all labor and all trade; which manipulates for its own benefit and its own purposes all the sources of supply, and which is powerfully represented in the councils of the State itself. On the other side there is the needy and powerless multitude, sore and suffering, always ready for disturbance. If working people can be encouraged to look forward to obtaining a share in the land, the result will be that the gulf between vast wealth and deep poverty will be bridged over, and the two orders will be brought nearer together. Another consequence will be the great abundance of the fruits of the earth. Men always work harder and more readily when they work on that which is their own; nay, they learn to love the very soil which yields in response to the labor of their hands not only food to eat, but an abundance of the good things for themselves and those that are dear to them. It is evident how such a spirit of willing labor would add to the produce of the earth and to the wealth of the community. And a third advantage would arise from this: men would cling to the country in which they were born; for no one would exchange his country for a foreign land if his own afforded him the means of living a tolerable and happy life. These three important benefits, however, can only be expected on the condition that a man's means be not drained and exhausted by excessive taxation. The right to possess private property is from nature, not from man; and the State has only the right to regulate its use in the interests of the public good, but by no means to abolish it altogether. The State is, therefore, unjust and

cruel, if, in the name of taxation, it deprives the private
owner of more than is just.

Workmen's Associations

36. In the first place—employers and workmen may themselves effect much in the matter of which We treat, by
means of those institutions and organizations which afford
opportune assistance to those in need, and which draw the
two orders more closely together. Among these may be
enumerated: societies for mutual help; various foundations
established by private persons for providing for the workman, and for his widow or his orphans, in sudden calamity,
in sickness, and in the event of death; and what are called
"patronages," or institutions for the care of boys and girls,
for young people, and also for those of more mature age.

The most important of all are Workmen's Associations; for
these virtually include all the rest. History attests what excellent results were affected by the Artificer's Guilds of a
former day. They were the means not only of many advantages to the workmen, but in no small degree of the advancement of art, as numerous monuments remain to prove.
Such associations should be adapted to the requirements of
the age in which we live—an age of greater instruction, of
different customs, and of more numerous requirements in
daily life. It is gratifyinng to know that there are actually in
existence not a few societies of this nature, consisting either
of workmen alone, or of workmen and employers together;
but it were greatly to be desired that they should multiply
and become more effective. We have spoken of them more
than once; but it will be well to explain here how much they
are needed, to show that they exist by their own right, and to
enter into their organization and their work.

37. The experience of his own weakness urges man to
call in help from without. We read in the pages of Holy
Writ: "It is better that two should be together than one; for
they have the advantage of their society. If one fall he shall
be supported by the other. Woe to him that is alone, for
when he falleth he hath none to lift him up." [32] And further:
"A brother that is helped by his brother is like a strong

[32] Eccles. iv. 9, 10.

city." [33] It is this natural impulse which unites men in civil society; and it is this also which makes them band themselves together in associations of citizen with citizen; associations which, it is true, cannot be called societies in the complete sense of the word, but which are societies nevertheless.

These lesser societies and the society which constitutes the State differ in many things, because their immediate purpose and end is different. Civil society exists for the common good, and, therefore, is concerned with the interests of all in general, and with the individual interests in their due place and proportion. Hence, it is called *public* society, because by its means, as St. Thomas of Aquin says, "Men communicate with one another in the setting up of a commonwealth." [34] But the societies which are formed in the bosom of the State are called *private*, and justly so, because their immediate purpose is the private advantage of the associates. "Now, a private society," says St. Thomas again, "is one which is formed for the purpose of carrying out private business; as when two or three enter into partnership with the view of trading in conjunction." [35]

38. Particular societies, then, although they exist within the State, and are each a part of the State, nevertheless cannot be prohibited by the State absolutely and as such. For to enter into a "society" of this kind is the natural right of man; and the State must protect natural rights, not destroy them; and if it forbids its citizens to form associations, it contradicts the very principle of its own existence; for both they and it exist in virtue of the same principle, viz., the natural propensity of man to live in society.

There are times, no doubt, when it is right that the law should interfere to prevent association; as when men join together for purposes which are evidently bad, unjust, or dangerous to the State. In such cases the public authority may justly forbid the formation of association, and may dissolve them when they already exist. But every precaution should be taken not to violate the rights of individuals, and not to make unreasonable regulations under the pretense of public benefit. For laws only bind when they are in accordance

[33] Prov. xviii. 19.
[34] *Contra impugnantes Dei cultum et religionem*, Cap. II.
[35] *Ibid.*

with right reason, and therefore with the eternal law of God.[36]

Violent Oppression

39. And here we are reminded of the Confraternities, Societies, and Religious Orders which have arisen by the Church's authority and the piety of the Christian people. The annals of every nation down to our own times testify to what they have done for the human race. It is indisputable on grounds of reason alone, that such associations, being perfectly blameless in their objects, have the sanction of the law of nature. On their religious side, they rightly claim to be responsible to the Church alone. The administrators of the State, therefore, have no rights over them, nor can they claim any share in their management; on the contrary, it is the State's duty to respect and cherish them, and, if necessary, to defend them from attack. It is notorious that a very different course has been followed, more especially in our own times. In many places the State has laid violent hands on these communities, and committed manifold injustice against them; it has placed them under the civil law, taken away their rights as corporate bodies, and robbed them of their property. In such property the Church had her rights, each member of the body had his or her rights, and there were also the rights of those who had founded or endowed them for a definite purpose, and of those for whose benefit and assistance they existed. Wherefore We cannot refrain from complaining of such spoliation as unjust and fraught with evil results; and with the more reason because, at the very time when the law proclaims that association is free to all, We see that Catholic societies, however peaceable and useful, are hindered in every way, whilst the utmost freedom is given to men whose objects are at once hurtful to Religion and dangerous to the State.

40. Associations of every kind, and especially those of working men, are now far more common than formerly. In

---

[36] "Human law is law only in virtue of its accordance with right reason: and thus it is manifest that it flows from the eternal law. And in so far as it deviates from right reason it is called an unjust law; in such case it is not law at all, but rather a species of violence." St. Thomas of Aquin, *Summa Theologica*, 1a 2æ Q. xciii. art. iii.

regard to many of these there is no need at present to inquire whence they spring, what are their objects or what means they use. But there is a good deal of evidence which goes to prove that many of these societies are in the hands of invisible leaders, and are managed on principles far from compatible with Christianity and the public well-being; and that they do their best to get into their hands the whole field of labor and to force workmen either to join them or starve. Under these circumstances the Christian workmen must do one of two things: either join associations in which their religion will not be exposed to peril or form associations among themselves—unite their forces and courageously shake off the yoke of an unjust and intolerable oppression. No one who does not wish to expose man's chief good to extreme danger will hesitate to say that the second alternative must by all means be adopted.

Principles of Organization

41. Those Catholics are worthy of all praise—and there are not a few—who, understanding what the times require, have, by various enterprises and experiments, endeavored to better the conditions of the working people without any sacrifice of principle. They have taken up the cause of the working man, and have striven to make both families and individuals better off; to infuse the spirit of justice into the mutual relations of employers and employed; to keep before the eyes of both classes the precepts of duty and the laws of the Gospel—that Gospel which, by inculcating self-restraint, keeps men within the bounds of moderation, and tends to establish harmony among the divergent interests and various classes which compose the State. It is with such ends in view that We see men of eminence meeting together for discussion, for the promotion of united action, and for practical work. Others, again, strive to unite working people of various kinds into associations, help them with their advice and their means, and enable them to obtain honest and profitable work. The Bishops, on their part, bestow their ready goodwill and support; and with their approval and guidance many members of the clergy, both secular and regular, labor assiduously on behalf of the spiritual and mental interests of the members of Associations. And there are not wanting

Catholics possessed of affluence, who have, as it were, cast
their lot with the wage-earners, and who have spent large
sums in founding and widely spreading Benefit and Insurance
Societies, by means of which the working man may without
difficulty acquire by his labor not only many present advantages, but also the certainty of honorable support in time
to come. How much this multiplied and earnest activity has
benefited the community at large is too well known to require Us to dwell upon it. We find in it the grounds of the
most cheering hope for the future; provided that the Associations We have described continue to grow and spread,
and are well and wisely administered. Let the State watch
over these societies of citizens united together in the exercise
of their right; but let it not thrust itself into their peculiar
concerns and their organization, for things move and live by
the soul within them, and they may be killed by the grasp
of a hand from without.

Religion First

42. In order that an Association may be carried on with a
unity of purpose and harmony of action, its organization and
government must be firm and wise. All such societies, being
free to exist, have the further right to adopt such rules and
organization as may best conduce to the attainment of their
objects. We do not deem it possible to enter into definite details on the subject of organization; this must depend on national character, on practice and experience, on the nature
and scope of the work to be done, on the magnitude of the
various trades and employments, and on other circumstances
of fact and of time—all of which must be carefully weighed.
Speaking summarily, we may lay it down as a general and
perpetual law, that Workmen's Associations should be so
organized and governed as to furnish the best and most suitable means for attaining what is aimed at, that is to say, for
helping each individual member to better his condition to
the utmost, in body, mind and property. It is clear that they
must pay special and principal attention to piety and
morality, and that their internal discipline must be directed
precisely by these considerations; otherwise they entirely
lose their special character, and come to be very little better
than those societies which take no account of Religion at

all. What advantage can it be to a workman to obtain by means of a society all that he requires, and to endanger his soul for want of spiritual food? "What doth it profit a man if he gain the whole world and suffer the loss of his own soul?" [37]

This, as Our Lord teaches, is the note or character that distinguishes the Christian from the heathen. "After all these things do the heathen seek. . . . Seek ye first the Kingdom of God and His justice, and all these things shall be added unto you." [38] Let our Associations, then, look first and before all to God; let religious instruction have therein a foremost place, each one being carefully taught what is his duty to God, what to believe, what to hope for, and how to work out his salvation; and let all be warned and fortified with especial solicitude against wrong opinions and false teaching. Let the working man be urged and led to the worship of God, to the earnest practice of Religion, and, among other things, to the sanctification of Sundays and festivals. Let him learn to reverence and love Holy Church the common Mother of us all; and so to obey the precepts and frequent the Sacraments of the Church, those Sacraments being the means ordained by God for obtaining forgiveness of sin and for leading a holy life.

Relation of Members

43. The foundations of the organization being laid in Religion, We next go on to determine the relations of the members, one to another, in order that they may live together in concord, and go on prosperously and successfully. The offices and charges of the society should be distributed for the good of the society itself, and in such manner that difference in degree or position should not interfere with unanimity and good-will. Office-bearers should be appointed with prudence and discretion, and each one's charge should be carefully marked out; thus no member will suffer wrong. Let the common funds be administered with strictest honesty, in such a way that a member receives assistance in proportion to his necessities. The rights and duties of employers should be the

[37] St. Matt. xvi. 26.
[38] St. Matt. vi. 32. 33.

subject of careful consideration as compared with the rights and duties of the employed. If it should happen that either a master or a workman deemed himself injured, nothing would be more desirable than that there should be a committee composed of honest and capable men of the Association itself, whose duty it should be, by the laws of the Association, to decide the dispute. Among the purposes of a society should be an effort to arrange for a continuous supply of work at all times and seasons; and to create a fund from which the members may be helped in their necessities, not only in case of accident, but also in sickness, old age, and misfortune.

Such rules and regulations, if obeyed willingly by all, will sufficiently ensure the well-being of poor people; whilst such Mutual Associations among Catholics are certain to be productive, in no small degree, of prosperity to the State. It is not rash to conjecture the future from the past. Age gives way to age, but the events of one century are wonderfully like those of another; for they are directed by the Providence of God, Who overrules the course of history in accordance with His purposes in creating the race of man. We are told that it was cast as a reproach on the Christians of the early ages of the Church, that the greater number of them had to live by begging or by labor. Yet, destitute as they were of wealth and influence they ended by winning over to their side the favor of the rich and the good-will of the powerful. They showed themselves industrious, laborious and peaceful, men of justice, and, above all, men of brotherly love. In the presence of such a life and such an example, prejudice disappeared, the tongue of malevolence was silenced, and the lying traditions of ancient superstition yielded little by little to Christian truth.

Honesty

44. At this moment the condition of the working population is the question of the hour; and nothing can be of higher interest to all classes of the State than that it should be rightly and reasonably decided. But it will be easy for Christian working men to decide it aright if they form Associations, choose wise guides, and follow the same path which with so much advantage to themselves and the com-

monwealth was trod by their fathers before them. Prejudice, it is true, is mighty, and so is the love of money; but if the sense of what is just and right be not destroyed by depravity of heart, their fellow-citizens are sure to be won over to a kindly feeling towards men whom they see to be so industrious and so modest, who so unmistakably prefer honesty to lucre, and the sacredness of duty to all other considerations.

And another great advantage would result from the state of things We are describing; there would be so much more hope and possibility of recalling to a sense of their duty those working men who have either given up their faith altogether, or whose lives are at variance with its precepts. These men, in most cases, feel that they have been fooled by empty promises and deceived by false appearances. They cannot but perceive that their grasping employers too often treat them with the greatest inhumanity, and hardly care for them beyond the profit their labor brings; and if they belong to an Association, it is probably one in which there exists, in place of charity and love, that internal strife which always accompanies unresigned and irreligious poverty. Broken in spirit and worn down in body, how many of them would gladly free themselves from this galling slavery! But human respect, or the dread of starvation, makes them afraid to take the step. To such as these, Catholic Associations are of incalculable service, helping them out of their difficulties, inviting them to companionship, and receiving the repentant to a shelter in which they may securely trust.

Conclusion

45. We have now laid before you, Venerable Brethren, who are the persons, and what are the means, by which this most difficult question must be solved. Every one must put his hand to work which falls to his share, and that at once and immediately, lest the evil which is already so great may by delay become absolutely beyond remedy. Those who rule the State must use the law and the institutions of the country; masters and rich men must remember their duty; the poor, whose interests are at stake, must make every lawful and proper effort; since Religion alone, as We said at the beginning, can destroy the evil at its root, all men must

be persuaded that the primary thing needful is to return to real Christianity, in the absence of which all the plans and devices of the wisest will be of little avail.

As far as regards the Church, its assistance will never be wanting, be the time or the occasion what it may; and it will intervene with great effect in proportion as its liberty of action is the more unfettered; let this be carefully noted by those whose office it is to provide for the public welfare. Every minister of holy Religion must throw into the conflict all the energy of his mind, and all the strength of his endurance; with your authority, Venerable Brethren, and by your example, they must never cease to urge upon all men of every class, upon the high as well as the lowly, the Gospel doctrines of Christian life; by every means in their power they must strive for the good of the people; and above all they must earnestly cherish in themselves, and try to arouse in others, Charity, the mistress and queen of virtues. For the happy results we all long for must be chiefly brought about by the plenteous outpouring of Charity; of that true Christian Charity which is the fulfilling of the whole Gospel law, which is always ready to sacrifice itself for other's sake, and which is man's surest antidote against worldly pride and immoderate love of self; that Charity whose office is described and whose God-like features are drawn by the Apostle St. Paul in these words: "Charity is patient, is kind, . . . seeketh not her own, . . . suffereth all things, . . . endureth all things." [39]

GRAVES DE COMMUNI
Christian Democracy*

January 18, 1901

The grave discussions on economical questions which for some time past have disturbed the peace of several countries of the world are growing in frequency and intensity to such

[39] I. Cor. xiii, 4–7.
* Official translation. The Vatican Polyglot Press.

a degree that the minds of thoughtful men are filled, and
rightly so, with worry and alarm. These discussions take their
rise in the bad philosophical and ethical teaching which is
now widespread among the people. The changes also which
the mechanical inventions of the age have introduced, the
rapidity of communication between places and the devices
of every kind for diminishing labor and increasing gain all
add bitterness to the strife; and lastly matters have been
brought to such a pass by the struggle between capital and
labor, fomented as it is by professional agitators, that the
countries where these disturbances most frequently occur,
find themselves confronted with ruin and disaster.

At the very beginning of Our Pontificate We clearly
pointed out what the peril was which confronted society on
this head, and We deemed it Our duty to warn Catholics,
in unmistakable language, how great the error was which
was lurking in the utterances of socialism, and how great
the danger was that threatened not only their temporal
possessions, but also their morality and religion. That was
the purpose of Our Encyclical Letter *Quod Apostolici
Muneris* which We published on the 28th of December in
the year 1878; but as these dangers day by day threatened
still greater disaster, both to individuals and the commonwealth, We strove with all the more energy to avert them.
This was the object of Our Encyclical *Rerum Novarum* of
the 15th May, 1891, in which We dwelt at length on the
rights and duties which both classes of society—those
namely, who control capital, and those who contribute labor
—are bound in relation to each other; and at the same time,
We made it evident that the remedies which are most useful
to protect the cause of religion, and to terminate the contest between the different classes of society, were to be found
in the precepts of the Gospel.

Nor, with God's grace, were Our hopes entirely frustrated.
Even those who are not Catholics, moved by the power
of truth, avowed that the Church must be credited with a
watchful care over all classes of society, and especially those
whom fortune had least favored. Catholics of course profited
abundantly by these Letters, for they not only received encouragement and strength for the admirable enterprises in
which they were engaged but also obtained the light which
they desired, by the help of which they were able with
greater safety and with more plentiful blessings to continue
the efforts which they had been making in the matter of

which We are now speaking. Hence it happened that the
differences of opinion which prevailed among them were
either removed or their acrimony diminished and the discussion laid aside. In the work which they had undertaken
this was effected, viz.: that in their efforts for the elevation of
the poorer classes, especially in those places where the trouble
is greatest, many new enterprises were set on foot; those
which were already established were increased and all reaped
the blessing of a greater stability imparted to them. Some of
these works were called *Bureaus of the People,* their object
being to supply information. Rural savings banks had been
established, and various associations, some for mutual aid,
others, of relief were organized. There were working men's
societies and other enterprises for work or beneficence. Thus
under the auspices of the Church, united action of Catholics
was secured as well as wise discrimination exercised in the
distribution of help for the poor who are often as badly
dealt with by chicanery and exploitation of their necessities,
as they are oppressed by indigence and toil. These schemes
of popular benevolence were, at first, distinguished by no
particular appellation. The name of *Christian Socialism* with
its derivatives which was adopted by some was very properly
allowed to fall into disuse. Afterwards some asked to have
it called *The Popular Christian Movement.* In the countries
most concerned with this matter, there are some who are
known as *Christian Socialists.* Elsewhere the movement is
described as *Christian Democracy,* and its partisans *Christian
Democrats,* in contradistinction to those who are designated
as *Socialists,* and whose system is known as *Social Democracy.* Not much exception is taken to the former, *i.e., Christian Socialism,* but many excellent men find the term
Christian Democracy objectionable. They hold it to be very
ambiguous and for this reason open to two objections. It
seems by implication to covertly favor popular government,
and to disparage other methods of political administration.
Secondly, it appears to belittle religion by restricting its
scope to the care of the poor, as if the other sections of
society were not of its concern. More than that, under the
shadow of its name, there might easily lurk a design to attack all legitimate power either civil or sacred. Wherefore,
since this discussion is now so widespread, so exaggerated
and so bitter, the consciousness of duty warns Us to put a
check on this controversy and to define what Catholics are to
think on this matter. We also propose to describe how the

movement may extend its scope and be made more useful to the commonwealth.

What *Social Democracy* is and what *Christian Democracy* ought to be, assuredly no one can doubt. The first, with due consideration to the greater or less intemperance of its utterance, is carried to such an excess by many as to maintain that there is really nothing existing above the natural order of things, and that the acquirement and enjoyment of corporal and external goods constitute man's happiness. It aims at putting all government in the hands of the people, reducing all ranks to the same level, abolishing all distinction of class, and finally introducing community of goods. Hence, the right of ownership is to be abrogated, and whatever property a man possesses, or whatever means of livelihood he has, is to be common to all.

As against this, *Christian Democracy*, by the fact that it is Christian, is built, and necessarily so, on the basic principles of divine faith, and provides for the betterment of the masses, with the ulterior object of availing itself of the occasion to fashion their minds for things which are everlasting. Hence, for *Christian Democracy* justice is sacred; it must maintain that the right of acquiring and possessing property cannot be impugned, and it must safeguard the various distinctions and degrees which are indispensable in every well-ordered commonwealth. Finally it must endeavor to preserve in every human society the form and the character which God ever impresses on it. It is clear, therefore, that there is nothing in common between *Social* and *Christian Democracy*. They differ from each other as much as the sect of Socialism differs from the profession of Christianity.

Moreover it would be a crime to distort this name of *Christian Democracy* to politics, for although democracy, both in its philological and philosophical significations, implies popular government, yet in its present application it is so to be employed that, removing from it all political significance, it is to mean nothing else than a benevolent and Christian movement in behalf of the people. For the laws of nature and of the Gospel, which by right are superior to all human contingencies, are necessarily independent of all modifications of civil government, while at the same time they are in concord with everything that is not repugnant to morality and justice. They are, therefore, and they must remain absolutely free from political parties, and have nothing to do with the various changes of administration which may occur in a nation; so that Catholics may and ought to be citizens according to the constitution of any State, guided as they are by those laws which command them to love God above all things, and their neighbors as themselves. This has always been the discipline of the Church. The Roman Pontiffs acted upon this principle, whenever they dealt with different countries, no matter what might be the character of their governments. Hence, the mind and the action of Catholics who are devoted to the amelioration of the working classes, can never be actuated with the purpose of favoring and introducing one government in place of another.

In the same manner, from *Christian Democracy*, We must remove another possible subject of reproach, namely: that while looking after the advantage of the working people they should act in such a manner as to forget the upper classes of society; for they also are of the greatest use in preserving and perfecting the commonwealth. As We have explained, the Christian law of charity will prevent Us from so doing. For it extends to all classes of society, and all should be treated as members of the same family, as children of the same heavenly Father, as redeemed by the same Saviour, and called to the same eternal heritage. Hence the doctrine of the Apostle who warns us that: "We are one body and one spirit called to the one hope in our vocation; one Lord, one Faith and one Baptism; one God and the Father of all who is above all, and through all, and in us all." Wherefore on account of the nature of the union which exists between the different classes of society and which Christian brotherhood makes still closer, it follows that no matter how great Our devotion may be in helping the people, We should all the more keep Our hold upon the upper classes, because association with them is proper and necessary, as We shall explain later on, for the happy issue of the work in which We are engaged.

Let there be no question of fostering under this name of *Christian Democracy* any intention of diminishing the spirit of obedience, or of withdrawing people from their lawful rulers. Both the natural and the Christian law command us to revere those who, in their various grades are above us in the State, and to submit ourselves to their just commands. It is quite in keeping with our dignity as men and Christians to obey, not only exteriorly but from the heart, as the Apostle expresses it, *for conscience' sake*, when he commands us to keep our soul subject to the higher powers. It is abhorrent to the profession of a Christian for any one to be unwilling to be subject and obedient to those who rule in the Church, and first of all to the bishops whom (without prejudice to the universal power of the Roman Pontiff) *the Holy Ghost has placed to rule the Church of God which Christ has purchased by His blood*.[1] He who thinks or acts otherwise is guilty of ignoring the grave precept of the Apostle who bids us to obey our rulers and to be subject to them, for they watch, having to give an account of our souls. Let the faithful everywhere implant these principles deep in their souls, and put them in practice in their daily life, and let the ministers of the Gospel meditate them profoundly, and incessantly labor not merely by exhortation but especially by example to make them enter into the souls of others.

We have recalled these matters which on other occasions We have made the subject of Our instructions, in the hope that all dissension about the name of *Christian Democracy* will cease and that all suspicion of any danger coming from what the name signifies will be put at rest. And with reason do We hope so; for neglecting the opinions of certain men, with regard to the power and the efficacy of this kind of *Christian Democracy*, which at times are exaggerated and are not free from error let no one however, condemn that zeal which, according to the natural and divine law, has this for its object, viz.: to make the condition of those who toil more tolerable; to enable them to obtain, little by little, those means by which they may provide for the future; to help them to practice in public and in private the duties which morality and religion inculcate; to aid them to feel that they are not animals but men, not heathens but Christians, and so to enable them to strive more zealously and more eagerly for the one thing which is necessary, viz.: that ultimate good for which we are all born into this world. This is the intention; this is the work of those who wish that the people should be animated by Christian sentiments and should be protected from the contamination of socialism which threatens them.

We have designedly made mention here of virtue and religion. For, it is the opinion of some, and the error is

[1] Acts xx. 28.

already very common, that the social question is merely an economic one, whereas in point of fact, it is above all a moral and religious matter, and for that reason must be settled by the principles of morality and according to the dictates of religion. For even though wages are doubled and the hours of labor are shortened and food is cheapened, yet if the working man hearkens to the doctrines that are taught on this subject, as he is prone to do, and is prompted by the examples set before him to throw off respect for God and to enter upon a life of immorality, his labors and his gain will avail him naught.

Trial and experience have made it abundantly clear that many a workman lives in cramped and miserable quarters, in spite of his shorter hours and larger wages, simply because he has cast aside the restraints of morality and religion. Take away the instinct which Christian virtue has planted and nurtured in men's hearts, take away prudence, temperance, frugality, patience, and other correct, natural habits, no matter how much he may strive, he will never achieve prosperity. That is the reason why We have incessantly exhorted Catholics to enter these associations for bettering the condition of the laboring classes, and to organize other undertakings with the same object in view; but We have likewise warned them that all this should be done under the auspices of religion, with its help and under its guidance.

The zeal of Catholics on behalf of the masses is especially noteworthy by the fact that it is engaged in the very field in which, under the benign inspiration of the Church, the active industry of charity has always labored, adapting itself in all cases to the varying exigencies of the times. For the law of mutual charity perfects, as it were, the law of justice, not merely by giving each man his due and in not impeding him in the exercise of his rights, but also by befriending him in case of need, "not with the word alone, or the lips, but in deed and in truth"; being mindful of what Christ so lovingly said to His own: "A new commandment I give unto you, that you love one another as I have loved you, that you love also one another. By this shall all men know that you are My disciples, if you have love one for the other." This zeal in coming to the rescue of Our fellow men should, of course, be solicitous, first for the imperishable good of the soul, but it must not neglect what is necessary and helpful for the body.

We should remember what Christ said to the disciples of

the Baptist who asked him: "Art Thou He that art to come or look we for another?" He invoked, as the proof of the mission given to Him among men, His exercise of charity, quoting for them the text of Isaias: *The blind see, the lame walk, the lepers are cleansed, the deaf hear, the dead rise again, the poor have the Gospel preached to them.*[2] And speaking also of the Last Judgment and of the rewards and punishments He will assign, He declared that He would take special account of the charity men exercised towards each other. And in that discourse there is one thing that especially excites our surprise, viz.: that Christ omits those works of mercy which comfort the soul and refers only to external works which, although done in behalf of men, He regards as being done to Himself. *For I was hungry and you gave Me to eat; I was thirsty and you gave Me to drink; I was a stranger and you took Me in; naked and you covered Me; sick and you visited Me; I was in prison and you came to Me.*[3]

To the teachings which enjoin the twofold charity of spiritual and corporal works, Christ adds His own example so that no one may fail to recognize the importance which He attaches to it. In the present instance we recall the sweet words that came from His paternal heart: *I have pity on the multitude,*[4] as well as the desire He had to assist them even if it were necessary to invoke His miraculous power. Of His tender compassion we have the proclamation made in Holy Writ, viz.: that *He went about doing good and healing all that were oppressed by the devil.*[5] This law of charity which He imposed upon His apostles, they in the most holy and zealous way put into practice; and after them those who embraced Christianity originated that wonderful variety of institutions for alleviating all the miseries by which mankind is afflicted. And these institutions carried on and continually increased their powers of relief and were the especial glories of Christianity and of the civilization of which it was the source, so that right-minded men never fail to admire those foundations, aware as they are of the proneness of men to concern themselves about their own and neglect the needs of others.

Nor are we to eliminate from the list of good works the

[2] Matt. xi. 5.
[3] Matt. xxv. 35.
[4] Mark vii. 2.
[5] Acts x. 38.

giving of money for charity, in pursuance of what Christ has said: *But yet that which remaineth, give alms.*[6] Against this, the Socialist cries out and demands its abolition as injurious to the native dignity of man. But if it is done in the manner which the Scripture enjoins, and in conformity with the true Christian spirit, it neither connotes pride in the giver nor inflicts shame upon the one who receives. Far from being dishonorable for man it draws closer the bonds of human society by augmenting the force of the obligation of the duties which men are under with regard to each other. No one is so rich that he does not need another's help; no one so poor as not to be useful in some way to his fellow man; and the disposition to ask assistance from others with confidence, and to grant it with kindness is part of our very nature. Thus justice and charity are so linked with each other, under the equable and sweet law of Christ, as to form an admirable cohesive power in human society and to lead all of its members to exercise a sort of providence in looking after their own and in seeking the common good as well.

As regards not merely the temporary aid given to the laboring classes, but the establishment of permanent institutions in their behalf, it is most commendable for charity to undertake them. It will thus see that more certain and more reliable means of assistance will be afforded to the necessitious. That kind of help is especially worthy of recognition which forms the minds of mechanics and labors to thrift and foresight so that in course of time they may be able, in part at least to look out for themselves. To aim at that is not only to dignify the duty of the rich towards the poor, but to elevate the poor themselves; for while it urges them to work for a better degree of comfort in their manner of living, it preserves them meantime from danger by checking extravagance in their desires, and acts as a spur in the practise of the virtues proper to their state. Since, therefore, this is of such great avail and so much in keeping with the spirit of the times, it is a worthy object for charity to undertake with all prudence and zeal.

Let it be understood, therefore, that this devotion of Catholics to comfort and elevate the mass of the people is in keeping with the spirit of the Church and is most conformable to the examples which the Church has always held up

6 Luke xi. 41.
7 Matt. vi. 2.

for imitation. It matters very little whether it goes under the name of *"The Popular Christian Movement,"* or *"Christian Democracy,"* if the instructions that have been given by Us be fully carried out with the submission that is due. But it is of the greatest importance that Catholics should be one in mind, will, and action in a matter of such great moment. And it is also of importance that the influence of these undertakings should be extended by the multiplication if men and means devoted to the same object.

Especially must there be appeals to the kindly assistance of those whose rank, worldly wealth, and culture give them importance in the community. If their help is excluded, scarcely anything can be done which will be of any assistance for the wants which now clamor for satisfaction in this matter of the well-being of the people. Assuredly the more earnestly many of those who are prominent in the State conspired effectively to attain that object the quicker and surer will the end be reached. We wish them to understand that they are not at all free to look after or neglect those who happen to be beneath them, but that it is a strict duty which binds them. For no one lives only for his personal advantage in a community; he lives for the common good as well, so that when others cannot contribute their share for the general object, those who can do so are obliged to make up the deficiency. The very extent of the benefits they have received increases the burden of their responsibility, and a stricter account will have to be rendered to God who bestowed those blessings upon them. What should also urge all to the fulfilment of their duty in this regard is the widespread disaster which will eventually fall upon all classes of society if this assistance does not arrive in time; and therefore is it that he who neglects the cause of the distressed poor is not doing his duty to himself or to the State.

If this social movement extends its scope far and wide in a true Christian fashion, and grows in its proper and genuine spirit, there will be no danger, as is feared, that those other institutions, which the piety of our ancestors have established and which are now flourishing, will decline or be absorbed by new foundations. Both of them spring from the same root of charity and religion, and not only do not conflict with each other, but can be made to coalesce and combine so perfectly as to provide by a union of their benevolent resources in a more efficacious manner against the

graver perils and necessities of the people which confront
us to-day.

The condition of things at present proclaims, and proclaims vehemently, that there is need for a union of brave
minds with all the resources they can command. The harvest
of misery is before Our eyes, and the dreadful projects of the
most disastrous national upheavals are threatening Us from
the growing power of the socialistic movement. They have
insidiously worked their way into the very heart of the State,
and in the darkness of their secret gatherings, and in the
open light of day, in their writings and their harangues, they
are urging the masses onward to sedition; they fling aside
religious discipline, they scorn duties and clamor only for
rights; they are working incessantly on the multitudes of the
needy which daily grow greater, and which, because of their
poverty, are easily deluded and hurried off into ways that
are evil. It is equally the concern of the State and of religion,
and all good men should deem it a sacred duty to preserve
and guard both in the honor which is their due.

That this most desirable agreement of wills should be
maintained, it is essential that all refrain from giving any
causes of dissension in hurting and alienating the minds of
others. Hence in newspapers and in speeches to the people,
let them avoid subtle and useless questions which are neither
easy to solve nor to understand except by minds of unusual
ability and only after the most serious study. It is quite natural for people to think differently in doubtful questions,
but those who address themselves to these subjects in a
proper spirit will preserve their mental calm and not forget
the respect which is due to those who differ from them. If
minds see things in another light it is not necessary to become alienated forthwith. To whatever opinion a man's
judgment may incline, if the matter is yet open to discussion
let him keep it, provided his mental attitude is such that he
is ready to yield if the Holy See should otherwise decide.

This Catholic action, of whatever description it may be,
will work with greater effect if all of the various associations,
while preserving their individual rights, move together under
one primary and directive force.

In Italy We desire that this directive force should emanate
from the Catholic Congresses and Reunions so often praised
by Us, to further which Our predecessor and We Ourselves
have ordered that these meetings should be controlled and
guided by the bishops of the country. So let it be for other

nations, in case there be any leading organization of this description to which this matter has been legitimately entrusted.

Now in all questions of this sort where the interests of the Church and the Christian people are so closely allied, it is evident what they who are in the sacred ministry should do, and it is clear how industrious they should be in inculcating right doctrine and in teaching the duties of prudence and charity. To go out and move among the people, to exert a healthy influence on them by adapting themselves to the present condition of things is what more than once in addressing the clergy We have advised. More frequently also in writing to the bishops and other dignitaries of the Church, and especially of late (to the Minister General of the Minorites, November 25, 1898) We have lauded this affectionate solicitude for the people and declared it to be the especial duty of both the secular and regular clergy. But in the fulfiment of this obligation let there be the greatest caution and prudence exerted, and let it be done after the fashion of the saints. Francis, who was poor and humble, Vincent of Paul, the Father of the afflicted classes, and very many others whom the Church keeps ever in her memory, were wont to lavish their care upon the people, but in such wise as not to be engrossed overmuch or to be unmindful of themselves or to let it prevent them from laboring with the same assiduity in the perfection of their own soul and the cultivation of virtue.

There remains one thing upon which We desire to insist very strongly, in which not only the ministers of the Gospel, but also all those who are devoting themselves to the cause of the people, can with very little difficulty bring about a most commendable result. That is to inculcate in the minds of the people, in a brotherly way and whenever the opportunity presents itself, the following principles, viz.: to keep aloof on all occasions from seditious acts and seditious men; to guard inviolate the rights of others; to show a proper respect to superiors; to willingly perform the work in which they are employed; not to grow weary of the restraint of family life which in many ways is so advantageous; to keep to their religious practices above all, and in their hardships and trials to have recourse to the Church for consolation. In the furtherance of all this, it is very efficacious to propose the splendid example of the Holy Family of Nazareth, and to advise the invocation of its protection, and it also helps to remind the people of the examples of sanctity which have shone in the midst of poverty, and to hold up before them the reward that awaits them in the better life to come.

Finally, We recur again to what We have already declared and We insist upon it most solemnly, viz.: that whatever projects individuals or associations form in this matter should be done with due regard to Episcopal authority and absolutely under Episcopal guidance. Let them not be led astray by an excessive zeal in the cause of charity. If it leads them to be wanting in proper submission it is not a sincere zeal; it will not have any useful result and cannot be acceptable to God. God delights in the souls of those who put aside their own designs and obey the rulers of His Church as if they were obeying Him; He assists them even when they attempt difficult things and benignly leads them to their desired end. Let them show also examples of virtue, so as to prove that a Christian is a hater of idleness and indulgence, that he gives willingly from his goods for the help of others, and that he stands firm and unconquered in the midst of adversity. Examples of that kind have a power of moving people to dispositions of soul that make for salvation, and have all the greater force as the condition of those who give them is higher in the social scale.

We exhort you, Venerable Brethren, to provide for all this, as the necessities of men and of places may require, according to your prudence and your zeal, meeting as usual in council to combine with each other in your plans for the furtherance of these projects. Let your solicitude watch and let your authority be effective in controlling, compelling, and also in preventing, lest any one under the pretext of good should cause the vigor of sacred discipline to be relaxed or the order which Christ has established in His Church to be disturbed. Thus by the correct, concurrent, and ever-increasing labor of all Catholics, the truth will flash out more brilliantly than ever, viz.: that truth and true prosperity flourish especially among those peoples whom the Church controls and influences: and that she holds it as her sacred duty to admonish every one of what the law of God enjoins to unite the rich and the poor in the bonds of fraternal charity, and to lift up and strengthen men's souls in the times when adversity presses heavily upon them.

Let Our commands and Our wishes be confirmed by the words which are so full of apostolic charity which the blessed Paul addressed to the Romans: "I beseech you therefore brethren, be reformed in the newness of your mind; he that giveth, with simplicity; he that ruleth, with carefulness; he that showeth mercy with cheerfulness. Let love be without dissimulation—hating that which is evil; clinging to that which is good; loving one another with the charity of brotherhood; with honor preventing one another; in carefulness, not slothful; rejoicing in hope; patient in tribulation; instant in prayer. Communicating to the necessities of the saints. Pursuing hospitality. Rejoice with them that rejoice; weep with them that weep; being of one mind to one another; to no man rendering evil for evil; providing good things not only in the sight of God but also in the sight of men."

As a pledge of these benefits receive the Apostolic Benediction which, Venerable Brethren, We grant most lovingly in the Lord to you and your clergy and people.

Chapter 2

A peace benefactor (1914-1922)

Benedict XV, on becoming pope on September 3, 1914,
before serving his long tenure
as a diplomat, arriving once Leo XIII and Cardinal Mariapolis
before becoming pope on September 3, 1914. His tragic
reign was given over to the problems of World War I, which
involved millions of Catholics on both sides. They naturally
guided him, that demonstrated his continuing concern as
the belligerents, and of refusing of unconditional sacrificial
head to peace. In the few years of his short Pontificate
(Gaspari, and his legalistic ... Cardinal
Mister Pope Pius XVII Benedict's role as ... reconciling
ing peace negotiations ... but none rejected it. He was
able to persuade both sides to a truce on Christmas Eve
during each of the war period and through the cooperation
of the neutral Swiss helped this to effect the exchange of
countless war prisoners, and to work for better care for the
wounded. He also helped establish an international organization for providing the families of lost soldiers with reliable
information. The three great demands of his reign are his
encyclical Ad Beatissimi (November 1, 1914), his historic
proposals for peace, Des le debut of August 1, 1917,
addressed to the belligerent peoples and to those leaders,
and the encyclical Pacem Dei munus of May 20, 1920 He
projected against the deprivation of French and Belgian
workmen to Germany, against German reprisals on prisoners
of war, against the bombardment of open towns and against

Chapter 2

✠

Benedict XV (1914-22)

BORN in Genoa on November 21, 1854, Giacomo della Chiesa was a nobleman who trained first as a lawyer before studying for the priesthood. He was then schooled as a diplomat, serving under Leo XIII and Cardinal Rampolla before becoming pope on September 2, 1914. His whole reign was given over to the problems of World War I, which involved millions of Catholics on both sides. Two principles guided him, that of maintaining strict neutrality toward all the belligerents, and of exploring all possibilities that might lead to peace. Through his secretary of state, Cardinal Gasparri, and his legate to Germany, Monsignor Pacelli (later Pope Pius XII) he offered both sides a basis for opening peace negotiations in 1917; but both rejected it. He was able to persuade both sides to a truce on Christmas Day during each of the war years; and through the co-operation of the neutral Swiss he was able to effect the exchange of countless war prisoners, and to work for better care for the wounded. He also helped establish an international organization for providing the families of dead soldiers with definite information. The three great documents of his reign are his encyclical *Ad Beatissimi* (November 1, 1914), his concrete proposals for peace, *Dès le début*, of August 1, 1917, addressed to the belligerent peoples and to their leaders, and the encyclical *Pacem Dei munus* of May 20, 1920. He protested against the deportation of French and Belgian workmen to Germany; against German reprisals on prisoners of war; against the bombardment of open towns, and against

71

the violations of international law by both Germany and Austria.

After the war, the pope was excluded from participating in the peace settlement, by a clause in the secret Treaty of London, made between the Allies and Italy in 1915, prior to Italy's entering the war.

Pope Benedict XV died of influenza on January 22, 1922.

AD BEATISSIMI*
Appeal for Peace

November 1, 1914

. . . It is not only the murderous struggle now going on that is ruining the nations, and filling Us with anxious alarm. There is another dreadful evil, which goes deep down in modern society, an evil that inspires fear in the minds of thoughtful men, because while it has already caused, and is threatening still to cause immense mischief to nations, it must also be recognised as the true source of the present deplorable conflict. Truly, as soon as the rules and dictates of Christian wisdom, which are the assured basis of stability and peace, came to be disregarded in the ordering of public life, the very structure of the State began to be shaken to its fall; and there has also ensued so great a change of thought and conduct, that, unless God comes to the rescue, the dissolution of human society itself would seem to be at hand. The more prominent disorders are these: the lack of mutual love among men; disregard for authority; unjust quarrels between the various classes; material prosperity become the absorbing object of human endeavor, as though there were nothing higher and better to be gained. These We regard as the four chief causes why the world is so terribly shaken. We must labour earnestly therefore, by putting in practice Christian principles, to remove such disorders from our midst, if indeed we have at heart the common peace and welfare. . . .

. . . Never perhaps was human brotherhood more preached

* Official translation. The Vatican Polyglot Press.

than now; nay, it is pretended that, without any help from the teaching of the Gospel, or from the work of Christ and the Church, the spirit of brotherhood has been one of the highest creations of modern civilisation. Yet the truth is that men never acted towards each other in less brotherly fashion than now. Race hatreds are becoming almost a frenzy; nation is divided from nation more by enmity and jealousy than by geographical position; in the same city, within the same walls, the different ranks are on fire with mutual envy; all take as their supreme law their own self-interest. . . .

ALLORCHÈ FUMMO
To the Belligerent Peoples and to Their Leaders*
July 28, 1915

. . . When We, though all unworthy, were called to succeed on the Apostolic Throne the meek Pius X, whose life of holiness and well-doing was cut short by grief at the fratricidal struggle that had just burst forth in Europe, We, too, on turning a fearful glance on the blood-stained battlefields, felt the anguish of a father who sees his homestead devastated and in ruins before the fury of the hurricane. And thinking with unspeakable regret of Our young sons, who were being mown down by death in thousands, We opened Our heart, enlarged by the charity of Christ, to all the crushing sorrow of the mothers, and of the wives made widows before their time, and to all the inconsolable laments of the little ones, too early bereft of a father's care. Sharing in the anxious fears of innumerable families, and fully conscious of the imperative duties imposed upon Us by the sublime mission of peace and of love, entrusted to Our care in days of so much sadness, We conceived at once the firm purpose of consecrating all Our energy and all Our power to the reconciling of the peoples at war: indeed, We made it a solemn promise to Our Divine Saviour, Who willed to make all men brothers at the cost of His Blood. . . .

* Official translation. The Vatican Polyglot Press.

In the holy name of God, and in the name of our heavenly Father and Lord, by the Blessed Blood of Jesus, Price of man's redemption, We conjure you, whom Divine Providence has placed over the nations at war, to put an end at last to this horrible slaughter, which for a whole year has dishonored Europe. It is the blood of brothers that is being poured out on land and sea. The most beautiful regions of Europe, this garden of the world, are sown with corpses and with ruin: there, where but a short time ago flourished the industry of manufactures and the fruitful labor of the fields, now thunders fearfully the cannon, and in its destructive fury it spares neither village nor city, but spreads everywhere havoc and death. You bear before God and man the tremendous responsibility of peace and war; give ear to Our prayer, to the fatherly voice of the Vicar of the Eternal and Supreme Judge, to Whom you must render an account as well of your public undertakings, as of your own individual deeds.

The abounding wealth, with which God, the Creator, has enriched the lands that are subject to you, allow you to go on with the struggle; but at what cost? Let the thousands of young lives quenched every day on the fields of battle make answer: answer, the ruins of so many towns and villages, of so many monuments raised by the piety and genius of your ancestors. And the bitter tears shed in the secrecy of home, or at the foot of altars where suppliants beseech—do not these also repeat that the price of the long-drawn-out struggle is great—too great?

Nor let it be said that the immense conflict cannot be settled without the violence of war. Lay aside your mutual purpose of destruction; remember that nations do not die; humbled and oppressed, they chafe under the yoke imposed upon them, preparing a renewal of the combat, and passing down from generation to generation a mournful heritage of hatred and revenge.

Why not from this moment weigh with serene mind the rights and lawful aspirations of the peoples? Why not initiate with a good will an exchange of views, directly or indirectly, with the object of holding in due account, within the limits of possibility, those rights and aspirations, and thus succeed in putting an end to the monstrous struggle, as has been done under other similar circumstances? Blessed be he who will first raise the olive-branch, and hold out his right hand to the enemy with an offer of reasonable terms of peace.

The equilibrium of the world, and the prosperity and assured tranquillity of nations, rest upon mutual benevolence and respect for the rights and the dignity of others, much more than upon hosts of armed men and the ring of formidable fortresses. . . .

DÈS LE DÉBUT
To the Belligerent Peoples and to Their Leaders*
August 1, 1917

. . . Since the beginning of Our Pontificate, in the midst of the horrors of the terrible war which has burst upon Europe, We have considered three things among others:

To maintain an absolute impartiality towards all belligerents, as becomes him who is the Common Father, and who loves all his children with an equal affection;

To endeavor continually to do the utmost good to all without distinction of persons, nationality or religion, in accordance not only with the universal law of charity, but also with the supreme spiritual duty laid upon Us by Christ; and

Finally, as is demanded by Our pacific mission to omit nothing, as far as in Our power lies, to contribute to hasten the end of this calamity by trying to bring the peoples and their leaders to more moderate resolutions in the discussion of means that will secure a "just and lasting peace."

Whoever has followed Our work during these three sorrowful years that have just ended has been able easily to recognize that, as We remained ever faithful to Our resolution of absolute impartiality and Our work of well-doing, so We have not ceased to exhort the belligerent peoples and Governments to become once again brothers, even though publicity was not given to all that We have done in order to attain this noble end.

Toward the end of the first year of war We addressed to the nations who are at grips the most earnest exhortations,

* Translation in John Eppstein, *The Catholic Tradition of the Law of Nations.* Washington, D.C.: The Catholic Association for International Peace, 1936, pp. 215–18. Published here with the permission of the Carnegie Endowment for International Peace.

and, further, We indicated the road to be followed in order to reach a peace which would be stable and honorable for all. Unhappily, Our appeal was not heard and the war continued desperately for another two years with all its horrors.

It became even more cruel, and spread upon the face of the earth, upon the sea, and even into the sky; and on defenseless cities, on tranquil villages, on their innocent populations, were seen to descend desolation and death.

And now anyone can imagine how the sufferings of all would be multiplied and aggravated if yet more months, or worse still, more years, were to be added to this blood-stained time. Must the civilized world be nothing more than a field of death, and shall Europe, so glorious and flourishing, rush to the abyss, as if dragged by some universal madness, and lend a hand in her own destruction? . . .

But that We may no longer limit Ourselves to general terms, as circumstances counseled Us in the past, We desire now to put forward some more concrete and practical propositions, and invite the Governments of the belligerents to come to some agreement on the following points, which seem to offer the bases of a just and lasting peace, though leaving to them the duty of adjusting and completing them: First of all, the fundamental point must be that the moral force of right shall be substituted for the material force of arms; thence must follow a just agreement of all for the simultaneous and reciprocal diminution of armaments, in accordance with rules and guarantees to be established here-after, in a measure sufficient and necessary for the maintenance, of public order in each State; next, as a substitute for armies, the institution of arbitration, with its high peace-making function, subject to regulations to be agreed on and sanctions to be determined against the State which should refuse either to submit international questions to arbitration or to accept its decision.

Once the supremacy of right is thus established, let all obstacles to the free intercourse of people be swept aside, in assuring, by means of rules, to be fixed in the same way, the true liberty of and common rights over the sea, which on the one hand would eliminate numerous causes of conflict, and, on the other, would open to all new sources of prosperity and progress.

As to the damage to be made good and the cost of the war, We see no other way of solving the question but to lay down, as a general principle, an entire and reciprocal con-

donation, justified moreover by the immense benefits which
will accrue from disarmament—the more so as the continuation of such carnage solely for economic reasons would
be inconceivable. If in certain cases there are, on the other
hand, particular reasons, let them be weighed justly and
equitably.

But these peaceful agreements, with the immense advantages which flow from them, are not possible without the
reciprocal restitution of territories at the moment occupied—
consequently, on the part of Germany, a total evacuation of
Belgium, with a guarantee of her complete political, military and economic independence, as against any other Power
whatever; similar evacuation of French territory; on the part
of other belligerent Powers a similar restitution of the German
Colonies.

As regards territorial questions—as, for instance, those
pending between Italy and Austria, and between Germany
and France—there is ground for hope that in view of the
immense advantages of a permanent peace with disarmament,
the disputants would feel disposed to examine them in a con-
ciliatory spirit, giving due weight, within the limits of justice
and feasibility, as We have said previously, to the aspirations
of the populations, and, on occasion, bringing their particular
interests into harmony with the general welfare of the great
community of mankind.

The same spirit of equity and justice must direct the examination of the remaining territorial and political questions, and particularly those which concern Armenia, the
Balkan States, and the territories which form part of the
former kingdom of Poland, which in particular, by reason of
her noble historical traditions and the sufferings endured,
especially during the present war, has a just claim on the
sympathies of all nations.

Such are the principal foundations on which We believe
that the future reorganization of the peoples must be built.
They are of a nature to make impossible the return of
similar conflicts, and to prepare the solution of the economic
question, which is so important for the material well-being
of all the belligerent States. . . .

Chapter 3

Pius XI (1922-)

A Ranuzzi V... in 1921 ... his doctorates in theology and canon law then became a curate in a country parish near Milan. Later librarian of the Ambrosian Library in Milan for thirty-eight years, he was an ecclesiastic important churchman ... was the first, but it was past the sport of science. ... from his titular diocese ... vicar of Bologna ... Pius XI, was nuncio, became nuncio ... Poland. ... 1921 and again Pius XI was most ...

... Christ, and he spoke to Cardinal Gasparri as Secretary of state, the first time a pope had taken at the apparatus of state of his predecessor. In 1929 he made his momentous move, Italy and the Vatican, by concluding the Treaty of the Lateran. He concluded peace treaties with Latvia, Poland, Estonia, Romania, Lithuania, Prussia, Spain, Germany, Austria, and Yugoslavia, and agreements with Portugal and Czechoslovakia. Diplomatic relations with Spain were improved, and a settlement about ecclesiastical property pending since 1904, and new Catholic universities were founded, as well as in Poland and Holland. He established a difficult Institute for Oriental studies and enlarged the significant importance of Leo XIII's Rerum Novarum with a new encyclical on labor questions, Quadragesimo Anno.

This pope early took the name Peter to the advantage of

Chapter 3

✠

Pius XI (1922-39)

A CHILLE Cardinal Ratti, who, as Pius XI, succeeded
Benedict XV in 1922, was born in Lombardy, the
fourth son of a silk weaver. Ordained in 1879, he took
his doctorates in theology and canon law then became a curate
in a country parish near Milan. Later librarian of the Ambrosian Library in Milan for thirty-eight years, he was an
enthusiastic mountain climber, and was the first Italian to
make the ascent of Monte Rosa from the Italian side.
Prefect of the Vatican Library from 1914 to 1918, when he
became nuncio to Poland, he became cardinal of Milan in
1921 and a year later was elected pope on February 6. He
chose as his motto "The peace of Christ in the reign of
Christ," and he kept on Cardinal Gasparri as his secretary of
state, the first time a pope had retained the secretary of state
of his predecessor. In 1929 he ended the impasse between
Italy and the Vatican by concluding the Treaty of the Lateran. He concluded concordats with Latvia, Poland, Bavaria,
Rumania, Lithuania, Prussia, Baden, Germany, Austria, and
Yugoslavia, and agreements with Portugal and Czechoslovakia. Diplomatic relations with France were improved (by
a settlement about ecclesiastical property pending since)
1904, and new Catholic universities were founded at Milan
and in Poland and Holland. He established pontifical institutes
for Oriental studies and celebrated the fortieth anniversary of
Leo XIII's *Rerum Novarum* with a new encyclical on labor
questions, *Quadragesimo Anno*.

This pope early faced the danger offered to the individual

soul and the human community by extreme nationalism, and condemned the *Action Française*, the organ of the French extreme right, in 1925. In *Non abbiamo bisogno* he made it clear that "no Catholic could be a genuine convinced Fascist," and on March 14, 1937, his encyclical *Mit brennender Sorge* denounced "the whole Nazi conception of life as utterly, and, necessarily, anti-Christian." *

Against the Soviet cruelities he was not less vehement, and in his great encyclical *Divini Redemptoris* of March 1, 1937, he made it abundantly clear that for the Catholic Church totalitarian regimes, whether of the right or of the left, are equally against that liberty which is man's first and greatest attribute, since it mirrors the divine liberty and is necessary to man for his pursuit of his true end. As Lord Acton put it, "When Christ said 'Render unto Caesar the things that are Caesar's and unto God the things that are God's' He gave to the civil power, under the protection of conscience, a sacredness it had never enjoyed, and bounds it had never acknowledged." These words were "the repudiation of absolutism and the inauguration of freedom. For our Lord not only delivered the precept, but created the force to execute it. To limit the power of the State became the perpetual charge of the universal Church," and of that supreme charge no pope has been more conscious than was Pius XI.

He died on February 10, 1939.

QUADRAGESIMO ANNO
On Reconstructing the Social Order †

May 15, 1931

Forty years have passed since Leo XIII's peerless Encyclical, *On the Condition of Workers*, first saw the light, and the whole Catholic world, filled with grateful recollection, is undertaking to commemorate it with befitting solem-

---

* Rev. Philip Hughes, *op. cit.*, p. 276.

† Translation in *Two Basic Social Encyclicals* (Washington, D.C.: Catholic University of America Press, 1943). Distributed by Benziger Brothers, New York.

nity. Other Encyclicals of Our Predecessor had in a way prepared the path for that outstanding document and proof of pastoral care: namely, those on the family and the holy Sacrament of matrimony as the source of human society, on the origin of civil authority and its proper relations with the Church, on the chief duties of Christian citizens, against the tenets of Socialism, against false teachings on human liberty, and others of the same nature fully expressing the mind of Leo XIII. Yet the Encyclical *On the Condition of Workers*, compared with the rest, had this special distinction that at a time when it was most opportune and actually necessary to do so, it laid down for all mankind the surest rules to solve aright that difficult problem of human relations, called "the social question."

For, toward the close of the nineteenth century, the new kind of economic life that had arisen and the new developments of industry had gone to the point in most countries that human society was clearly becoming divided more and more into two classes. One class, very small in number, was enjoying almost all the advantages which modern inventions so abundantly provided; the other, embracing the huge multitude of working people, oppressed by wretched poverty, was vainly seeking escape from the straits wherein it stood.

Quite agreeable, of course, was this state of things to those who thought it, in their abundant riches, the result of inevitable economic laws and, accordingly, as if it were for charity to veil the violation of justice which lawmakers not only tolerated but at times sanctioned, wanted the whole care of supporting the poor committed to charity alone. The workers, on the other hand, crushed by their hard lot, were barely enduring it and were refusing longer to bend their necks beneath so galling a yoke; and some of them, carried away by the heat of evil counsel, were seeking the overturn of everything, while others, whom Christian training restrained from such evil designs, stood firm in the judgment that much in this had to be wholly and speedily changed. . . .

. . . The Supreme Pastor, . . . grieving that so large a portion of mankind should "live undeservedly in miserable and wretched conditions," took it upon himself with great courage to defend "the cause of the workers whom the present age had handed over, each alone and defenseless, to the inhumanity of employers and the unbridled greed of competitors." He sought no help from either Liberalism or

Socialism, for the one had proved that it was utterly unable to solve the social problem aright, and the other, proposing a remedy far worse than the evil itself, would have plunged human society into greater dangers.

Since a problem was being treated "for which no satisfactory solution" is found "unless religion and the Church have been called upon to aid," the Pope, clearly exercising his right and correctly holding that the guardianship of religion and the stewardship over those things that are closely bound up with it had been entrusted especially to him and relying solely upon the unchangeable principles drawn from the treasury of right reason and Divine Revelation, confidently and *as one having authority*, declared and proclaimed "the rights and duties within which the rich and the proletariat —those who furnish material things and those who furnish work—ought to be restricted in relation to each other," and what the Church, heads of States and the people themselves directly concerned ought to do.

The Apostolic voice did not thunder forth in vain. On the contrary, not only did the obedient children of the Church hearken to it with marveling admiration and hail it with the greatest applause, but many also who were wandering far from the truth, from the unity of the Faith, and nearly all who since then, either in private study or in enacting legislation, have concerned themselves with the social and economic question. Feeling themselves vindicated and defended by the Supreme Authority on earth, Christian workers received this Encyclical with special joy. . . .

And so, with Leo's Encyclical pointing the way and furnishing the light, a true Catholic social science has arisen, which is daily fostered and enriched by the tireless efforts of those chosen men whom We have termed auxiliaries of the Church. . . .

Nor is the benefit that has poured forth from Leo's Encyclical confied within these bounds; for the teaching which *On the Condition of Workers* contains has gradually and imperceptibly worked its way into the minds of those outside Catholic unity who do not recognize the authority of the Church. Catholic principles on the social question have, as a result, passed little by little into the patrimony of all human society. . . .

Meanwhile, as Leo's teachings were being widely diffused in the minds of men, with learned investigations leading the way, they have come to be put into practice. In the first place, zealous efforts have been made, with active good-will, to lift up that class which, on account of the modern expansion of industry, had increased to enormous numbers but not yet had obtained its rightful place or rank in human society and was, for that reason, all but neglected and despised—the workers. . . .

With regard to civil authority, Leo XIII, boldly breaking through the confines imposed by Liberalism, fearlessly taught that government must not be thought a mere guardian of law and of good order, but rather must put forth every effort so that "through the entire scheme of laws and institutions . . . both public and individual well-being may develop spontaneously out of the very structure and administration of the State." Just freedom of action must, of course, be left both to individual citizens and to families, yet only on condition that the common good be preserved and wrong to any individual be abolished. The function of the rulers of the State, moreover, is to watch over the community and its parts; but in protecting private individuals in their rights, chief consideration ought to be given to the weak and the poor. . . .

However, in spite of such great agreement, there were some who were no little disturbed; and so it happened that the teaching of Leo XIII, so noble and lofty and so utterly new to worldly ears, was held suspect by some, even among Catholics, and to certain ones it even gave offense. For it boldly attacked and over-turned the idols of Liberalism, ignored long-standing prejudices, and was in advance of its time beyond all expectation, so that the slow of heart disdained to study this new social philosophy and the timid feared to scale so lofty a height. There were some also who stood, indeed, in awe at its splendor, but regarded it as a kind of imaginary ideal of perfection more desirable than attainable.

Our Predecessor of happy memory strongly defended the right of property against the tenets of the Socialists of his time by showing that its abolition would result, not to the advantage of the working class, but to their extreme harm. Yet since there are some who calumniate the Supreme Pontiff and the Church herself, as if she had taken and were still taking the part of the rich against the non-owning workers—certainly no accusation is more unjust than that—and since Catholics are at variance with one another concerning the true and exact mind of Leo, it has seemed best to vindicate this, that is, the Catholic teaching on this matter, from calumnies and safeguard it from false interpretations.

First, then, let it be considered as certain and established that neither Leo nor those theologians who have taught under the guidance and authority of the Church have ever denied or questioned the twofold character of ownership, called usually individual or social according as it regards either separate persons or the common good. For they have always unanimously maintained that nature, rather the Creator Himself, has given man the right of private ownership not only that individuals may be able to provide for themselves and their families but also that the goods which the Creator destined for the entire family of mankind, may, through this institution, truly serve this purpose. All this can be achieved in no wise except through the maintenance of a certain and definite order.

Accordingly, twin rocks of shipwreck must be carefully avoided. For, as one is wrecked upon, or comes close to, what is known as "individualism" by denying or minimizing the social and public character of the right of property, so by rejecting or minimizing the private and individual character of this same right, one inevitably runs into "collectivism" or at least closely approaches its tenets. Unless this is kept in mind, one is swept from his course upon the shoals of moral, juridical and social modernism. . . .

In order to place definite limits on the controversies that have arisen over ownership and its inherent duties, there must be first laid down as a foundation a principle established by Leo XIII: the right of property is distinct from its use. That justice called commutative commands sacred respect for the division of possessions and forbids invasion of others' rights through the exceeding of the limits of one's own property; but the duty of owners to use their property only in a right way does not come under this type of justice, but under other virtues, obligations of which "cannot be enforced by legal action." Therefore, they are in error who assert that ownership and its right use are limited by the same boundaries; and it is much farther still from the truth to hold that a right to property is destroyed or lost by reason of abuse or non-use. . . .

It follows from what We have termed the individual and at the same time social character of ownership that men must consider in this matter not only their own advantage but also the common good. To define these duties in detail, when necessity requires and the natural law has not done so, is the function of those in charge of the State. Therefore, public authority, under the guiding light always of the natural and divine law, can determine more accurately upon consideration of the true requirements of the common good, what is permitted and what is not permitted to owners in the use of their property. . . .

Labor, as Our Predecessor explained well in his Encyclical, is not a mere commodity. On the contrary, the worker's human dignity in it must be recognized. It, therefore, cannot be bought and sold like a commodity. Nevertheless, as the situation now stands, hiring and offering for hire in the so-called labor market separate men into two divisions, as into battle lines, and the contest between these divisions turns the labor market itself almost into a battlefield where face to face the opposing lines struggle bitterly. Everyone understands that this grave evil which is plunging all human society to destruction must be remedied as soon as possible. But complete cure will not come until this opposition has been abolished and well-ordered members of the social body —industries and professions—are constituted in which men may have their place, not according to the position each has in the labor market but according to the respective social functions which each performs. For under nature's guidance it comes to pass that just as those who are joined together by nearness of habitation establish towns, so those who follow the same industry or profession—whether in the economic or other field—form guilds or associations, so that many are wont to consider these self-governing organizations, if not essential, at least natural to civil society.

The teaching of Leo XIII on the form of political government, namely, that men are free to choose whatever form they please, provided that proper regard is had for the requirements of justice and of the common good, is equally applicable in due proportion, it is hardly necessary to say, to the guilds of the various industries and professions. Moreover, just as inhabitants of a town are wont to found associations with the widest diversity of purposes, which each is quite free to join or not, so those engaged in the same industry or profession will combine with one another into associations equally free for purposes connected in some manner with the pursuit of the calling itself. Since these free associations are clearly and lucidly explained by Our Predecessor of illustrious memory, We consider it enough to emphasize this one point: People are quite free not only to found such associations, which are a matter of private order and private right, but also in respect to them "freely to adopt the organization and the rules which they judge most appropriate to achieve their purpose." The same freedom must be asserted for founding associations that go beyond the boundaries of individual callings. . . .

Attention must be given also to another matter that is closely connected with the foregoing. Just as the unity of human society cannot be founded on an opposition of classes, so also the right ordering of economic life cannot be left to a free competition of forces. For from this source, as from a poisoned spring, have originated and spread all the errors of individualist economic teaching. Destroying through forgetfulness or ignorance the social and moral character of economic life, it is held that economic life must be considered and treated as altogether free from and independent of public authority, because in the market, that is, in the free struggle of competitors, it would have a principle of self-direction which governs it much more perfectly than through the intervention of any created intellect. But free competition, while justified and certainly useful, provided it is kept within certain limits, clearly cannot direct economic life—a truth which the outcome of the application in practice of the tenets of this evil individualistic spirit has more than sufficiently demonstrated. Therefore, it is most necessary that economic life be again subjected to and governed by a true and effective directing principle. This function is one that the economic dictatorship which has recently displaced free competition can still less perform, since it is a headstrong power and a violent energy that, to benefit people, needs to be strongly curbed and wisely ruled. But it cannot curb and rule itself. Loftier and nobler principles—social justice and social charity—must, therefore, be sought whereby this dictatorship may be governed firmly and fully. Hence, the institutions themselves of peoples, and particularly those of all social life, ought to be penetrated with this justice, and it is most necessary that it be truly effective, that is, establish a juridical and social order which will, as it were, give form and shape to all economic life. . . .

The civil authority itself constitutes the syndicate as a juridical personality in such a manner as to confer on it simultaneously a certain monopoly-privilege, since only such a syndicate when thus approved, can maintain the rights (according to the type of syndicate) of workers or employers, and since it alone can arrange for the placement of labor and conclude the so-termed labor agreements. Anyone is free to join a syndicate or not, and only within these limits can this kind of syndicate be called free; for syndical dues and special assessments are exacted of absolutely all members of every specified calling or profession, whether they are workers or employers; likewise all are bound by the labor agreements made by the legally recognized syndicate. Nevertheless, it has been officially stated that this legally recognized syndicate does not prevent the existence, without legal status, however, of other associations made up of persons following the same calling. . . .

With the diffusion of modern industry throughout the whole world, the "capitalist" economic regime has spread everywhere to such a degree, particularly since the publication of Leo XIII's Encyclical, that it has invaded and pervaded the economic and social life of even those outside its orbit and is unquestionably impressing on it its advantages, disadvantages and vices, and, in a sense, is giving it its own shape and form.

Accordingly, when directing Our special attention to the changes which the capitalist economic system has undergone since Leo's time, We have in mind the good not only of those who dwell in regions given over to "capital" and industry, but of all mankind. In the first place, it is obvious that not only is wealth concentrated in our times but an immense power and despotic economic dictatorship is consolidated in the hands of a few, who often are not owners but only the trustees and managing directors of invested funds which they administer according to their own arbitrary will and pleasure.

This dictatorship is being most forcibly exercised by those who, since they hold the money and completely control it, control credit also and rule the lending of money. Hence, they regulate the flow, so to speak, of the lifeblood whereby the entire economic system lives, and have so firmly in their grasp the soul, as it were, of economic life, that no one can breathe against their will.

This concentration of power and might, the characteristic mark, as it were, of contemporary economic life, is the fruit that the unlimited freedom of struggle among competitors has of its own nature produced, and which lets only the strongest survive, which is often the same as saying,

those who fight the most violently, those who give least heed
to their conscience.

This accumulation of might and of power generates in
turn three kinds of conflict. First, there is the struggle for
economic supremacy itself; then there is the bitter fight to
gain supremacy over the State in order to use in economic
struggles its resources and authority; finally, there is conflict
between States themselves, not only because countries employ
their power and shape their policies to promote every economic advantage of their citizens, but also because they seek
to decide political controversies that arise among nations
through the use of their economic supremacy and strength.

The ultimate consequences of the individualist spirit in
economic life are these: free competition has destroyed itself; economic dictatorship has supplanted the free market;
unbridled ambition for power has likewise succeeded greed
for gain; all economic life has become tragically hard, inexorable and cruel. To these are to be added the grave evils that
have resulted from an intermingling and shameful confusion
of the functions and duties of public authority with those of
the economic sphere. . . . And as to international relations,
two different streams have issued from the one fountain-
head: On the one hand, economic nationalism or even economic imperialism; on the other, a no less deadly and ac-
cursed internationalism of finance or international imperialism whose country is where profit is. . . .

Since the present system of economy is founded chiefly
upon ownership and labor, the principles of right reason, that
is, of Christian social philosophy, must be kept in mind in
theory regarding ownership and labor and their association together, and must be put into actual practice. . . .

MIT BRENNENDER SORGE

On the Present Position of the Catholic Church in the German Empire[*]

March 14, 1937

It is with deep anxiety and growing surprise that We have long been following the painful trials of the Church and the increasing vexations which afflict those who have remained loyal in heart and action in the midst of a people that once received from St. Boniface the bright message and the Gospel of Christ and God's Kingdom. . . .

When, in 1933, We consented, Venerable Brethren, to open negotiations for a concordat, which the Reich Government proposed on the basis of a scheme of several years' standing; and when, to your unanimous satisfaction, We concluded the negotiations by a solemn treaty, We were prompted by the desire, as it behooved Us, to secure for Germany the freedom of the Church's beneficent mission and the salvation of the souls in her care, as well as by the sincere wish to render the German people a service essential for its peaceful development and prosperity. Hence, despite many and grave misgivings, We then decided not to withhold Our consent, for We wished to spare the Faithful of Germany, as far as it was humanly possible, the trials and difficulties they would have had to face, given the circumstances, had the negotiations fallen through. . . .

. . . Whoever has left in his soul an atom of love for truth, and in his heart a shadow of a sense of justice, must admit that, in the course of these anxious and trying years following upon the conclusion of the concordat, every one of Our words, every one of Our acts, has been inspired by the binding law of treaties. At the same time, anyone must acknowledge, not without surprise and reprobation, how the other contracting party emasculated the terms of the treaty, distorted their meaning, and eventually considered its more or less official violation as a normal policy. The moderation We showed in spite of all this was not inspired by motives of

[*] Official English Text as issued by *The London Tablet*, 1937.

worldly interest, still less by unwarranted weakness, but merely by Our anxiety not to draw out the wheat with the cockle; not to pronounce open judgment, before the public was ready to see its force; not to impeach other people's honesty, before the evidence of events should have torn the mask off the systematic hostility leveled at the Church. Even now that a campaign against the confessional schools, which are guaranteed by the concordat, and the destruction of free election, where Catholics have a right to their children's Catholic education, afford evidence, in a matter so essential to the life of the Church, of the extreme gravity of the situation and the anxiety of every Christian conscience; even now Our responsibility for Christian souls induces Us not to overlook the last possibilities, however slight, of a return to fidelity to treaties, and to any arrangement that may be acceptable to the episcopate. We shall continue without failing, to stand before the rulers of your people as the defender of violated rights, and in obedience to Our Conscience and Our pastoral mission, whether We be successful or not, to oppose the policy which seeks, by open or secret means, to strangle rights guaranteed by a treaty. . . .

True Faith in God

Take care, Venerable Brethren, that above all, faith in God, the first and irreplaceable foundation of all religion, be preserved in Germany pure and unstained. The believer in God is not he who utters the name in his speech, but he for whom this sacred word stands for a true and worthy concept of the Divinity. Whoever identifies, by pantheistic confusion, God and the universe, by either lowering God to the dimensions of the world, or raising the world to the dimensions of God, is not a believer in God. Whoever follows that so-called pre-Christian Germanic conception of substituting a dark and impersonal destiny for the personal God, denies thereby the Wisdom and Providence of God. . . .

Whoever exalts race, or the people, or the State, or a particular form of State, or the depositories of power, or any other fundamental value of the human community—however necessary and honorable be their function in worldly things —whoever raises these notions above their standard value and divinizes them to an idolatrous level, distorts and perverts an order of the world planned and created by God: he is far from the true faith in God and from the concept of life which that faith upholds.

Beware, Venerable Brethren, of that growing abuse, in speech as in writing, of the name of God as though it were a meaningless label, to be affixed to any creation, more or less arbitrary, of human speculation. Use your influence on the Faithful, that they refuse to yield to this aberration. Our God is the Personal God, supernatural, omnipotent, infinitely perfect, one in the Trinity of Persons, tri-personal in the unity of divine essence, the Creator of all existence, Lord, King and ultimate Consummator of the history of the world, who will not, and cannot, tolerate a rival god by His side.

This God, this Sovereign Master, has issued commandments whose value is independent of time and space, of country and race. As God's sun shines on every human face, so His law knows neither privilege nor exception. Rulers and subjects, crowned and uncrowned, rich and poor, are equally subject to His word. From the fulness of the Creator's right there naturally arises the fulness of His right to be obeyed by individuals and communities, whoever they are. This obedience permeates all branches of activity in which moral values claim harmony with the law of God, and pervades all integration of the ever-changing laws of man into the immutable laws of God.

None but superficial minds could stumble into concepts of a national God, of a national religion; or attempt to lock within the frontiers of a single people, within the narrow limits of a single race, God, the Creator of the universe, King and Legislator of all nations, before whose immensity they are "as a drop of a bucket" (Isaiah xl, 15). . . .

Recognition of Natural Rights

Such is the rush of present-day life that it severs from the divine foundation of Revelation, not only morality, but also theoretical and practical rights. We are especially referring to what is called the natural law, written by the Creator's hand on the tablet of the heart (Rom. ii. 14) and which reason, not blinded by sin or passion, can easily read. It is in the light of the commands of this natural law, that all positive law, whoever be the lawgiver, can be gauged in its moral content, and hence, in the authority it wields over conscience. Human laws in flagrant contradiction with the natural law are vitiated with a taint which no force, no power can mend. In the light of this principle one must judge the axiom, that "right is common utility," a proposition which may be given a correct significance: it means that what is morally indefensible, can never contribute to the good of the people. But ancient paganism acknowledged that the axiom, to be entirely true, must be reversed and be made to say: "Nothing can be useful, if it is not at the same time morally good" (Cicero, De Off. ii. 30). Emancipated from this moral rule, the principle would in international law carry a perpetual state of war between nations; for it ignores in national life, by confusing right and utility, the basic fact that man as a person possesses rights he holds from God, and which any collectivity must protect against denial, suppression or neglect. To overlook this truth is to forget that the real common good ultimately takes its measure from man's nature, which balances personal rights and social obligations, and from the purpose of society, established for the benefit of human nature. Society was intended by the Creator for the full development of individual possibilities, and for the social benefits, which by a give and take process, everyone can claim for his own sake and that of others. Higher and more general values, which collectivity alone can provide, also derive from the Creator for the good of man, and for the full development, natural and supernatural, and the realization of his perfection. To neglect this order is to shake the pillars on which society rests, and to compromise social tranquillity, security and existence.

The believer has an absolute right to profess his Faith and live according to its dictates. Laws which impede this profession and practice of Faith are against natural law.

Parents who are earnest and conscious of their educative duties, have a primary right to the education of the children God has given them in the spirit of their Faith, and according to its prescriptions. Laws and measures which in school questions fail to respect this freedom of the parents go against natural law, and are immoral. The Church, whose mission it is to preserve and explain the natural law, as it is divine in its origin, cannot but declare that the recent enrolment into schools organized without a semblance of freedom, is the result of unjust pressure, and is a violation of every common right.

To the Youth

. . . If the State organizes a national youth, and makes this organization obligatory to all, then, without prejudice to rights of religious associations, it is the absolute right of youths as well as of parents to see to it that this organization is purged of all manifestations hostile to the Church and Christianity. These manifestations are even today placing Christian parents in a painful alternative, as they cannot give to the State what they owe to God alone.

No one would think of preventing young Germans establishing a true ethnical community in a noble love of freedom and loyalty to their country. What We object to is the voluntary and systematic antagonism raised between national education and religious duty. That is why We tell the young: Sing your hymns to freedom, but do not forget the freedom of the children of God. Do not drag the nobility of that freedom in the mud of sin and sensuality. He who sings hymns of loyalty to his terrestrial country should not, for that reason, become unfaithful to God and His Church, or a deserter and traitor to His heavenly country. You are often told about heroic greatness, in lying opposition to evangelical humility and patience. Why conceal the fact that there are heroisms in moral life? That the preservation of baptismal innocence is an act of heroism which deserves credit? . . .

To the Faithful of the Laity

We visualize the immense multitudes of Our faithful children, Our sons and daughters, for whom the sufferings of the Church in Germany and their own have left intact their devotion to the cause of God, their tender love for the Father of Christendom, their obedience to their pastors, their joyous resolution to remain ever faithful, happen what may, to the sacred inheritance of their ancestors. To all of them We send Our paternal greetings. And first to the members of those religious associations which, bravely and at the cost of untold sacrifices, have remained faithful to Christ and have stood by the rights which a solemn treaty had guaranteed to the Church and to themselves according to the rules of loyalty and good faith.

We address Our special greetings to the Catholic parents. Their rights and duties as educators, conferred on them by God, are at present the stake of a campaign pregnant with consequences. The Church cannot wait to deplore the devastation of its altars, the destruction of its temples, if an education, hostile to Christ, is to profane the temple of the child's soul consecrated by baptism, and extinguish the eternal light of the faith in Christ for the sake of counterfeit light alien to the Cross. Then the violation of temples is nigh, and it will be every one's duty to sever his responsibility from the opposite camp, and free his conscience from guilty cooperation with such corruption. The more the enemies attempt to disguise their designs, the more a distrustful vigilance will be needed, in the light of bitter experience. Religious lessons maintained for the sake of appearances, controlled by unauthorized men, within the frame of an educational system which systematically works against religion, do not justify a vote in favor of non-confessional schools. We know, dear Catholic parents, that your vote was not free, for a free and secret vote would have meant the triumph of the Catholic schools. Therefore, We shall never cease frankly to represent to the responsible authorities the iniquity of the pressure brought to bear on you and the duty of respecting the freedom of education. Yet do not forget this: none can free you from the responsibility God has placed on you over your children. None of your oppressors, who pretend to relieve you of your duties, can answer for you to the eternal Judge, when He will ask: "Where are those I confided to you?" May every one of you be able to answer: "Of them whom thou hast given me, I have not lost any one" (John xviii. 9). . . .

DIVINI REDEMPTORIS
On Atheistic Communism*

March 28, 1937

1. The promise of a Redeemer brightens the first page of the history of mankind, and the confident hope aroused by this promise softened the keen regret for a paradise which had been lost. It was this hope that accompanied the human race on its weary journey, until in the fullness of time the expected Saviour came to begin a new universal civilization, the Christian civilization, far superior even to that which up to this time had been laboriously achieved by certain more privileged nations.

2. Nevertheless, the struggle between good and evil remained in the world as a sad legacy of the original fall. Nor has the ancient tempter ever ceased to deceive mankind with false promises. It is on this account that one convulsion following upon another has marked the passage of the centuries, down to the revolution of our own days. This modern revolution, it may be said, has actually broken out or threatens everywhere, and it exceeds in amplitude and violence anything yet experienced in the preceding persecutions launched against the Church. Entire peoples find themselves in danger of falling back into a barbarism worse than that which oppressed the greater part of the world at the coming of the Redeemer.

3. This all too imminent danger, Venerable Brethren, as you have already surmised, is bolshevistic and atheistic communism, which aims at upsetting the social order and at undermining the very foundations of Christian civilization. . . .

8. The communism of today, more emphatically than similar movements in the past, conceals in itself a false messianic idea. A pseudo-ideal of justice, of equality and fraternity in labor impregnates all its doctrine and activity with a deceptive mysticism, which communicates a zealous and contagious

---

* Official translation. The Vatican Polyglot Press.

enthusiasm to the multitudes entrapped by delusive promises. This is especially true in an age like ours, when unusual misery has resulted from the unequal distribution of the goods of this world. This pseudo-ideal is even boastfully advanced as if it were responsible for a certain economic progress. As a matter of fact, when such progress is at all real, its true causes are quite different, as for instance the intensification of industrialism in countries which were formerly almost without it, the exploitation of immense natural resources, and the use of the most brutal methods to insure the achievement of gigantic projects with a minimum of expense.

9. The doctrine of modern communism, which is often concealed under the most seductive trappings, is in substance based on the principles of dialectical and historical materialism previously advocated by Marx, of which the theoreticians of bolshevism claim to possess the only genuine interpretation. According to this doctrine there is in the world only one reality, matter, the blind forces of which evolve into plant, animal and man. Even human society is nothing but a phenomenon and form of matter, evolving in the same way. By a law of inexorable necessity and through a perpetual conflict of forces, matter moves towards the final synthesis of a classless society. In such a doctrine, as is evident, there is no room for the idea of God; there is no difference between matter and spirit, between soul and body; there is neither survival of the soul after death nor any hope in a future life. Insisting on the dialectical aspect of their materialsm, the communists claim that the conflict which carries the world towards its final synthesis can be accelerated by man. Hence they endeavor to sharpen the antagonisms which arise between the various classes of society. Thus the class struggle with its consequent violent hate and destruction takes on the aspect of a crusade for the progress of humanity. On the other hand, all other forces whatever, as long as they resist such systematic violence, must be annihilated as hostile to the human race.

10. Communism, moreover, strips man of his liberty, robs human personality of all its dignity, and removes all the moral restraints that check the eruptions of blind impulse. There is no recognition of any right of the individual in his relations to the collectivity; no natural right is accorded to human personality, which is a mere cog-wheel in the communist system. In man's relations with other individuals,

besides, communists hold the principle of absolute equality, rejecting all hierarchy and divinely constituted authority, including the authority of parents. What men call authority and subordination is derived from the community as its first and only font. Nor is the individual granted any property rights over material goods or the means of production, for inasmuch as these are the source of further wealth, their possession would give one man power over another. Precisely on this score, all forms of private property must be eradicated, for they are at the origin of all economic enslavement.

11. Refusing to human life any sacred or spiritual character, such a doctrine logically makes of marriage and the family a purely artificial and civil institution, the outcome of a specific economic system. There exists no matrimonial bond of a juridico-moral nature that is not subject to the whim of the individual or of the collectivity. Naturally, therefore, the notion of an indissoluble marriage tie is scouted. Communism is particularly characterized by the rejection of any link that binds woman to the family and the home, and her emancipation is proclaimed as a basic principle. She is withdrawn from the family and the care of her children, to be thrust instead into public life and collective production under the same conditions as man. The care of home and children then devolves upon the collectivity.

Finally, the right of education is denied to parents, for it is conceived as the exclusive prerogative of the community, in whose name and by whose mandate alone parents may exercise this right.

12. What would be the condition of a human society based on such materialistic tenets? It would be a collectivity with no other hierarchy than that of the economic system. It would have only one mission: the production of material things by means of collective labor, so that the goods of this world might be enjoyed in a paradise where each would "give according to his powers" and would "receive according to his needs." Communism recognizes in the collectivity the right, or rather, unlimited discretion, to draft individuals for the labor of the collectivity with no regard for their personal welfare; so that even violence could be legitimately exercised to dragoon the recalcitrant against their wills. In the communistic commonwealth morality and law would be nothing but a derivation of the existing economic order, purely earthly in origin and unstable in character. In a word, the communists claim to inaugurate a new era and a new

civilization which is the result of blind evolutionary forces culminating in a "humanity without God."

13. When all men have finally acquired the collectivisit mentality in this Utopia of a really classless society, the political State, which is now conceived by communists merely as the instrument by which the proletariat is oppressed by the capitalists, will have lost all reason for its existence and will "wither away." However, until that happy consummation is realized, the State and the powers of the State furnish communism with the most efficacious and most extensive means for the achievement of its goal.

14. Such, Venerable Brethren, is the new gospel which bolshevistic and atheistic communism offers the world as the glad tidings of deliverance and salvation! It is a system full of errors and sophisms. It is in opposition both to reason and to divine Revelation. It subverts the social order, because it means the destruction of its foundations; because it ignores the true origin and purpose of the State; because it denies the rights, dignity and liberty of human personality. . . .

19. . . . Where communism has been able to assert its power—and here We are thinking with special affection of the people of Russia and Mexico—it has striven by every possible means, as its champions openly boast, to destroy Christian civilization and the Christian religion by banishing every remembrance of them from the hearts of men, especially of the young. Bishops and priests were exiled, condemned to forced labor, shot and done to death in inhuman fashion: laymen suspected of defending their religion were vexed, persecuted, dragged off to trial and thrown into prison. . . .

22. . . . For the first time in history we are witnessing a struggle, cold-blooded in purpose and mapped out to the least detail, between man and "all that is called God." Communism is by its nature antireligious. It considers religion as "the opiate of the people" because the principles of religion which speak of a life beyond the grave dissuade the proletariat from the dream of a soviet paradise which is of this world.

23. But the law of nature and its Author cannot be flouted with impunity. Communism has not been able, and will not be able, to achieve its objectives even in the merely economic sphere. It is true that in Russia it has been a contributing factor in rousing men and materials from the inertia of centuries, and in obtaining by all manner of means, often with-

out scruple, some measure of material success. Nevertheless We know from reliable and even very recent testimony that not even there, in spite of slavery imposed on millions of men, has communism reached its promised goal. After all, even the sphere of economics needs some morality, some moral sense of responsibility, which can find no place in a system so thoroughly materialistic as communism. Terrorism is the only possible substitute, and it is terrorism that reigns today in Russia, where former comrades in revolution are exterminating each other. Terrorism, having failed despite all to stem the tide of moral corruption, cannot even prevent the dissolution of society itself.

24. In making these observations it is no part of Our intention to condemn *en masse* the peoples of the Soviet Union. For them We cherish the warmest paternal affection. We are well aware that not a few of them groan beneath the yoke imposed on them by men who in very large part are strangers to the real interests of the country. We recognize that many others were deceived by fallacious hopes. We blame only the system, with its authors and abettors who considered Russia the best-prepared field for experimenting with a plan elaborated decades ago, and who from there continue to spread it from one end of the world to the other.

29. . . . In the plan of the Creator, society is a natural means which man can and must use to reach his destined end. Society is for man and not vice versa. This must not be understood in the sense of liberalistic individualism, which subordinates society to the selfish use of the individual; but only in the sense that by means of an organic union with society and by mutual collaboration the attainment of earthly happiness is placed within the reach of all. In a further sense, it is society which affords the opportunities for the development of all the individual and social gifts bestowed on human nature. These natural gifts have a value surpassing the immediate interests of the moment, for in society they reflect the divine perfection, which would not be true were man to live alone. But on final analysis, even in this latter function society is made by men, that he may recognize the reflection of God's perfection, and refer it in praise and adoration to the Creator. Only man, the human person, and not society in any form is endowed with reason and a morally free will.

30. Man cannot be exempted from his divinely imposed obligations toward civil society, and the representatives of authority have the right to coerce him when he refuses with-

out reason to do his duty. Society, on the other hand, cannot defraud man of his God-granted rights, the most important of which We have indicated above. Nor can society systematically void these rights by making their use impossible. It is therefore according to the dictates of reason that ultimately all material things should be ordained to man as a person, that through his mediation they may find their way to the Creator. . . .

33. In view of this organized common effort towards peaceful living, Catholic doctrine vindicates to the State the dignity and authority of a vigilant and provident defender of those divine and human rights on which the Sacred Scriptures and the Fathers of the Church insist so often. It is not true that all have equal rights in civil society. It is not true that there exists no lawful social hierarchy. . . . The enslavement of man despoiled of his rights, the denial of the transcendental origin of the State and its authority, the horrible abuse of public power in the service of a collectivistic terrorism, are the very contrary of all that corresponds with natural ethics and the will of the Creator. Both man and civil society derive their origin from the Creator, Who has mutually ordained them one to the other. Hence neither can be exempted from their correlative obligations, nor deny or diminish each other's rights. The Creator Himself has regulated this mutual relationship in its fundamental lines, and it is by an unjust usurpation that communism arrogates to itself the right to enforce, in place of the divine law based on the immutable principles of truth and charity, a partisan political program which derives from the arbitrary human will and is replete with hate. . . .

36. . . . It was Christianity that first affirmed the real and universal brotherhood of all men of whatever race and condition. This doctrine she proclaimed by a method, and with an amplitude and conviction, unknown to preceding centuries; and with it she potently contributed to the abolition of slavery. Not bloody revolution, but the inner force of her teaching made the proud Roman matron see in her slave a sister in Christ. It is Christianity that adores the son of God, made Man for love of man, and become not only the "Son of a Carpenter" but Himself a "Carpenter." It was Christianity that raised manual labor to its true dignity. . . .

38. It may be said in all truth that the Church, like Christ, goes through the centuries doing good to all. There would be today neither socialism nor communism if the rulers of the

nations had not scorned the teachings and maternal warnings of the Church. On the bases of liberalism and laicism they wished to build other social edifices which, powerful and imposing as they seemed at first, all too soon revealed the weakness of their foundations, and today are crumbling one after another before our eyes, as everything must crumble that is not grounded on the one corner stone which is Christ Jesus. . . .

39. . . . The most urgent need of the present day is therefore the energetic and timely application of remedies which will effectively ward off the catastrophe that daily grows more threatening. . . .

41. As in all the stormy periods of the history of the Church, the fundamental remedy today lies in a sincere renewal of private and public life according to the principles of the Gospel by all those who belong to the Fold of Christ, that they may be in truth the salt of the earth to preserve human society from total corruption.

43. . . . There is still much to be done in the way of spiritual renovation. Even in Catholic countries there are still too many who are Catholics hardly more than in name. . . . The Catholic who does not live really and sincerely according to the Faith he professes will not long be master of himself in these days when the winds of strife and persecution blow so fiercely, but will be swept away defenceless in this new deluge which threatens the world. And thus, while he is preparing his own ruin, he is exposing to ridicule the very name of Christian. . . .

51. . . . Now it is of the very essence of social justice to demand from each individual all that is necessary for the common good. But just as in the living organism it is impossible to provide for the good of the whole unless each single part and each individual member is given what it needs for the exercise of its proper functions, so it is impossible to care for the social organism and the good of society as a unit unless each single part and each individual member—that is to say, each individual man in the dignity of his human personality—is supplied with all that is necessary for the exercise of his social functions. If social justice be satisfied, the result will be an intense activity in economic life as a whole, pursued in tranquillity and order. This activity will be proof of the health of the social body, just as the health of the human body is recognized in the undisturbed regularity and perfect efficiency of the whole organism.

52. But social justice cannot be said to have been satisfied as long as workingmen are denied a salary that will enable them to secure proper sustenance for themselves and for their families; as long as they are denied the opportunity of acquiring a modest fortune and forestalling the plague of universal pauperism; as long as they cannot make suitable provision through public or private insurance for old age, for periods of illness and unemployment. . . .

54. If, therefore, We consider the whole structure of economic life, as We have already pointed out in Our Encyclical *Quadragesimo anno*, the reign of mutual collaboration between justice and charity in social-economic relations can only be achieved by a body of professional and interprofessional organizations, built on solidly Christian foundations. . . .

58. . . . Communism is intrinsically wrong, and no one who would save Christian civilization may collaborate with it in any undertaking whatsoever. Those who permit themselves to be deceived into lending their aid towards the triumph of communism in their own country, will be the first to fall victims of their error. . . .

75. It must likewise be the special care of the State to create those material conditions of life without which an orderly society cannot exist. The State must take every measure necessary to supply employment, particularly for the heads of families and for the young. To achieve this end demanded by the pressing needs of the common welfare, the wealthy classes must be induced to assume those burdens without which human society cannot be saved nor they themselves remain secure. However, measures taken by the State with this end in view ought to be of such a nature that they will really affect those who actually possess more than their share of capital resources, and who continue to accumulate them to the grievous detriment of others.

76. The State itself, mindful of its responsibility before God and society, should be a model of prudence and sobriety in the administration of the commonwealth. Today more than ever the acute world crisis demands that those who dispose of immense funds, built up on the sweat and toil of millions, keep constantly and singly in mind the common good. State functionaries and all employees are obliged in conscience to perform their duties faithfully and unselfishly, imitating the brilliant example of distinguished men of the past and of our own day, who with unremitting labor sacrificed their

all for the good of their country. In international trade relations let all means be sedulously employed for the removal of those artificial barriers to economic life which are the effects of distrust and hatred. All must remember that the peoples of the earth form but one family in God.

77. At the same time the State must allow the Church full liberty to fulfil her divine and spiritual mission, and this in itself will be an effectual contribution to the rescue of nations from the dread torment of the present hour. Everywhere today there is an anxious appeal to moral and spiritual forces; and rightly so, for the evil we must combat is at its origin primarily an evil of the spiritual order. From this polluted source the monstrous emanations of the communistic system flow with satanic logic. Now, the Catholic Church is undoubtedly pre-eminent among the moral and religious forces of today. Therefore the very good of humanity demands that her work be allowed to proceed unhindered. . . .

THE HIERARCHY'S RESPONSE

Excerpts from the comments of the French hierarchy on Divini Redemptoris *are included below:* *

Catholics and Communist Propaganda

THEY MUST AVOID IT AS FAR AS POSSIBLE

The Holy Office in its decision once again expressly warns Catholics against communist propaganda. Not only does it forbid them to participate in the editing or distribution of publications and newspapers which favor the policies or actions of the Communist Party, but it even forbids Catholics to read them. We consider it useful to emphasize the adequate reasons for this general prohibition, which the insidious tricks used by newspapers of the Communist Party to attract the Catholic masses have made necessary. In our country where the party assumes the appearance of a political party similar

* From *The Catholic Mind*, December, 1949, pp. 754–756.

to the others, it is to be feared that Catholics, because of their
desire to clarify their opinions as citizens and voters, may
allow themselves to become involved in too closely following
communist propaganda publications and in submitting, unwittingly, to their insidious arguments. If they know how to
yield, in a spirit of faith, to the decision of the Holy Office,
they will escape from this grave peril to their souls.

THEY MUST NOT COLLABORATE IN ANY WAY IN MANIFESTATIONS OF THIS PROPAGANDA

With all the more reason we hope, then, that no Catholic
may be found who, claiming to be an obedient son of the
Church, will nevertheless lend his aid to the numerous publications and public displays of communist propaganda. To
put at its service his reputation and talents as a writer or
speaker, be it in the field of literature, music or sports, is
to contribute to the maintenance of a dangerous confusion
by favoring the tactics of a party, the most adroit of all in
seducing minds.

DANGER VERY REAL

Be quite sure that, as much in France as in every other
country, the danger of communism is not imaginary. Against
it, our filial obedience to the dictates of the Sovereign Pontiff
will make us stronger. May the merits of our fidelity preserve
the Church in our country from the persecution which our
brothers in countries under the domination of communist
parties are enduring with such courage.

Meanings Not to Be Given to the Holy Office's Decree

Such are, dear brethren, the meaning and the scope of the
decree that the Holy Office has issued against communism.
No Catholic must allow himself to be led into the error of
giving it any other meaning if he wants to remain truly
obedient to the thought of his religious leaders.

The Church Is Not Embarking Upon An "Anti-communist Crusade"

A Catholic, therefore, will carefully refrain from saying

that, in the midst of the conflict in which the communist powers are pitted against the anti-communist powers, the Church has joined the ranks of one of the two sides. The Church refuses to enter into a "crusade" where so many rivalries and interests of the temporal and economic order are involved. The Church knows that such a course would compromise the purity of her mission, which is essentially spiritual. No more today than in the last world war does the Church desire that condemnations of a doctrinal nature, which she has had to issue against the dominant ideology of a state, constitute a weapon that she has given to one of the combatants to use against its enemy.

The Church Does Not Support Capitalism

In regard to the decree of the Holy Office, no Catholic should fall into that all too frequently conceived illusion that an unfavorable judgment by the Holy See on one doctrine signifies its approval of the opposing doctrine. By condemning the actions of communist parties, the Church does not support the capitalist regime. It is most necessary that it be realized that in the very essence of capitalism—that is to say, in the absolute value that it gives to property without reference to the common good or to the dignity of labor—there is a materialism rejected by Christian teaching. Whatever their rank in society or their power in the economic life of the various nations, Catholics whose pride of class or atttachment to worldy riches induces them to object to any change in the social structure are certainly not acting in the spirit of Jesus Christ. They are, without doubt, accomplices of the enemies of His Church and serve as the forerunners of communist revolution.

While Condemning Atheistic Communism, the
Church Shares the Anguish and Hopes of the
Working Class and, Faithful to Its Doctrine,
Earnestly Seeks to Serve the Workingman's Cause

We understand very well the suffering that could be felt by workingmen because of the condemnation of communism.

We know that they see in it, above all, an aggressive party resolved to suppress the social injustices from which they suffer and to give to workers their place as free men, in their professions as well as in civil life. We are also deeply moved by their misery and mean, with all our hearts, to rid them of their painful impression that the Church remains insensible to their sufferings and hopes. For such is not the case.

After, as before, the Holy Office's decree, the Church clearly takes their side in the social conflict. For more than fifty years now, the Popes have not ceased to teach that the status of workers under present working conditions is not just. It is not just under capitalism; it is no more just under communism, which does no more than concentrate in the hands of an all-powerful government the privileges it has taken from private capital. Man must not be an instrument for the profit of either private interests or the state. He must enjoy personal freedom, see his dignity as a worker respected and have his just share in the prosperity he helps to create.

That is why the Church does not cease to encourage priests and militant Christian workers who, in the Catholic Action movement and the Christian labor unions, are in contact with the spiritual and material needs of the working classes and who, as Cardinal Suhard, our colleague of most blessed memory, wrote shortly before his death, "share their uncertainties, their worries and their hopes."

Far from letting themselves be intimidated by the attacks leveled against the decree of the Holy Office, let workers be absolutely certain of this, and let them say so boldly: the Church, through her steadfastness against the communist error, wants to be the workers' best ally in their efforts to realize the ideals of the workers' cause. Indeed, the true value of men and the dignity of labor could not be found in a society where freedom does not exist. But without God, the origin and end of man, freedom is but an empty word. Atheism, which is at the root of communism, and which one finds as an active ferment wherever communist economic and social teachings have been realized, leads logically to the crushing of men. In sum, atheistic communism can offer to humanity no other ideal than the anthill, where the individual is destined to do a job whose why, how and wherefore he cannot see.

When the communist error will have lost the hold it has today on too many minds, humanity will recognize that the Church of Jesus Christ, heroically aligned against her persecutors, will have saved the true idea of man and his dignity.

The decree of the Holy Office, because it defends the truth, constitutes for Christians, and with them all men, a decisive act of liberation.

We renew to you, very dear brethren, the assurance of our paternal devotion in Our Lord.

ACHILLE CARDINAL LIENART,
Bishop of Lille;

PIERRE-MARIE CARDINAL GERLIER,
Archbishop of Lyon;

JULES CARDINAL SALIEGE,
Archbishop of Toulouse;

EMILE CARDINAL ROQUES,
Archbishop of Rennes.

The Australian hierarchy also commented on Divini Redemptoris. *Below are excerpts from their statement:* *

Socialization

The effect of the Second World War upon the people of every nation may be measured not only by the length of the casualty lists, but by the degree to which the normal economic life of entire communities has been dislocated. Material destruction in European countries has been so great that governments have been compelled to intervene in economic life to an extent heretofore unknown.

Even in countries like Australia, which have been spared the devastation visited on Europe, the war has given a strong impetus to the idea that the government should take a far more direct part in economic affairs. In some quarters, the claim has been made that the government should directly assume the ownership and control of the land and of industry. This claim has in turn given rise to a widespread demand that the teaching of the Church on this question should be set forth with greater clarity and detail.

In such a complex matter it is most important that the

* From *The Catholic Mind*, May, 1949, pp. 305–320.

terms which are used should be clearly defined. Words like "Communism," "Socialism," "Socialization," are used indiscriminately as if their meanings were identical. In reality their meanings differ.

Communism is a political philosophy which is based on materialism. Its economic aim is the complete control and operation of all the economic resources of the nation by the government and its agencies. Its political objective is the dictatorship of one party, achieved by the use of revolutionary violence, the destruction of all other parties and the suppression of all other political opinions.

Communism is completely opposed to Christianity and between the two there can be no compromise.

Socialism, in its strict sense, is a theory which advocates that the State should take over and operate the entire machinery of production, distribution and exchange. It differs from Communism in that its adherents generally believe that Socialism can be achieved by peaceful rather than by violent means.

Socialism in this strict sense has a Marxist basis and is repugnant to Christian social principles.

Socialization is a word to which two different meanings are commonly attributed.

By some it is defined in the same terms as Socialism has been defined in the preceding paragraph. Whether this theory is called "Socialization" or "Socialism" it is equally opposed to Christian social teaching.

On other occasions "Socialization" is held to mean State ownership of public utilities like the railways and the electricity supply, and State ownership or control of basic industries and monopolies which cannot safely be left in private hands.

In this latter usage of the term, "Socialization," as such, is not offensive to Christian principles.

LIMITS OF INTERVENTION

It should be made clear from the outset that the Church will always resolutely refuse to intervene in any matter which is purely political or purely economic. In the case of any projected law, where the aim which a government sets itself is morally sound, and where the political means by which it proposes to achieve that aim do not violate any moral principle, the Church will not intervene. Furthermore, the Church recognizes the complete freedom of her children to support or to oppose such a measure.

However, where a particular law goes beyond the limits of what is legitimate and moral; where a law tends to weaken or destroy the basic Christian institution of the family; where it attempts to arrogate all power to the State, at the expense of the human person, of the family, and of many smaller associations which men and women have freely formed so as to achieve legitimate objectives; then the Church has a duty to intervene, since the good of souls is endangered. By such laws man's earthly objective—to know, love and serve God —may be made more difficult and in some cases impossible of achievement.

For this reason the Church has constantly expounded the moral principles which must govern the social order. Successive Popes have explained the principles which must govern dealings between nations, relationships between governments and the governed, between employers and wage-earners, between trade unions, employers' associations and the community on the one hand, and their own members on the other. Pope Pius XII declared:

> By disposition of Divine Providence, the Catholic Church has formulated and promulgated its social doctrine. She points out the path to be followed, and no hope of achieving temporal gain, or fear of losing possessions, or of appearing less in harmony with modern civilization, or less national or social, could authorize true Christians to deviate even a hair's breadth from this path.[1]

Hence the teaching of the Church on the question of socialization springs not from temporary political considerations, but rather from the Church's vision of a social order which is in conformity with the nature and destiny of man.

The teaching of the Church in relation to socialization can be understood only if certain more fundamental principles are appreciated beforehand. It is necessary to depict the type of economy which the Church regards as normal. It is necessary also to understand the various forms which State intervention may take.

The proper aim of all legislation, of all social and economic measures and systems, is simply the public welfare. The public welfare is measured, however, not only by the economic wealth of the community, or of particular classes

---

[1] Address to College of Cardinals on Feast of St. Eugene, 1947, *Catholic Mind*, Aug. 1947, p. 454.

in it, but by social, moral and political considerations as well. In measuring the degree of well-being which exists within a community at any particular time the true Christian considers many factors:

Are the institutions of marriage and the family strong?

Are material goods equitably divided between the different classes, granted the functions which each performs?

Is religion a strong and vital force?

Is the human person free, and secure in the enjoyment of his inviolable rights?

The well-being of an individual is not measured only by his bank balance. In the same way all of these factors are at least equal in importance to the financial wealth of the community in measuring the common good.

Although the primary task of a government is to promote the common good, this does not mean that a government has either the duty or the right to regulate in detail the life of the individual or of the family. The task of the government is rather to secure the conditions in which both the individual and the family can fulfill their proper functions.

I. THE NORMAL ECONOMIC ORDER

The basic institution within the community is the family. The family comes before the State. One of the most important functions of the State is to assist the family to fulfill its purpose. "Since the family is the cornerstone of society, it should not be a temporary association bound to dispersion once the parents die and the children grow up. It must be a continuous factor, it must reckon its age not in years, but in generations. Yet the most firmly established family becomes dispersed very quickly, unless endowed with property handed down from father to son." [2]

The institution of the family defended by the Church is far removed, however, from the emasculated version to which the modern world has become accustomed. In Christian thought "the home is at once an economic and industrial center preparing goods for family use; a school in which the young are introduced to the universe; a sanctuary for rest and relaxation; a temple dedicated to the praise of God." [3] The only type of economic order which is acceptable to

[2] Dobozynski: *The Economics of Charity*, p. 41. (F. Mildner & Sons, London).

[3] Janet Kalven: *The Task of Women in the Modern World*, p. 9 (Pamphlet). Grailville, Loveland, Ohio.

Christians is one in which it is possible for family life to be regulated in accordance with this Christian ideal.

In the economic sphere, it is therefore a most important task of government to encourage that type of economic organization in which the family and the home may prosper. The normal economic order—that order which is best adapted to the real needs of mankind—is one in which the majority of men are working proprietors; that is to say, where they earn a living for themselves and their families by working their own property, whether that property is a farm, a shop, a workshop, or a factory. This is the best economic order precisely because the institution of the family is strongest while this system prevails.

This type of economic order may be adapted to enterprises which require more capital than one family can contribute. Where the amount of capital actually needed for the conduct of a business is greater than one man can supply, the necessary capital is best made up in the form of a partnership in which each of the partners has an effective share of control.

Where the technical equipment required for certain operations is so complex and expensive that small and medium-sized firms are unable to finance its purchase or operation—as for example in the assembling or other finishing processes of manufacture—co-operative enterprises operated by small firms operating in the industry appear to be the natural organizations to carry on the work.

The Church recognizes that even in the economic order which is thus organized on a Christian basis there will always be a certain proportion of wage-earners. These will be made up in part of young men who are working for others during the years before they marry and assume family responsibilities. This group may also recruit its members from those who do not wish to assume the obligations of ownership. The fact that there is a number of wage-earners in the community is not in itself a source of instability so long as this group does not become so numerous that society is substantially divided into two classes, as it is today; and so long as there are real and ample opportunities for those who wish to become working proprietors to do so.

TWO KINDS OF PROPERTY

While the Church desires that the working proprietor should become the characteristic figure of the nation's economy, it does not believe that all property should be in

private hands. Certain forms of property should be owned
and operated by public authorities, local or national. These
are the forms of property which "carry with them a
dominating power so great that they cannot, without grave
danger, be entrusted to private individuals." [4] Even in these
cases, however, it should not be supposed that the proper
controlling authority should always be the central government. Where these types of property can be operated by
municipalities, shires and regions, it is better that these
subordinate bodies should control them than that the central government should do so.

As one writer has well expressed it: "Essentially the State
will be one in which though a certain number will work for
employers, and a certain number for the government, the
principal type of work will be to make a living by using one's
own means of production; and those who work for employers, or for the government, will know that they can
readily obtain an opportunity for working as independent
proprietors if they wish. Emphatically it will not be recognized as the normal thing for the main body of the working
population to have to earn their living by working for employers (as under Capitalism) or for the Government (as
under Communism)." [5]

A PRACTICAL PROGRAM

This vision of a normal economic order has always been
presented by the Church as the aim which all peoples and
governments set themselves. It is advanced not as a Utopian
ideal but as a practical program. It is definitely opposed to
the system of industrial capitalism which the community
actually experiences today. It is definitely opposed to the
system promised by the exponents of Communism. It is
sound, both in principle and in practice.

The Church places such strong emphasis upon the private ownership, control and operation of productive property
for two reasons. In the first place, she regards a strong
family structure as the cornerstone of a Christian society
and of civic liberty. Secondly, she realizes that the ownership, control and operation of productive property is the
economic bastion of personal freedom and of a virile family
life.

[4] *Quadragesimo Anno*, America Press ed., p. 37.
[5] Colin Clark: *Property and Economic Progress*, p. 6.

It is precisely because the community has failed to establish a social order in which the ownership of productive property is so widespread as to set the "tone" of society, that the nation is riven by the great spasms of class warfare. The Supreme Pontiffs have never failed to point out that a community cannot be stable if in effect it is divided into two classes—the tiny few who control the vast bulk of the means of production, and the very many who own nothing.

The attitude of the Church to philosophies like Communism, which elevates class-warfare to a principle of action, has been made abundantly clear.[6] The Church, however, does not restrict its condemnation to the agents of revolution. At the same time she condemns in equal measure the social system of monopoly capitalism which has denied property to the masses and thus created the division of classes on which all class warfare is based.

NO DEFENSE OF INDUSTRIAL CAPITALISM

In defending the Church's demand that the ownership, control and operation of productive property should be extended as widely as possible, the present Pope, Pius XII, has not hesitated to condemn the economic principles of monopoly capitalism.

In his Fifth Anniversary Message, His Holiness uttered a strong rebuke not only to those who, like the Communists, deny the right of private property, but to those who, at the other extreme, hold that the right to private property is unlimited, and should not be subordinated to the common good.

With clear insight the Holy Father emphasized the evil results which follow when productive property is concentrated in the hands of the few, so that the worker is confronted with the "virtual impossibility of effectively acquiring private property of his own."

As a result of this development, said the Pope, "We see the small and medium proprietors lose their value in human society, and compelled to take part in an increasingly bitter struggle for existence, without hope of success." The fear of insecurity has led men to barter away their freedom, to "throw themselves at the feet of any political party, as slaves

6 See "Peace in Industry" (Social Justice Statement, 1947).

to anyone who might promise them, in some way, bread and
security."

In conclusion the Holy Father made it clear that the
Church's defense of private property was not to be inter-
preted as a defense of capitalism:

> In defending the principle of private property, the Church
> pursues a high ethical and social purpose. She does not in-
> tend to defend the present state of affairs, absolutely and
> simply, as if she saw in it the expression of God's will, or to
> defend as a matter of principle the rich and the plutocrats
> against the poor and the needy. . . .[7]

The Church desired that the large majority of families
rather than a tiny minority should own productive property,
since this ownership was in itself an "incentive to work to
the achievement of life's purpose here and hereafter, and
an instrument of the liberty and dignity of man."[8]

This, then, is the kernel of the Christian social program
—the development of an economic system in which great
numbers of individual men, now without a stake in the
country, shall again become the owners, controllers and the
operators of productive property, be it in the form of a farm,
a shop, a workshop or a factory.

"Christian thought" declares the present Pontiff, "insists
. . . on the rehabilitation of the proletariat."[9]

II. ECONOMIC POLICY OF A CHRISTIAN STATE

In our day it is commonly believed that the "iron law" of
economics makes bigger farms and larger factories inevitable
because these productive units alone are efficient. Nevertheless, an examination of the true position provides justification for those who propose that the class of working proprietors should be strengthened, as the stronghold of true freedom in the life of the community.

The fact that the class of independent proprietors is particularly strong in the sphere of agriculture is so commonly
known as to need little further exposition. In Australia, there
are some hundreds of thousands of farmers owning and
operating their own farms. It is true that the stability of

[7] Pius XII, Fifth Anniversary Message. cf. *Catholic Mind*, Oct.,
1944, p. 580.

[8] *Ibid.*

[9] *Ibid.*

this class of farm owners is imperiled by many factors [10] particularly by the overwhelming political and economic power of big cities. Yet, throughout the world, its members have proved enduring and resourceful in the face of their many enemies.

The Holy Father has pointed out that the holding "on which the family lives and from the products of which it draws all or part of its subsistence," [11] is the most perfect form of private property. It is the family holding alone which provides the permanent bond joining together different generations of the same family.

Accordingly, it is a primary duty of public authorities to encourage agriculture and to create all the conditions in which the small agricultural holdings can flourish and extend. This may well involve drastic legal and financial measures, and a display of moral strength in face of a public opinion which is accustomed to think of progress almost exclusively in terms of more industries and of bigger cities. Yet it is well to remember that no civilization has endured which has allowed its tradition of land husbandry to be destroyed.

WORKING PROPRIETORSHIP IN MANUFACTURE

Recent official figures issued by the Commonwealth Statistician indicate that more than 22,000 working proprietors are actively occupied in manufacturing industries. Approximately 29,000 factories were in operation in the year 1945; of these no less than 23,000 employed twenty workers or less. [12]

These facts are brought forward to dispose of the belief that the working proprietor and the small industrial units are outdated, and that industrial efficiency demands the large industrial unit and the complex apparatus of the highly capitalized company. In fact, despite all the political, economic, legal and social advantages which large-scale industry has enjoyed for many years past, the working proprietor and the small industrial unit play a most important part in the economic life of the Commonwealth.

NON-ECONOMIC FACTORS

Nevertheless, the trend to big industry still exists. Yet it

[10] See "The Land Is Your Business." (Social Justice Statement, 1945).

[11] Pius XII: "La Solennita," *Catholic Mind*, June 8, 1941, p. 13.

[12] "Production." Bulletin No. 39. Part 1 (1944-5) p. 21.

is clear that this trend is due more to legal, social and political advantages—capable of being controlled and countered
—than to the strict demands of economic efficiency.

Every kind of production has its "natural" dimensions.
When the financial and technical requirements of the industries concerned are examined, there seems no valid reason
why the majority of manufactured goods needed in every-
day life should not be manufactured in small and medium-
sized workshops. "Clothing, textiles, shoes, hosiery, laces,
millinery; toilet articles, household-ware, pottery, furniture,
prints, baking and confectionery, tinned food, electrical and
wireless gear, watches, articles of small engineering, chemical
products such as soap, pastes, shoe polish and so on," [13]
are typical of the manufactures which can be produced
economically by small firms.

The public authorities should neither set up huge industrial concerns to produce these commodities nor permit
their production to fall into the hands of large-scale private
industrial enterprises.

As time passes, an ever-greater proportion of the working
population is employed in industries of this type. It is precisely in this field that small and medium-sized enterprises
can operate efficiently.

In this field it is only the "assembling" or "finishing" processes of manufacturing which may prove unsuitable for
small-scale operation. In principle it is better that these processes should be conducted by co-operatives of producers
already in the industry rather than by private big business or
by the State. The suggestion that co-operative associations
should be developed to serve as the buttress of small industry
was made by the present Holy Father in July, 1947.[14] Examples of this type of co-operative organization already exist in
Europe, for instance in the manufacture of optical glass.[15]

The possibility of organizing many of the "finishing" and
"assembling" processes of manufacture by means of producers' co-operatives is proved by the experience of the
Australian engineering industry in war and peace. The largest
corporations undertake huge projects—the manufacturer of
motor vehicles, or refrigerators and similar complex products.

[13] Dobozynski: *The Economics of Charity.* (p. 82).

[14] Pius XII: Letter to Charles Flory, *Catholic Mind,* Nov. 1947,
p. 681.

[15] Paul Derrick: *Lost Property,* p. 40. (Dobson, London).

In many cases the manufacture of the constituent parts of these articles is "contracted out" to small firms. These small "sub-contractors" return the individual part to the large corporation, which assembles and markets the product.

This method of production indicates that the small firms can function effectively in an industrial society. Under the present system, however, small firms are scarcely independent. They function in a state of economic servitude to the big corporations, which also absorb the greater proportion of the profit of manufacture.

At present the large corporation carries out three essential functions. It organizes the work; it performs the assembling and finishing processes; it markets the product. These functions can be carried out equally well by co-operative organizations of small producers financed by their own co-operative industrial banks.

By wise and prudent action, the State, as guardian of the common good, can ensure that this substantial and growing sector of the nation's economy shall be restored to the working proprietor, to the craftsman, and to the small industrial unit. In this endeavor it will have the support of the Church, because such a policy follows logically from the natural law. In the words of the present Holy Father:

> The small workshops of the craftsmen still preserve their family character. The relationship between the Church and the small craftsman has a basis . . . deeper and more essential than the mere fact that they have been associated throughout history. For the Church wishes to impose a definite limit on the subordination of Man to the Machine.
>
> Small craftsmen as a class may be regarded as a militia chosen to defend the personal dignity and character of the worker, But, for more than a century, they have had to fight for their existence against great industrial enterprises. In this struggle, the small craftsmen have shown strength, resistance, vigor and life. Even in the most heavily industrialized regions, where great factories are found in abundance, they have gained new ground. The small craftsman can look to the future with a true sense of confidence.[16]

INTERVENTION BY THE STATE

It is one of the duties of the government to supervise the

---

[16] Pius XII: Address to the First National Congress of the Christian Association of Small Craftsmen. (Oct. 1947).

economic life of the nation. It should intervene to break down monopoly and the concentration of the means of production in few hands wherever these factors exist, and wherever they are not technically indispensable. This is the primary form which government intervention should take.

The necessity for measures of this kind is apparent in view of the growing degree of concentration of industry. Although the relatively large number of working proprietors and of small workshops indicates both the desire and the ability of "small" men to operate industrial enterprises, in recent times the trend has been to the larger factory. Employing wage-labor on a large scale, these units are conducted not by working proprietors but by impersonal companies with their complex apparatus of shareholders, boards of directors, managers, technicians and other salaried officers.

DRIFT TO MONOPOLY

Should the present trend continue, the healthy developments which we have already noted will not only be stifled, but the Australian economy may, with disastrous results, become a replica of the American economy, which is dominated by huge companies, trusts and combines.

It will be an evil day for our nation when an Australian statesman is able to describe our economy in the words with which the late President Roosevelt characterized the economic structure of his own country. In 1933 he wrote:

> Our economic life is dominated by some six hundred odd corporations, which control two-thirds of American industry. Ten million small businessmen divide the other third. More striking still, it appears that if the process of concentration goes on at the same rate, at the end of the century we shall have all American industry controlled by a dozen corporations and run by perhaps a hundred men.[17]

In this condition of monopoly, it will be useless for businessmen in particular, and for the community in general, to bemoan the decline of "free enterprise" and the taking over of industry by the State. "Free enterprise" will have been effectively destroyed already and the community will see no moral evil in the substitution of government monopoly for private monopoly.

[17] Franklin D. Roosevelt: *Looking Forward*, p. 31. (Day, New York).

CONCENTRATION NOT INEVITABLE

It is not true that this concentration of ownership is inevitable, and that nothing can be done to avoid the domination of the life of men by the huge enterprise and the great machine. Pope Pius XI, in his great Encyclical *Quadragesimo Anno*, listed the causes which led to these serious developments in the social order, under the following heads: concentration of men's attention upon business to the exclusion of all else; speculation; the abuses of the company form under which modern business is generally organized; excessive advertising.[18]

REMEDIES

The first of these ills—namely the focusing of men's attention exclusively upon business and money-making—can only be cured by spiritual remedies. No man can be truly a Christian and at the same time act as if business came first in his life and business relationships were outside the moral law. It is the task of the Church constantly to recall to all men engaged in economic life that their true purpose in life extends beyond business. It is her duty to warn them that an exaggerated devotion to business is, in itself, a form of materialism which cannot be reconciled with the Christian spirit.

The other factors named by the Holy Father must, however, be countered by the wise laws of the public authority.

CORPORATIONS

A limit must be placed on the operation of business by public companies. "Only too often," declared Pope Pius XI, "by hiding under the shelter of a joint name, the worst of injustices and frauds are perpetrated; and . . . directors of business companies, forgetful of their trust, betray the rights of those whose savings they have undertaken to administer." [19]

Existing laws encouraging the organization of public companies encourage the concentration of productive property into fewer and fewer hands. A person who in one way or another has amassed savings which he should invest in business operations of his own, only too often surrenders the

---

[18] *Quadragesimo Anno*, p. 43.
[19] *Ibid.*

active control of his property by purchasing shares in public companies. He thus diminishes his own status as a man and at the same time inordinately increases the power of a small class of financiers and administrators. These, even if they are not nominally the owners of the property which they administer, are in fact its real controllers.

The strongest measures of all should be taken against the technique of the "holding" company which enables the same group of men to spread their control over many fields of production.

The energies of the State authority should be directed not only to corporate organizations which might come into existence in the future, but to those bodies which already exist, and which are already spreading their hold. A limit must be placed on the number and variety of enterprises which one individual or one group is permitted to conduct.

THE PROBLEM OF EXCESSIVE ADVERTISING

In his Encyclical letter *Quadragesimo Anno* the late Holy Father directed his attention to the problem of advertising in the modern world—and none too soon.[20] Much modern advertising places a premium on dishonesty. Modern advertising too often trades in immorality and preys on man's baser passions. The millions of pounds which are spent annually on advertising even in a relatively small industrial community like our own add substantially to the cost of living. In addition, great corporate enterprises use the immense funds at their disposal to secure a nation-wide distribution for their goods, thus limiting local markets for the products of smaller enterprises. It is difficult to find moral or even economic justification for the structure of modern advertising.

In a Christian society, there will be a place only for certain small varieties of advertising. At the present time, advertising expenditure is an "allowable deduction" under the taxation laws. If it were removed from this category, the first and most obvious step towards a solution of this problem would have been taken.

SCIENTIFIC RESEARCH FOR SMALL PRODUCERS

The State can powerfully assist the widespread diffusion of productive property by organizing bureaus of scientific

[20] *Quadragesimo Anno*, p. 43.

research, especially for small producers. With the vast funds which they control, the great public companies are able to develop their own scientific research organizations and almost to monopolize the economic benefits of human invention. The small producers alone are unable to afford similar facilities.

It is the task of the State to supply this deficiency to ensure that modern technical processes such as electric power, which can so greatly assist the spread of small industry, are not transformed into buttresses of large-scale production.

This then is the primary kind of intervention in economic life which the public authority should undertake—to free the community from the fetters of giant industrial concerns, to allow the working proprietor to function as the normal unit of our economy, to provide a framework in which the small industrial unit can flourish and expand.

Over the major portion of economic life this is a better type of intervention than nationalization. For nationalization of an industry in itself does not alter the status of the workers employed in it. They still remain in the proletarian condition in which they were before the industry was taken over by the State.

III. THE SPHERE OF NATIONALIZATION

In the light of this general statement of the principles which should govern the distribution of property in our present-day community, the attitude of the Church to the general question of nationalization can be more easily understood. By nationalization, we mean the specific act whereby the government compulsorily substitutes public ownership for private ownership in a particular industry.

Normally it is not the function of the government to engage in business. We recognize, however, that we are living in abnormal times. The disorder in our economic life has progressed to such a degree that the government is called upon to fulfill many functions which would be alien to it in a Christian economic order. Furthermore, it is clear that the needs of Australian development in the past have justified a greater degree of direct business activity on the part of the public authority than would be considered desirable in other countries. Our immense areas, our tiny population, the weakness of private economic resources made it inevitable that the government should develop communications and utilities which, in other countries, have been developed by private interest.

The following governing principles concerning nationalization are therefore set down for the guidance of Catholics:

WRONG IN PRINCIPLE

A. While the nationalization of certain industries may be justified under certain conditions, it is quite clear that the nationalization of all the means of production is absolutely wrong in principle and cannot be held by Catholics. It is equally wrong whether its achievement is proposed by peaceful or by violent means, whether it is to be achieved piecemeal or at one stage.

Not only would a system based on such a principle destroy the economic basis of family life; but, as is shown by the bitter experience of the totalitarian nations, it woud be accompanied by the complete destruction of human freedom. Wholesale nationalization is the economic basis of a totalitarian tyranny.

In our own times, the complete nationalization of the means of production is the economic basis of the barbaric tyranny which prevails in the Soviet Union. Again, in the case of Nazi Germany, while the expedient of complete nationalization was not adopted, the overwhelming power of the pagan State was built upon the merciless destruction of the class of artisans and small farmers, and the concentration of all economic power in the government.

B. A system which, while avoiding complete nationalization, extends public ownership far beyond what is required by the common good, is opposed to Christian teaching.

An official publication of the Labor Party of Great Britain, "A Guide to the Elements of Socialism," illustrates how a statement of principle which is quite compatible with the social doctrines of Christianity may be applied in a way which is totally out of harmony with the Christian tradition.

"Socialists," declares this publication, "are fully prepared to recognize private property in the means of production where that is the best way of providing for the use of resources for the general benefit, and on condition that it is not made a means to the exploitation of labor or monopoly at the consumers' expense. Socialists do not want to 'nationalize' all industries and services, but only those which it is necessary to bring under public ownership in the general interest." [21]

As a statement of principle this is in accord with Christian doctrine. Yet when this principle is applied to concrete instances, it is held to justify "public ownership and operation" not only of banks, insurance companies, public utilities and of basic industries like iron and steel, but of the land itself, of road transport, the major part of housing construction, the boot and shoe industry, among others.[22]

It is quite clear that in these latter cases the precise method by which the government should intervene should not be nationalization, but the dispersion of ownership, in the manner which has already been indicated. The nationalization of industries which are capable of being conducted in small units cannot be reconciled with Christian thought.

As far as the land is concerned, whether the legal title granted by the State is freehold or leasehold, the individual is entitled to possess certain rights over a quantity of land sufficient to provide a secure living for himself and his family. These rights include the right to use one's land freely but in accordance with the canons of good husbandry, the right to sell the land at a fair price, varying with the improvements made to it but not necessarily including a speculative profit, and the right to bequeath the property to one's heirs. So long as these conditions are preserved, it matters little whether the tenure under which they are enjoyed is entitled freehold or leasehold.

Today, even in certain democratic countries, nationalization is being carried beyond the bounds laid down by the moral law. It is becoming apparent even to Socialists, however, that a democracy which is limited to the political sphere provides no necessary guarantee of real freedom once the government begins to monopolize economic power. It is becoming apparent that such a system can operate only when there is open or hidden "direction of labor" or "industrial conscription." Under such a system the worker is deprived of his inalienable right freely to choose his vocation. Under these circumstances, the freedom of the person is an illusion; and the family becomes in fact the serf or chattel of the State.

[21] G. D. H. Cole: "A Guide to the Elements of Socialism" (p. 4).
[22] Ibid, p. 4.

PUBLIC CONTROL

C. The Church recognizes that, under present conditions, there are certain forms of enterprise and industry which are of quite extraordinary importance to the community, and which may legitimately come under public control in one form or another, although not necessarily by means of nationalization.

Among these are banking and insurance; the manufacture of steel and heavy chemicals; rail, sea and air transport; public utility services (electricity, gas, tramways); armaments. The public utility services and a section of the transport industry are already generally under some form of public control in Australia, whether operated by Federal, State or by municipal bodies. The other industries are, at the moment, generally owned and operated by great private corporations.

Some of these concerns are no doubt efficiently conducted, but the question of efficiency is of secondary importance only. These are the industries which, if they remain in the hands of uncontrolled private bodies, confer upon those bodies the "dominating power" referred to by Pius XI. This power is "so great that it cannot without danger to the general welfare be entrusted to private individuals." [23] It is beyond doubt that the companies which operate in these fields, few in number and extensive in power, are in a position often to dominate alike their customers, their suppliers, their employes, their potential competitors, and, at times, even the public authority.

Crude iron and steel and basic chemicals are the primary materials without which a multitude of other industries cannot exist. Those who exercise a monopolistic control over the supply of these commodities possess a virtually unlimited power over the nation's economy.

In the present stage of technical development, however, it is impossible to produce these commodities by methods of small-scale production. The production of these commodities is best carried on by corporations controlling extensive natural resources and operating very large plants. These are therefore the very types of industry referred to by Pope Pius XI. If not publicly owned, they should at least be placed under very strict government supervision.

It is also out of harmony with Christian thought that the

[23] Pius XI.—*Quadragesimo Anno*, p. 37.

control of credit policy—as distinct from the administration
of credit—should be in private hands. This is a basic function of the public authority. Whether credit is dispensed by
banks or by insurance companies—which are today often
more powerful financially than the banks—it is opposed to
right order that the sovereign economic power which rests in
formulating the credit policy of the nation should be in
the hands of private individuals.

The nationalization of the trading banks is not, in itself,
opposed to the principles of social morality. It becomes so
only if intended as one step advancing a system of total
Socialism.

It is therefore the Christian view that so long as these
particular forms of industry and enterprise endure, they
should be under public control. Whether public control is
exercised by way of nationalization, or in some other way,
depends upon all the circumstances of each individual case.

D. Among the industries which should be publicly controlled there are some which may legitimately be nationalized. In the words of the present Holy Father, "these are the
cases in which it is evident that (nationalization) is really
required by the common good—that is to say, that when it
is apparent that it is the only method which will effectively
remedy an abuse or avoid a wastage of the productive resources of the country; and which will ensure the organic
development of these very resources, and which will direct
them so as to benefit the economic interests of the nation . . ."

However, since nationalization is not the only way, nor
even the primary way, in which the government should intervene in industry, recourse should be had to it only if and
insofar as other less drastic measures have been shown by
experience to be insufficient.

Thus while it is admitted that the control of the nation's
credit policy should be in the hands of the central government, merely to state this principle does not finally answer
the question whether this control is best achieved by the
complete nationalization of the banks.

The real issue in the matter of bank nationalization rests
in these questions: "Is other less drastic legislation sufficiently comprehensive to achieve the same objective? If it is
sufficiently comprehensive, is it sufficiently safe from legal
or political challenge to make nationalization unnecessary?"

Once the principles have been stated, and once the issues

have thus been clarified, the answer to these latter questions is a matter of political judgment in which the Church is necessarily silent, and in which her children have the right to form their own reasoned judgments.

E. Even if in a particular case nationalization proves to be justifiable, it is an expedient which may have dangerous results. "Instead of diminishing the mechanical character of life and work . . ." writes the present Holy Father, "nationalization, even when morally legitimate, is more likely to increase it."

This undesirable development comes about in two ways. In the first place, the nationalized industries will always be large industries with a tendency to keep on increasing in size. The larger the industrial unit the greater the inclination to value the worker as a mere cog in the productive machine.

On the other hand, the fact that the government sinks millions of pounds into a nationalized industry will inevitably mean that it will fight to preserve its monopoly, even when new technical methods make it possible for the industry to be run by small units operated by working proprietors.

A concrete illustration of this danger is the battle which is today being fought between the Government-controlled railway systems and road transport, controlled often by small private operators. The small road transport firms can often handle goods and passengers more efficiently than the railways. Since governments have invested tremendous sums in rail transport, they are driven to extreme measures to defend their investment and to crush out their competitors.

F. Hence, even when the State does justly nationalize some enterprise, it would be a mistake for it to conduct that enterprise as a centralized monopoly. For this would be simply to substitute State capitalism for private capitalism, a process without any advantage to the community.

This principle makes clear the real significance of the suggestion that, should the private banks be taken over by the government, the day-to-day administration of the banking system should not be conducted exclusively by the branches of the one nationalized bank, but by co-operative credit societies.

Properly regulated by legislation, these co-operative credit societies would do much to avert the evils of monopoly. So long as they were backed by the credit of the State, but at the same time allowed to enjoy an independent life of their own, they would enable individuals and industrial enterprises to preserve their freedom from the direct control of a government instrumentality.

While maintaining the sovereignty of the government in the field of credit policy, co-operative credit societies would ensure that the central government would not become a colossus threatening the freedom of its subjects, because of its direct control over their individual finances. By decentralizing the administration of credit, they would ensure that this freedom would be preserved in day-to-day business relationships.

The proposal that co-operatives should be introduced wherever nationalization operates is one which extends beyond the sphere of banking. It should be investigated always and applied in every possible case.

G. In the case of the nationalization of a particular enterprise, it is obvious that a just compensation should be paid.

As to the amount of compensation, it is clear that it would vary in individual cases and that, in each case, all the circumstances should be taken into consideration. The market value of the property taken over is not necessarily the only criterion of the compensation which should be paid.

CONCLUSION

The attitude of the Catholic Church to the various systems which demand the intervention of the government in social and economic life may be summarized as follows:

(a) The philosophy and program of Communism cannot under any circumstances be reconciled with Christian teaching.

(b) The philosophy and program of strict Socialism—the taking over and operation by the State of the entire machinery of production, distribution and exchange—are Marxist in origin, and cannot be reconciled with Christian teaching.

(c) Where the meaning which is given to the program of socialization is the same as that given above to Socialism strictly so called—socialization, in that sense, cannot be reconciled with Christian teaching.

(d) Where the meaning which is given to the program of socialization is simply that the State has the right to place under public control those industries which are too vital to the common good to be left safely in private hands, then in that sense socialization is not opposed to Christian teaching.

(e) The nationalization of any particular industry within this particular and restricted group is not opposed to Christian teaching, so long as it is not intended as one step on the road to total Socialism.

(f) Citizens should always seek to determine whether the nationalization of an individual industry is legitimate or whether it is really only one part of a more far-reaching plan. There are three methods by which this can be done. They should constantly question their parliamentary representatives as to the real aim of their policies. They should constantly study the published programs of political parties. Above all they should endeavor to discover whether the over-all result of a government's policy has been to extend the ownership of productive property or to restrict it. In the former case, the nationalization of a particular industry is far less suspect than in the latter.

(g) On the other hand, the nationalization of an industry in which numerous small firms operate, or which is capable of being run by small units, is not legitimate.

(h) At all times the purpose of government policy should be, as far as possible, to break up big productive units, particularly monopolies and near monopolies, so that industries may be operated by small and medium-sized firms. In all industries in which this is possible, it is the only program fully in accord with Christian teaching.

Chapter 4

✠

Pius XII (1939-1958)

EUGENIO Cardinal Pacelli was born March 2, 1876, the son of the dean of the Vatican lawyers. An aristocrat, he studied at the Capranica, and was ordained in 1899. Appointed professor of law at the Roman Seminary, he left to enter the papal secretariat of state at Cardinal Gasparri's invitation. Throughout World War I he supervised the work of exchanging prisoners, moving the wounded to hospitals, etc. In May, 1917, he was sent as papal nuncio to Bavaria, and stayed in Munich during revolutionary outbreaks in which his life was threatened. In 1925, after concluding a Concordat with Bavaria, Archbishop Pacelli was sent to Berlin. Recalled to Rome in 1929, he succeeded his teacher and friend, Cardinal Gasparri, as secretary of state. He traveled to South America as legate to the Eucharistic Congress in Buenos Aires in 1934, and was in the United States in 1936. The conclave of 1939 which elected him pope on the first ballot was the shortest since 1623. Cardinal Pacelli was the first secretary of state to be elected pope since 1775.

Pius XII spoke seven languages fluently, and during World War II he made no fewer than thirty appeals in the first sixteen months of the war. He was above all the Pope of the Mystical Body; yet his encyclical *Mystici Corporis* is but one of the many he addressed to all kinds and conditions of men. Through his radio addresses and television appearances, no less than his encyclicals, this pope strove to bring the Church's message to every human creature.

He died on October 8, 1958.

SUMMI PONTIFICATUS

On the Function of the State in the Modern World[*]

October 20, 1939

. . . What age has been, for all its technical and purely civic progress, more tormented than ours by spiritual emptiness and deep-felt interior poverty?

16. As Vicar of Him Who in a decisive hour pronounced before the highest earthly authority of that day, the great words: "For this was I born, and for this came I into the world; that I should give testimony to the truth. Every one that is of the truth, heareth my voice." (*St. John* xviii: 37), We feel We owe no greater debt to Our office and to Our time than to testify to the truth with Apostolic firmness: "to give testimony to the truth." This duty necessarily entails the exposition and confutation of errors and human faults; for these must be made known before it is possible to tend and to heal them, "you shall know the truth, and the truth shall make you free" (*St John* viii: 32). . . .

23. . . . Before all else, it is certain that the radical and ultimate cause of the evils which We deplore in modern society is the denial and rejection of a universal norm of morality as well for individual and social life as for international relations; We mean the disregard, so common nowadays, and the forgetfulness of the natural law itself, which has its foundation in God, Almighty Creator and Father of all, supreme and absolute Lawgiver, all-wise and just Judge of human actions. When God is hated, every basis of morality is undermined; the voice of conscience is stilled or at any rate grows very faint, that voice which teaches even to the illiterate and to uncivilized tribes what is good and what is bad, what lawful, what forbidden, and makes men feel themselves responsible for their actions to a Supreme Judge.

24. The denial of the fundamentals of morality had its origin, in Europe, in the abandonment of that Christian teaching of which the Chair of Peter is the depository and ex-

[*] Official translation. The Vatican Polyglot Press.

ponent. That teaching had once given spiritual cohesion to a
Europe which, educated, ennobled and civilized by the Cross,
had reached such a degree of civil progress as to become the
teacher of other peoples, of other continents. But, cut off
from the infallible teaching authority of the Church, not a
few separated brethren have gone so far as to overthrow
the central dogma of Christianity, the Divinity of the Saviour,
and have hastened thereby the progress of spiritual decay. . . .

29. Among the many errors which derive from the poisoned source of religious and moral agnosticism, We would
draw your attention, Venerable Brethren, to two in particular,
as being those which more than others render almost impossible or at least precarious and uncertain, the peaceful intercourse of peoples.

30. The first of these pernicious errors, widespread
today, is the forgetfulness of that law of human solidarity
and charity which is dictated and imposed by our common
origin and by the equality of rational nature in all men, to
whatever people they belong, and by the redeeming Sacrifice
offered by Jesus Christ on the Altar of the Cross to His
Heavenly Father on behalf of sinful mankind. . . .

37. In the light of this unity of all mankind, which exists
in law and in fact, individuals do not feel themselves
isolated units, like grains of sand, but united by the very
force of their nature and by their internal destiny, into an
organic, harmonious mutual relationship which varies with
the changing of times.

38. And the nations, despite a difference of development
due to diverse conditions of life and of culture, are not
destined to break the unity of the human race, but rather to
enrich and embellish it by the sharing of their own peculiar
gifts and by that reciprocal interchange of goods which can
be possible and efficacious only when a mutual love and a
lively sense of charity unite all the sons of the same Father
and all those redeemed by the same Divine Blood.

39. The Church of Christ, the faithful depository of the
teaching of Divine Wisdom, cannot and does not think of
deprecating or disdaining the particular characteristics which
each people, with jealous and intelligible pride, cherishes and
retains as a precious heritage. Her aim is a supernatural
union in all-embracing love, deeply felt and practiced, and
not the unity which is exclusively external and superficial
and by that very fact weak. . . .

43. In accordance with these principles of equality, the

Church devotes her care to forming cultured native clergy and gradually increasing the number of native Bishops. And in order to give external expression to these, Our intentions, We have chosen the forthcoming Feast of Christ the King to raise to the Episcopal dignity at the Tomb of the Apostles twelve representatives of widely different peoples and races. In the midst of the disruptive contrasts which divide the human family, may this solemn act proclaim to all Our sons, scattered over the world, that the spirit, the teaching and the word of the Church can never be other than that which the Apostle of the Gentiles preached: "putting on the new [man], him who is renewed unto knowledge, according to the image of him that created him. Where there is neither Gentile nor Jew, circumcision nor uncircumcision, Barbarian nor Scythian, bond nor free. But Christ is all, and in all" (*Colossians* iii: 10, 11).

44. Nor is there any fear lest the consciousness of universal brotherhood aroused by the teaching of Christianity, and the spirit which it inspires, be in contrast with love of traditions or the glories of one's fatherland, or impede the progress of prosperity or legitimate interests. For that same Christianity teaches that in the exercise of charity we must follow a God-given order, yielding the place of honor in our affections and good works to those who are bound to us by special ties. Nay, the Divine Master Himself gave an example of this preference for His Own country and fatherland, as He wept over the coming destruction of the Holy City. But legitimate and well-ordered love of our native country should not make us close our eyes to the all-embracing nature of Christian charity, which calls for consideration of others and of their interests in the pacifying light of love. . . .

47. But there is yet another error no less pernicious to the well-being of the nations and to the prosperity of that great human society which gathers together and embraces within its confines all races. It is the error contained in those ideas which do not hesitate to divorce civil authority from every kind of dependence upon the Supreme Being—First Source and absolute Master of man and of society—and from every restraint of a Higher Law derived from God as from its First Source. Thus they accord the civil authority an unrestricted field of action that is at the mercy of the changeful tide of human will, or of the dictates of casual historical claims, and of the interests of a few.

48. Once the authority of God and the sway of His law

are denied in this way, the civil authority as an inevitable result tends to attribute to itself that absolute autonomy which belongs exclusively to the Supreme Maker. It puts itself in the place of the Almighty and elevates the State or group into the last end of life, the supreme criterion of the moral and juridical order, and therefore forbids every appeal to the principles of natural reason and of the Christian conscience. . . .

54. . . . It is the noble prerogative and function of the State to control, aid and direct the private and individual activities of national life that they converge harmoniously towards the common good. That good can neither be defined according to arbitrary ideas nor can it accept for its standard primarily the material prosperity of society, but rather it should be defined according to the harmonious development and the natural perfection of man. It is for this perfection that society is designed by the Creator as a means.

55. To consider the State as something ultimate to which everything else should be subordinated and directed, cannot fail to harm the true and lasting prosperity of nations. This can happen either when unrestricted dominion comes to be conferred on the State as having a mandate from the nation, people, or even a social order, or when the State arrogates such dominion to itself as absolute master, despotically, without any mandate whatsoever. If, in fact, the State lays claim to and directs private enterprises, these, ruled as they are by delicate and complicated internal principles which guarantee and assure the realization of their special aims, may be damaged to the detriment of the public good, by being wrenched from their natural surroundings, that is, from responsible private action. . . .

59. True courage and a heroism worthy in its degree of admiration and respect, are often necessary to support the hardships of life, the daily weight of misery, growing want and restrictions on a scale never before experienced, whose reason and necessity are not always apparent. Whoever has the care of souls and can search hearts knows the hidden tears of mothers, the resigned sorrow of so many fathers, the countless bitternesses of which no statistics tell or can tell. He sees with sad eyes the mass of sufferings ever on the increase; he knows how the powers of disorder and destruction stand on the alert ready to make use of all these things for their dark designs. No one of good-will and vision will think of refusing the State, in the exceptional conditions of the

world of today, correspondingly wider and exceptional rights to meet the popular needs. But even in such emergencies, the moral law, established by God, demands that the lawfulness of each such measure and its real necessity be scrutinized with the greatest rigor according to the standards of the common good.

60. In any case, the more burdensome the material sacrifices demanded of the individual and the family by the State, the more must the rights of conscience be to it sacred and inviolable. Goods, blood it can demand; but the soul redeemed by God, never. The charge laid by God on parents to provide for the material and spiritual good of their offspring and to procure for them a suitable training saturated with the true spirit of religion, cannot be wrested from them without grave violation of their rights. . . .

64. The idea which credits the State with unlimited authority is not simply an error harmful to the internal life of nations, to their prosperity, and to the larger and well-ordered increase in their well-being, but likewise it injures the relations between peoples, for it breaks the unity of supranational society, robs the law of nations of its foundation and vigor, leads to violation of others' rights and impedes agreement and peaceful intercourse.

65. A disposition, in fact, of the divinely sanctioned natural order divides the human race into social groups, nations or States, which are mutually independent in organization and in the direction of their internal life. But for all that, the human race is bound together by reciprocal ties, moral and juridical, into a great commonwealth directed to the good of all nations and ruled by special laws which protect its unity and promote its prosperity.

66. Now no one can fail to see how the claim to absolute autonomy for the State stands in open opposition to this natural way that is inherent in man—nay, denies it utterly—and therefore leaves the stability of international relations at the mercy of the will of rulers, while it destroys the possibility of true union and fruitful collaboration directed to the general good.

67. So, Venerable Brethren, it is indispensable for the existence of harmonious and lasting contacts and of fruitful relations, that the peoples recognize and observe these principles of international natural law which regulate their normal development and activity. Such principles demand respect for corresponding rights to independence, to life and to the

possibility of continuous development in the paths of civilization; they demand, further, fidelity to compacts agreed
upon and sanctioned in conformity with the principles of
the law of nations.

68. The indispensable presupposition, without doubt, of
all peaceful intercouse between nations, and the very soul of
the juridical relations in force among them, is mutual trust:
the expectation and conviction that each party will respect its
plighted word; the certainty that both sides are convinced
that "Better is wisdom, than weapons of war" (*Ecclesiastes*
ix: 18), and are ready to enter into discussion and to avoid
recourse to force or to threats of force in case of delays,
hindrances, changes or disputes, because all these things can
be the result not of bad-will, but of changed circumstances
and of genuine interests in conflict.

69. But on the other hand, to tear the law of nations from
its anchor in Divine law, to base it on the autonomous will
of States, is to dethrone that very law and deprive it of its
noblest and strongest qualities. Thus it would stand abandoned to the fatal drive of private interest and collective
selfishness exclusively intent on the assertion of its own rights
and ignoring those of others.

70. Now, it is true that with the passage of time and
the substantial change of circumstances, which were not
and perhaps could not have been foreseen in the making of a
treaty, such a treaty or some of its clauses can in fact become, or at least seem to become, unjust, impracticable or
too burdensome for one of the parties. It is obvious that
should such be the case, recourse should be had in good
time to a frank discussion with a view to modifying the treaty
or making another in its stead. But to consider treaties on
principle as ephemeral and tacitly to assume the authority of
rescinding them unilaterally when they are no longer to one's
advantage, would be to abolish all mutual trust among
States. In this way, natural order would be destroyed and
there would be seen dug between different peoples and nations
trenches of division impossible to refill.

71. Today, Venerable Brethren, all men are looking with
terror into the abyss to which they have been brought by the
errors and principles which We have mentioned, and by their
practical consequences. Gone are the proud illusions of limitless progress. . . .

CHRISTIANITY AND THE WORLD CRISIS*

... We, therefore, who in these bitter times of warring upheaval are tortured by your tortures and sorrowed by your sorrow, We who live with you under the awful incubus of a scourge, which is tearing at humanity for still a third year, wish to speak to you from Our paternal heart on this vigil of the solemn feast of Christmas to exhort you to remain always strong in your Faith and to share with you the comfort of that very real, superabundant and elevating hope and certainty which radiates from the crib of the newborn Saviour. . . .

The necessary premises for such a new order are as follows:

(1) Victory over the hatred which divides the nations today and the disappearance of systems and actions which breed this hatred. As a matter of fact, in some countries an unbridled propaganda is to be seen: it does not recoil from methodical distortion of the truth in order to show the enemy nations in a falsified and vilifying light. He, however, who really wants the good of the people and wants to contribute to the future cooperation of nations and to preserve this cooperation from incalculable damage, will consider it as his sacred duty to uphold the natural ideals of Truth, Justice and Charity.

(2) Victory over distrust which exerts a paralyzing pressure on international law and makes all honest understanding impossible. Therefore, return to the principle of mutual trust. Return to the loyalty for treaties without which the secure cooperation of nations and especially, the living side by side of strong and weak nations, are inconceivable. The foundation of justice is loyalty, reliability and truth of the pledged word, and of the understanding which has been reached.

(3) Victory over the dismal principle that utility is the foundation and aim of law, and that might can create right.

* Christmas message, 1941. As delivered on Vatican Radio.

This principle is bound to upset all international relations and is inacceptable to all weaker nations. This conception does not exclude the desire for the honourable improvement of conditions or the right to defend oneself if peaceful life has been attacked, or to repair the damage sustained thereby.

(4) Victory over those potential conflicts arising out of the disequilibrium of world economy. Therefore, a new economic order was to be gradually evolved which gives all nations the means to secure for their citizens an appropriate standard of life.

(5) Victory over the kind of egoism which, relying on its own power, aims at impairing the honour and liberty of individuals. This egoism has to be replaced by a genuine Christian solidarity of a legal and economic character, and by a brotherly-cooperation of the nations, the sovereignty of which has been duly secured. . . .

Nations' Resources Depleted

It is with that same anguish that We look upon the depleted resources of nations and upon the millions of people who are being hurled into a state of misery and total exhaustion by this conflict and by its brutal violence.

And while the strength and health of a great part of youth which was in the process of maturing are being weakened through the privations imposed by the present scourge, the war expenditures and debts are rising to levels never dreamed of before.

Such large-scale disbursements, giving rise as they must to contraction of the forces of production in the civil and social field, cannot but be the basis for serious anxiety on the part of those who turn their thoughts with pre-occupation toward the future.

The very idea of force stifles and perverts the rule of law, offers the possibility and free opportunity to individuals and to social or political groups to violate the property and the rights of others and permits all other destructive forces to upset and agitate the civil atmosphere until it becomes a raging tempest, and you shall see the notions of good and evil, or right and injustice, lose their well-defined outlines, become blunted and confused finally threaten to disappear.

Those who, by virtue of the Pastoral Ministry, are enabled to penetrate the depths of men's hearts, know and see what an accumulation of sorrows and unspeakable anxieties take root in many souls and diminish therein the longing for the enjoyment of labor and life; sorrows and anxieties which suffocate men's spirits and render them silent and indolent, suspecting, and almost devoid of hope in the face of the events and requirements of the times.

No Visible Road to Accord

These are anxieties of the soul which no one may take lightly if he has at heart the genuine good of peoples and desires to promote a return in the near future to normal and ordered conditions of life and action. Faced with this view of the present, men sense a feeling of bitter disappointment which has invaded their very hearts, especially since there appears today to be no open road to agreement between the belligerent parties whose reciprocal war aims and programs would seem to be irreconcilable. . . .

Let us burrow deeply into the conscience of modern society. Let us seek out the root of the evil. Where does it thrive? Here again, of course, We do not wish to withdraw the praise due to the wisdom of those rulers who either favored always, or who desired, and were capable of restoring to their place of honor, to the advantage of the people, the values of Christian civilization in the amicable relations between Church and State, in the safeguard of the sanctity of marriage, in the religious education of youth.

But We cannot close Our eyes to the sad spectacle of the progressive de-christianization, both individual and social, which from moral laxity has developed into a general state of weakness and brought about the open denial of truth and of those influences whose function it is to illuminate our minds in the matter of good and evil and to fortify family life, private life and the public life of the State.

Religious Anemia Grips World

A religious anemia, like a spreading contagion, has so

afflicted many peoples of Europe and of the world and has created in their souls such a moral void that no spurious and pharisaical religious organization and no national or international mythology will serve to fill this emptiness.

Is it not true that for decades and centuries past men have directed their every thought, word and deed, to their sworn objective of tearing from the hearts of our young and old alike their faith in God, the Creator and Father of all, rewarder of good and avenger of evil? And have they not striven for the accomplishment of this goal through a process of radical change in education and instruction, opposing and oppressing by every act and means the diffusion of the spoken and printed word, and by the abuse of scientific knowledge and political power the religion and the Church of Christ?

For the human spirit, overwhelmed in the confusion of this moral abyss, by its alienation from God and Christian practices, no other course remained but that of turning all its thoughts, purposes and enterprises and every evaluation of men's possessions, actions and labor and directing them to the material world, striving and sweating with might and main to spread out in space, to surpass all previous accomplishments in the attainment of riches and power, to engage in a competition of speed, to produce in greater quantity everything that material advancement and progress seemed to require.

Effect of Material Striving

Hence, We witnessed in the political sphere the prevalence of an unrestrained impulse toward expansion and mere political advantage, to the disregard of moral principles; in the field of economics the domination of great gigantic enterprises and trusts; in social life, the uprooting, and crowding of masses of the people in distressing and excessive concentration in the great cities and centers of industry and commerce, with all the uncertainty which is an inevitable consequence when men in large numbers change their home and residence, their country and trade, their attachments and friendships.

It has followed from this, then, that the contact and relationship between men in their social life took on a character that was purely physical and mechanical, with a contemptuous disregard for every reasonable moderation and consideration. The rule of external compulsion, mere possession of power, overruled the norms of right and order governing human associations and community life, which emanating from God, determine the natural and supernatural relationship that should prevail in the co-existence of law and love as applied to the individual and to society.

The majesty and dignity of the particular social groups became a dead letter, degraded and suppressed by the idea that might makes right. The right to private property became, for some, a power to be used for the exploitation of the labor of their fellowmen; in others that right enkindled a spirit of jealousy, intolerance and hatred, and the organization that resulted therefrom was conflict by the contending parties to gain the advantage of their particular interests.

Bondage of the Individual

To some countries a godless and anti-Christian conception of the State bound the individual to itself with its vast tentacles in such a way as to almost deprive him of all independence, and this no less in his private than in his public life.

Who today can be surprised that such radical opposition to the principles of Christian teaching has finally found its outlet in so intense a clash of internal and external enmities as to lead to the extermination of human lives and the destruction of worldly goods?

The spectacle which we are now beholding with such profound sorrow is the unhappy consequence and fruit of the social condition we have described. The way, far from arresting this influence and development, promotes it, accelerates it and spreads it with increasing ruin the longer it endures, rendering the catastrophe ever more general.

From Our words, directed against the materialism of the past century and of the present time, it would be wrong to deduce a condemnation of technical progress.

No, We do not condemn that which is a gift of God, Who just as He causes the bread-yielding wheat to rise from the sod of the earth, has also hidden in the bowels of the earth from the time of the world's creation treasures of fire, of metals, of precious stones to be uncovered by the hand of man for his needs, for his works and for his progress.

The Church, mother of so many universities of Europe, while continuing to exalt and gather together the most fearless masters of the sciences and explorers of nature, does not fail at the same time to bear in mind that all God's gifts and the very freedom of the human will itself can be used in a way to merit praise and reward, or blame and condemnation. Thus, it has happened that the spirit and the tendency with which technical progress was often put to use have brought it about that in our time technology must expiate its error and be, as it were, its own avenger by producing instruments of destruction which destroy today what it has erected yesterday.

Sole Indicated Remedy

In the face of the enormity of the disaster which has had its origin in errors, We have indicated there is no other remedy than that of a return to the altars, at the foot of which numberless generations of the Faithful in former times drew down upon themselves Divine blessings and moral strength for the fulfillment of their duties, a return to the Faith which enlightened individuals and society as a whole, and indicated to them their respective rights and duties, a return to the wise and unshakable norms of the social order which, in affairs of national as well as international import, erected an efficacious barrier against the abuse of liberty and against the misuse of power.

But the recall of these beneficent sources must be especially loud, persistent and universal in that hour when the old order will be about to give way and cede its place to the new.

The future reconstruction will present and offer very valuable opportunities to advance the forces of good but it will also be fraught with the danger of a lapse into errors which will favor the forces of evil and there will be demanded prudent sincerity and mature reflection, not only by reason of the gigantic difficulty of the task but also because of the grave consequences which in the case of failure, would result in both material and spiritual spheres.

There will be required broad intellects and will, strong in their purposes; men of courage and enterprise, but above and before all, there must be consciences which in their planning, in their deliberations and in their actions, are animated, moved and sustained by a lively sense of responsibility and which do not shrink from submission to the holy laws of God.

Judgment of Saint Augustine

For if, to the vigor which shapes the material order, there be not united in the moral order the highest reflection and sincere purpose, then, undoubtedly, we will see verified the judgment of Saint Augustine: "They run well but they have left the track; the farther they run the greater is their error for they are going ever farther from their course."

Nor would it be the first time that men who, in the expectation of being crowned at war's end with the laurel wreath of victory, have dreamed of giving to the world a new order by pointing out new ways which in their opinion lead to well-being, prosperity and progress. Yet whenever they have yielded to the temptation of imposing their own interpretation, contrary to the dictates of reason, moderation, justice and the nobility of man, they have found themselves disheartened and stupified in the contemplation of the ruins of deluded hopes and miscarried plans.

Thus history teaches that treaties of peace stipulated in a spirit and with conditions opposed both to the dictates of morality and to genuine political wisdom has had but a wretched and short-lived existence, and so have revealed and testified to an error of calculation. Human, indeed, but fatal nonetheless.

Cooperation for Peace

Now the destruction brought about by the present war is on so vast a scale that it is imperative that there be not added to it also the further ruin of a frustrated and deluded peace. In order to avoid so great a calamity it is fitting that in the formulation of that peace there should be assured the cooperation, with sincerity of will and energy, with the purpose of a generous participation not only of this or that party, not only of this or that people, but of all people, yea, rather of all humanity. It is a universal undertaking for the common good which requires the collaboration of all Christendom in the religious and moral aspects of the new edifice that is to be constructed.

We are, therefore, making use of Our right, or better, We are fulfilling Our duty as today, on this eve of the Holy Feast of Christmas, the Divine dawn of hope and of peace for the world, with all the authority of Our apostolic ministry, and with the fervent impulse of Our heart, We direct the attention and the consideration of the entire world to the dangers which lie in wait to threaten a peace which is to be the well-prepared basis for a truly new order and which is to fulfill the expectation and desires of all peoples for a more tranquil future.

New Order of Moral Law

Such a new order, which all peoples desire to see brought into being after the trials and the ruins of this war, must be founded on that immovable and unshakable rock, the moral law which He has engraved with indelible characters in the hearts of men: that moral law whose observance must be inculcated and fostered by the public opinion of all nations and of all States with such a unanimity of voice and energy that no one may dare to call into doubt or weaken its binding force.

Like a shining beacon, this moral law must direct by the light of its principles the course of action of men and of States, and they must all follow its admonishing, salutary and profitable precepts if they do not wish to abandon to the tempest and to ultimate shipwreck every labor and every effort for the establishment of a new order.

Consequently, recapitulating and integrating what We have expounded on other occasions, We insist once again on certain fundamental conditions essential for an international order which will guarantee for all peoples a just and lasting peace and which will be a bountiful source of well-being and prosperity.

Within the limits of a new order founded on moral principles there is no room for the violation of the freedom, integrity and security of other States, no matter what may be their territorial extension or their capacity for defense.

Duty of the Powerful States

It is inevitable that the powerful States should, by reason of their greater potentialities and their power, play leading roles in the formation of economic groups comprising not only of themselves but also smaller and weaker States as well, it is, nevertheless, indispensable that in the interests of the common good they, as all others, respect the rights of those smaller States to political freedom, to economic development and to the adequate protection, in the case of conflicts between nations, of that neutrality which is theirs according to the natural, as well as international, law.

In this way, and in this way only, shall they be able to obtain a fitting share of the common good and assure the material and spiritual welfare of the peoples concerned.

Within the limits of a new order founded on moral principles, there is no place for open or occult oppression of the cultural and linguistic characteristics of national minorities, for the hindrance or restriction of their economic resources, for the limitation or abolition of their natural fertility. The more conscientiously the government of the State respects the rights of minorities, the more confidently and the more effectively can it demand from its subjects a loyal fulfillment of those civil obligations which are common to all citizens.

Resources Must be Shared

Within the limits of a new order founded on moral principles, there is no place for that cold and calculating egoism which tends to hoard the economic resources and materials destined for the use of all to such an extent that the nations less favored by nature are not permitted access to them.

In this regard, it is for Us a source of great consolation to see admitted the necessity of a participation of all in the natural riches of the earth, even on the part of those nations which in the fulfillment of this principle belong to the category of "givers" and not to that of "receivers."

It is, however, conformity with the principles of equity that the solution to a question so vital to the world economy should be arrived at methodically and in easy stages, with the necessary guarantees, drawing useful lessons from the omissions and mistakes of the past.

If, in the future peace, this point were not to be courageously dealt with, there would remain in the relations between peoples a deep and far-reaching root, blossoming forth into bitter dissensions and burning jealousies, and which would lead eventually to new conflicts. It must, however, be noted how closely the satisfactory solution to this problem is connected with another fundamental point which We shall treat next.

No Place for Total War

Within the limit of a new order founded on moral principles, once the more dangerous sources of armed conflicts have been eliminated, there is no place for a total warfare or for a mad rush to armaments. The calamity of a world war, with the economic and social ruins and the moral dissolution and breakdown which follow in its trail, should not be permitted to envelop the human race for a third time.

In order that mankind be preserved from such a misfortune it is essential to proceed with sincerity and honesty to a progressive limitations of armaments. The lack of equilibrium between the exaggerated armaments of the powerful States and the limited armaments of the weaker ones is a menace to harmony and peace among nations and demands that an ample and proportionate limit be placed upon production and possession of offensive weapons in proportion to the degree in which disarmament is effected.

Means must be found which will be appropriate, honorable and efficacious in order that the norm "pacts must be observed" will once again enjoy its vital and moral function in the juridical relations between States.

Such a norm has undergone many serious crises and has suffered undeniable violations in the past and has met with an incurable lack of trust among the various nations and among their respective rulers. To procure the rebirth of mutual trust, certain institutions must be established which will merit the respect of all and which will dedicate themselves to the most noble office of guaranteeing the sincere observance of treaties and of promoting, in accordance with the principles of law and equity, necessary corrections and revisions of such treaties.

Difficulties to be Overcome

We are well aware of the tremendous difficulties to be overcome and the almost superhuman strength and good will required on all sides if the double task We have outlined is to be brought to a successful conclusion. But this work is so essential for a lasting peace that nothing should prevent responsible statesmen from undertaking it, and cooperating in it with abundant good will so that, by bearing in mind the advantages to be gained in the future, they will be able to triumph over the painful remembrances of similar efforts doomed to failure in the past and will not be daunted by the knowledge of the gigantic strength required for the accomplishment of their objective.

Within the limits of a new order founded on moral principles, there is no place for the persecution of religion and of the Church. From a lively faith in a personal and transcendent God, there springs a sincere and unyielding moral strength which informs the whole course of life; for faith is not only a virtue, it is also the Divine gate by which all the virtues enter the temple of the soul and it constitutes that strong and tenacious character which does not falter before the rigid demands of reason and justice.

This fact always holds true, but it should be even more evident when there is demanded of the statesmen, as of the least of his citizens, the maximum of courage and moral strength for the reconstruction of a new Europe and a new world on the ruins accumulated by the violence of the World War and by the hatred and bitter disunity among men regarding the social question which will be present in the postwar period in a form more acute than ever.

Faith in a Personal God

Our predecessors, and We ourselves, have set forth principles for its solution. It is, however, well to bear in mind that these principles can be followed in their entirety and bear their fullest fruit only when statesmen and peoples, employers, are animated by faith in a personal God, the Legislator and Judge to whom they must one day give an account of their actions; for while unbelief which arrays itself against God, the Ruler of the universe, is the most dangerous enemy of a new order that would be just, on the other hand, every man who believes in God is numbered among his partisans and paladins.

Those who have faith in Christ, in His divinity, in His law, in work of love and of brotherhood among men, will make a particularly valuable contribution to the reconstruction of the social order.

All the more priceless, therefore, will be the contribution of statesmen who show themselves ready to open the gates and smooth the path for the Church of Christ so that, free and unhindered, it may bring its supernatural influence to bear in the conclusion of a peace among nations and may cooperate with its zeal and love in the immense task of finding remedies for the evils which the war will leave in its wake.

For this reason We are unable to explain why it is that in some parts of the world countless legislative dispositions bar the way to the message of the Christian faith while free and ample scope is given to a propaganda that opposes it, youth is withdrawn from the beneficent influence of the Christian family, alienated from the Church, educated in a spirit contrary to the teachings of Christ and imbued with ideas, maxims and practices which are anti-Christian, the work of the Church for the care of souls and for charitable enterprises is rendered arduous and less efficacious while its moral influence on individuals and on society is disregarded and rejected.

All these forms of resolute opposition, far from being mitigated or eliminated in the course of the war, have, on the contrary, in many respects become even more marked.

Spirit of Church's Foes

That all this, and even more, should be continued in the midst of the sufferings of the present time is a sad commentary on the spirit which animates the enemies of the Church in imposing upon the Faithful, already bearing many heavy sacrifices, the irksome and the troublesome burden of a bitter anxiety which weighs upon their consciences.

We love, and in this We call upon God to be Our witness, We love with equal affection all peoples, without any exception whatsoever, and in order to avoid even the appearance of being moved by partisanship, We have maintained hitherto the greatest reserve.

But the measures directed against the Church and their scope are of such a nature that We feel obliged, in the name of truth, to say a word about it, if only to eliminate the danger of unfortunate misunderstandings amongst the Faithful. We behold today, beloved children, the God Man, born in a manger to restore man to the greatness from which he had fallen through his own fault and to place him once again on the throne of liberty, of justice and of honor which centuries of error and untruth had denied him.

The foundations of that throne shall be Calvary. It shall be enriched, not with gold or silver, but with the blood of Christ, the Divine Blood which has overflowed upon the world for twenty centuries to give a scarlet hue to the cheeks of His spouse, the Church, and which, in purifying, consecrating, sanctifying and glorifying its children, takes on the brilliance of heaven.

O Christian Rome, that Blood is your life. By reason of that Blood, you are great and even the ancient ruins of your pagan greatness are seen in a new light and the codices of the juridical wisdom of the praetors and the Caesars are purified and consecrated. You are the mother of higher and more human justice which does honor to you, to your See, and to those who hear your voice.

You are the beacon of civilization and civilized Europe and all the world owes to you all that is most sacred and most saintly, all that is most wise and most honorable.

In the exalted tradition and proud history of their people, you are the mother of charity. Your splendor, your monuments, your hospices, your monasteries, your convents, your heroes and your heroines, your voyages, and your missions, your generations and your centuries, with their schools and universities, all bear testimony to the triumphs of your charity, that charity which embraces all, suffers all, hopes for all, becoming all things to all men, consoling and comforting all, curing all and recalling them to that liberty given them by Christ, uniting all peoples in the peace of brotherly love, that charity which brings together all men, regardless of country, language or custom, into one united family and makes of the entire world one common fatherland.

From this Rome, center, rock and teacher of Christianity, from this city called eternal by reason of its relation with the living Christ rather than because of its association with the passing glory of the Caesars; from this Rome, in Our ardent and intense longing for the welfare of individual nations and of all humanity, We direct Our appeal to all beseeching and exhorting that the day be not delayed in which, wherever today hostility against God and Christ is dragging men to temporal and eternal ruin, a fuller religious consciousness and new higher objectives may prevail, and that on that day there may shine resplendently over the manger of the new order among peoples, the guiding star of Bethlehem, herald of a new order that will rouse all mankind to sing with the angels, "Glory to God in the highest," and to proclaim as the gift bestowed at last by Heaven upon the nations of the earth, "Peace to men of good-will." . . .

THE INTERNAL ORDER OF STATES AND PEOPLE*

International Relations and Order Within the Nations

In our last Christmas Message, We expounded the principles which Christian thought suggest, for the establishment of an international order of friendly relations and col-

* Christmas message, 1942. As delivered on Vatican Radio.

laboration such as to conform to the demands of God's Law. Today We shall, with the consent, We feel, and the interested attention of all upright men, pause to consider very carefully and with equal impartiality, the fundamental laws of the internal order of the States and peoples.

International relations and internal order are intimately related. International equilibrium and harmony depend on the internal equilibrium and development of the individual States in the material, social and intellectual spheres. A firm and steady peace policy towards other nations is, in fact, impossible without a spirit of peace within the nation which inspires trust. It is only, then, by striving for an integral peace, a peace in both fields, that people will be freed from the cruel nightmare of war, and the material and psychological causes of further discord and disorder will be diminished in a desire for peace, and hence aims at attaining peace, that "tranquil living together in order" in which St. Thomas finds the essence of peace. Two primary elements, then, regulate social life, a living together in order, and a living together in tranquility.

Living Together in Order

Order, which is fundamental in an association of men (of beings, that is, who strive to attain an end appropriate to their nature) is not merely external linking up of parts which are numerically distinct. It is rather, and must be, a tendency and an even more perfect approach to an internal union; and this does not exclude differences founded in fact and sanctioned by the will of God or by supernatural standard.

A clear understanding of the genuine fundamentals of all social life has a capital importance today as never before, when mankind, impregnated by the poison of error and social aberrations, tormented by the fever of discordant desires, doctrines, and aims, is excitedly tossing about in the disorder which it has itself created, and is experiencing the destructive force of false ideas, that disregard the Law of God or are opposed to it. And since disorder can only be overcome by an order which is not merely superimposed and fictitious (just as darkness with its fearful and depressing effects can only be driven away by light and not by will o'the wisps); so security, reorganizations, progressive improvement cannot be expected and cannot be brought about unless by a return of large and influential sections to correct notions about security.

It is a return which calls for the Grace of God in large measure, and for a resolute will, ready and prepared for sacrifice on the part of good farseeing men. From these influential circles who are more capable of penetrating and appreciating the beauty of just social norms, there will pass on and infiltrate into the masses the clear knowledge of the true, divine, spiritual origin of social life. Thus the way will be cleared for the reawakening, the growth and the fixing of those moral principles without which even the proudest achievements create but a babel in which the citizens, though they live inside the same walls, speak different and incoherent languages.

God, The First Cause and Ultimate Foundation of Individual and Social Life

From individual and social life we should rise to God, the First Cause and Ultimate Foundation, as He is the Creator of the first conjugal society, from which we have the society which is the family, and the society, of peoples and of nations. As an image, albeit imperfect, of its Exemplar, the One and Tribune God, Who through the Mystery of the Incarnation, redeemed and raised human nature, life in society, in its ideals and in its end, possesses by the light of reason and of revelation a moral authority and an absoluteness which transcend every temporal change.

It has a power of attraction that, far from being weakened or lessened by delusions, errors, failures, draws irresistibly the noblest and most faithful souls to the Lord, to take up with renewed energy, with added knowledge, with new studies, methods and means, the enterprises which in other times and circumstances were tried in vain.

Development and Perfection of the Human Person

The origin and the primary scope of social life is the conservation, development and perfection of the human person, helping him to realize accurately the demands and values of religion and culture set by the Creator for every man and for all mankind, both as a whole and in its natural ramifications.

A social teaching or a social reconstruction program which denies or prescinds from this internal essential relation to God of everything that regards men, is on a false course; and while it builds up with one hand, it prepares with the other the materials which sooner or later will undermine and destroy the whole fabric. And when it disregards the respect due to the human person and to the life which is proper to that person, and gives no thought to it in its organization, in legislative and executive activity, then instead of serving society, it harms it; instead of encouraging and stimulating social thought, instead of realizing its hopes and expectations, it strips it of all real value and reduces it to a utilitarian formula which is openly rejected by constantly increasing groups.

If social life implies intrinsic unity, it does not, at the same time, exclude differences which are founded in fact and nature. When we hold fast to God, the Supreme Controller of all that relates to man, then the similarities no less than the differences of men find their allotted place in the fixed order of being, of values, and hence also of morality. When, however, this foundation is removed, there is a dangerous lack of cohesion in the various spheres of culture; the frontier of true value becomes uncertain and shifting, even to the point where mere external factors, and often blind instincts, come to determine, according to the prevalent fashion of the day, who is to have control of this or that direction.

After the fateful economy of the past decades, during which the lives of all citizens were subordinated to the stimulus of gain, there now succeeds another and no less fateful policy which, while it considers everybody with reference to the State, excludes all thought of ethics or religion. This is a fatal travesty, a fatal error. It is calculated to bring about far-reaching consequences for social life, which is never nearer to losing its noblest prerogatives than when it thinks it can deny or forget with impunity the external source of its own dignity: God.

Reason, enlightened by faith, assigns to individuals and to particular societies in the social organization a definite and exalted place. It knows, to mention only the most important, that the whole political and economic activity of the State is directed to the permanent realization of the common good.

In a conception of society which is pervaded and sanctioned by religious thought, the influence of economics and of every other sphere of cultural activity represents a universal and most exalted center of activity, very rich in its variety and coherent in its harmony, in which men's intellectual equality and diversity of occupation come into their own and secure adequate expression. When this is not so, work is depreciated and the worker is belittled.

Juridical Order of Society and Its Aims

That social life, such as God willed it, may attain its scope, it needs a juridical order to support it from without, to defend and protect it. The function of this juridical order is not to dominate but to serve, to help the development and increase of society's vitality in the rich multiplicity of its ends, leading all the individual energies to their perfection in peaceful competition, and defending them with appropriate and honest means against all that may militate against those who only by this means can be held within the noble discipline of social life. But in the just fulfillment of this right, an authority which is truly worthy of the name will always be painfully conscious of its responsibility in the sight of the Eternal Judge, before Whose Tribunal every wrong judgment, and especially every revolt against the order established by God, will receive without fail its sanction and its condemnation.

The precise, bedrock, basic rules that govern society cannot be prejudiced by the intervention of human agency. They can be denied, overlooked, despised, transgressed, but they can never be overthrown with legal validity. It is true indeed that, as time goes on, conditions of life change. But there is never a complete break or a complete discontinuity between the law of yesterday and that of today, between the disappearance of old powers and constitutions and the appearance of a new order. In any case, whatever be the change or transformation, the scope of every social life remains identical, sacred, obligatory; it is the development of the personal values of man as the image of God; and the obligation remains with every member of the human family to realize his unchangeable destiny, whosoever be the legislator and the authority whom he obeys.

In consequence, there always remains, too, his inalienable right, which no opposition can nullify—a right which must be respected by friend and foe—to a legal order and practice which appreciate and understand that it is their essential duty to serve the common good.

The juridical order has, besides, the high and difficult scope of insuring harmonious relations both between individuals and between societies, and within these. This scope will be reached if legislators will abstain from following those perilous theories and practices, so harmful to communities to their spirit of union, which derive their origin and promulgation from false postulates. Among such postulates We must count the juridical positivism which attributes a deceptive majesty to the setting up of purely human laws, and which leaves the way open for a fatal divorce of law from morality.

There is, besides, the conception which claims for particular nations, or classes, the juridical instinct as the final imperative and the norm from which there is no appeal; finally, there are those various theories which, differing among themselves, and deriving from opposite ideologies, agree in considering the State, or a group which represents it, as an absolute and supreme entity, exempt from control and from criticism even when its theoretical and practical postulates result in, and offend by, their open denial of essential tenets of the human Christian conscience.

Anyone who considers with an open and penetrating mind the vital connection between social order and a genuine juridical order, and who is conscious of the fact that internal order in all its complexity depends on the predominance of spiritual forces, on the respect of human dignity in oneself and in others, on the love of society and of its God-given ends, cannot wonder at the sad effects of juridical conceptions which, far from the royal road of truth, proceed on the insecure ground of materialistic postulates. But he will realize at once the urgent need of a return to a conception of law which is spiritual and ethical, serious and profound, vivified by the warmth of true humanity and illumined by the splendor of the Christian Faith, which bids us seek in the juridical order an outward refraction of the social order willed by God, a luminous product of the spirit of man which is in turn the image of the Spirit of God.

On this organic conception which alone is living, in which the noblest humanity and the most genuine Christian spirit flourish in harmony, there is marked the Scripture thought, expounded by the great Aquinas: *Opus Justitiae Pax*—The work of justice shall be peace—a thought which is as applicable to the internal as to the external aspect of social life. It admits of neither contrast nor alternative such as expressed in the disjunction, love or right, but of the fruitful synthesis, love and right. In the one as in the other, since both radiate from the same Spirit of God, We read the program and the seal of the human spirit; they complement one another, give each other life and support, walk hand in hand along the road of concord and pacification, while right clears the way for love and love makes right less stern, and gives it a higher meaning. Both elevate human life to that social atmosphere where, even amid the failings, the obstacles and the difficulties of this earth a fraternal community of life is made possible.

But once let the baneful spirit of materialist ideas predominate; let the urge for power and for predominance take in its rough hands the direction of affairs; you shall then find its disruptive effects appearing daily in greater measure; you shall see love and justice disappear; all this as the sad foretaste of the catastrophes that menace society when it abandons God. . . .

The World of Labor

In one field of social life, where for a whole century there was agitation and bitter conflict, there is today a calm, at least on the surface. We speak of the vast and evergrowing world of labor, of the immense army of workers, of breadwinners and dependents. If we consider the present with its wartime exigencies, as an admitted fact, then this calm may be called a necessary and reasonable demand; but if we look at the present situation in the light of justice, and with reference to a legitimately regulated labor movement, then the tranquillity will remain only apparent, until the scope of such a movement be attained.

Always moved by religious motives, the Church has condemned the various forms of Marxist Socialism; and she condemns them today, because it is her permanent right and duty to safeguard men from currents as thought and influences that jeopardize their external salvation. But the

Church cannot ignore or overlook the fact that the worker in his efforts to better his lot, is opposed by a machinery which is not only not in accordance with nature, but is at variance with God's plan and with the purpose He had in creating the goods of earth.

In spite of the fact that the ways they followed were and are false and to be condemned, what man, and especially what priest or Christian, could remain deaf to the cries that rise from the depths and call for justice and a spirit of brotherly collaboration in a world ruled by a just God? Such silence would be culpable and unjustifiable before God, and contrary to the inspired teaching of the Apostle, who, while he inculcates the need of resolution in the fight against error, also knows that we must be full of sympathy for those who err, and open-minded in our understanding of their aspirations, hopes and motives.

When He blessed our first parents, God said: "Increase and multiply and fill the earth and subdue it." And to the first father of a family, He said later: "In the sweat of thy face shalt thou eat bread." The dignity of the human person, then, requires normally as a natural foundation of life the right to the use of the goods of the earth. To this right corresponds the fundamental obligation to grant private ownership of property, if possible, to all. Positive legislation regulating private ownership may change and more or less restrict its use. But if legislation is to play its part in the pacification of the community, it must prevent the worker, who is or will be a father of a family, from being condemned to an economic dependance and slavery which is irreconcilable with his rights as a person. Whether this slavery arises from the exploitation of private capital or from the power of the state, the result is the same. Indeed, under the pressure of a State which dominates all and controls the whole field of public and private life, even going into the realm of ideas and beliefs and of conscience, this lack of liberty can have the more serious consequences, as experience shows and proves.

Five Fundamental Points for the Order and Pacification of Human Society

Anyone who considers in the light of reason and of faith the foundations and the aims of social life, which we have

traced in broad outline, and contemplates them in their
purity and moral sublimity, and in their benefits in every
sphere of life, cannot but be convinced of the powerful
contribution to order and pacification which efforts directed
towards great ideals and resolved to face difficulties, could
present, or better, could restore to a world which is internally
unhinged, when once they had thrown down the intellectual
and juridical barriers, created by prejudice, errors, indif-
ferences, and by a long tradition of secularization of thought,
feeling, action which succeeded in detaching and subtracting
the early city from the light and force of the City of God.
Today, as never before, the hour has come for reparation,
for rousing the conscience of the world from the heavy
torpor into which the drugs of false ideas, widely diffused,
have sunk it. This is all the more so because in this hour of
material and moral disintegration the appreciation of the
emptiness and inconsistency of every purely human order is
beginning to disillusion even those who, in days of apparent happiness, were not conscious of the need of contact
with the eternal in themselves or in society, and did not
look upon its absence as an essential defect in their constitutions. What was clear to the Christian, who in his deeply
founded faith was pained by the ignorance of others, is
now presented to us in dazzling clearness by the din of appalling catastrophe which the present upheaval brings to
man and which portrays all the terrifying lineaments of a
general judgment even for the tepid, the indifferent, the
frivolous. It is indeed, an old truth which comes out in ever
new forms and thunders through the ages and through the
nations from the mouth of the Prophet: "All that forsake
thee shall be confounded; they who depart from thee,
shall be written in the earth; because they have forsaken the
Lord, the Vein of Living Waters."

The call of the moment is not lamentation but action; not
lamentation over what has been, but reconstruction of what
is to arise and must arise for the good of society. It is for the
best and most distinguished members of the Christian family,
filled with the enthusiasm of Crusaders, to unite in the
spirit of truth, justice and love to the call; God wills it,
ready to serve, to sacrifice themselves, like the Crusaders of
old.

If the issue was then the liberation of the land hallowed
by the life of the Incarnate Word of God, the call today
is, if We may so express Ourselves, to traverse the sea of

errors of our day and to march on to free the holy land of
the spirit, which is destined to sustain in its foundations the
unchangeable norms and laws on which will rise a social
construction of solid internal consistency . . . the first five
stones of which bear chiselled on them the following
maxims:

I. DIGNITY AND RIGHTS OF THE HUMAN PERSON

He who would have the Star of Peace shine out and stand
over society should cooperate, for his part, in giving back
to the human person the dignity given to it by God from
the very beginning; should oppose the excessive herding of
men, as if they were a mass without a soul; their economic,
social, political, intellectual and moral inconsistency; their
dearth of solid principles and strong convictions, their sur-
feit of instinctive sensible excitement and their fickleness.

He should favor, by every lawful means, in every sphere
of life, social institutions in which a full personal responsibility is assured and guaranteed both in the early and the
eternal order of things. He should uphold respect for and
the practical realization of the following fundamental personal rights; the right to maintain and develop one's corporal,
intellectual and moral life and especially the right to religious
formation and education; the right to worship God in private and public and to carry on religious works of charity;
the right to marry and to achieve the aim of married life;
the right to conjugal and domestic society; the right to
work, as the indispensable means towards the maintenance
of family life; the right to free choice of state of life, and
hence, too, of the priesthood or religious life; the right to
the use of material goods; in keeping with his duties and
social limitations.

II. DEFENSE OF SOCIAL UNITY AND ESPECIALLY OF THE FAMILY IN PRINCIPLE

He who would have the Star of Peace shine out and stand
over society should reject every form of materialism which
sees in the people only a herd of individuals who, divided
and without any internal cohesion, are considered as a mass
to be lorded over and treated arbitrarily; he should strive

to understand society as an intrinsic unity, which has grown up and matured under the guidance of Providence, a unity which within the bounds assigned to it and according to its own peculiar gifts—tends, with the collaboration of the various classes and professions, towards the eternal and ever new aims of culture and religion.

He should defend the indissolubility of matrimony; he should give to the family—that unique cell of the people—space, light and air so that it may attend to its mission of perpetuating new life, and of educating children in a spirit corresponding to its own true religious convictions, and that it may preserve, fortify and reconstitute, according to its powers, its proper economic, spiritual, moral and juridic unity. He should take care that the material and spiritual advantages of the family be shared by the domestic servants; he should strive to secure for every family a dwelling where a materially and morally healthy family life may be seen in all its vigor and worth; he should take care that the place of work be not so separated from the home as to make the head of the family and educator of the children a virtual stranger to his own household; he should take care above all that the bond of trust and mutual help should be re-established between the family and the public school, that bond which in other times gave such happy results, but which now has been replaced by mistrust where the school, influenced and controlled by the spirit of materialism, corrupts and destroys what the parents have instilled into the minds of the children.

III. Dignity and Prerogative of Labor

He who would have the Star of Peace shine out and stand over society should give to work the place assigned to it by God from the beginning. As an indispensable means towards gaining over the world that mastery which God wishes, for His glory, all work has an inherent dignity and at the same time a close connection with the perfection of the person; this is the noble dignity and privilege of work which is not in any way cheapened by the fatigue and the burden, which have to be borne as the effect of original sin, in obedience and submission to the will of God.

Those who are familiar with the great Encyclicals of Our predecessors and Our Own previous messages know well that

the Church does not hesitate to draw the practical con-
clusions which are derived from the moral nobility of work,
and to give them all the support of her authority. These
exigencies include, besides a just wage which covers the
needs of the worker and his family, the conversation and
perfection of a social order which will make possible an
assured, even if modest, private property for all classes
of society, which will promote higher education for the
children of the working class who are especially endowed
with intelligence and good will, will promote the care and
the practice of the social spirit in one's immediate neigh-
borhood, in the district, the province, the people and the
nation, a spirit which, by smoothing over friction arising
from privileges or class interests, removes from the workers
the sense of isolation through the assuring experience of a
genuinely human, and fraternally Christian, solidarity.

The progress and the extent of urgent social reforms depend on the economic possibilities of single nations. It is only
through an intelligent and generous sharing of forces between the strong and the weak that it will be possible to effect
a universal pacification in such wise as not to leave behind
centers of conflagration and infection from which new dis-
asters may come. There are evident signs which go to show
that, in the ferment of all the prejudices and feelings of
hate, those inevitable but lamentable offspring of the war
psychosis, there is still aflame in the people the consciousness of their intimate mutual dependence for good or for
evil, nay, that this consciousness is more alive and active.
It is not true that deep thinkers see ever more clearly in the
renunciation of egoism and national isolation, the way to
general salvation, ready as they are to demand of their peoples a heavy participation in the sacrifices necessary for social wellbeing in other peoples?

May this Christmas Message of Ours, addressed to all
those who are animated by a good and generous heart, encourage and increase the legions of these social crusades in
every nation. And may God deign to give to their peaceful
cause the victory of which their noble enterprise is worthy.

IV. THE REHABILITATION OF JURIDICAL ORDER

He who would have the Star of Peace shine out and stand
over social life should collaborate towards a complete re-

habilitation of the juridical order. The juridic sense of today is often altered and overturned by the profession and the practice of positivism and a utilitarianism which are subjected and bound to the service of determined groups, classes and movements, whose programs direct and determine the course of legislation and the practices of the courts. The cure of this situation becomes feasible when we awaken again the consciousness of a juridical order resting on the supreme dominion of God, and safeguarded from all human whims; a consciousness of an order which stretches forth its arm, in protection or punishment, over the unforgettable rights of man and protects them against the attacks of every human power.

From the juridical order, as willed by God, flows man's inalienable right to juridical security, and by this very fact to a definite sphere of rights, immune from all arbitrary attack. The relations of man to man, of the individual to society, to authority, to civil duties; the relations of society and of authority to the individual, should be placed on a firm juridic footing and be guarded, when the need arises, by the authority of the courts. This supposes:

(A) A tribunal and a judge who take their directions from a clearly formulated and defined right.

(B) Clear juridical norms which may not be overturned by unwarranted appeals to a supposed popular sentiment or by merely utilitarian considerations.

(C) The recognition of the principle that even the State and the functionaries and organizations depend on it are obliged to repair and to withdraw measures which are harmful to the liberty, property, honor, progress of health of the individuals.

V. THE CONCEPTION OF THE STATE ACCORDING TO THE CHRISTIAN SPIRIT

He who would have the Star of Peace shine out and stand over human society should cooperate towards the setting up of a State conception and practice founded on reasonable discipline, exalted kindliness and a responsible Christian spirit. He should help to restore the State and its power to the service of human society, to the full recognition of the respect due to the human person and his efforts to attain his eternal destiny. He should apply and devote himself to dis-

pelling the errors which aim at causing the State and its authority to deviate from the path of morality, at severing them
from the eminently ethical bond which links them to individual and social life, and at making them deny or in practice
ignore their essential dependence on the will of the Creator.
He should work for the recognition and diffusion of the
truth which teaches, even in matters of this world, that the
deepest meaning, the ultimate moral basis and the universal validity of "reigning" lies in "serving."

Consideration on The World War and the Renovation of Society

Beloved Children, may God grant that while you listened
to Our voice your heart may be profoundly stirred and
moved by the deeply felt seriousness, the loving solicitude,
the unremitting insistence, with which We drive home
these thoughts, which are meant as an appeal to the conscience of the world, and a rallying-cry to all those who are
ready to ponder and weigh the grandeur of their mission
and responsibility by the vastness of this universal disaster.

A great part of mankind, and, let Us not shirk from saying it, not a few who call themselves Christians, have to
some extent their share in the collective responsibility for
the growth of error and for the harm and the lack of moral
fibre in the society of today.

What is this world war, with all its attendant circumstances, whether they be remote or proximate causes, its
progress and material, legal and moral effects? What is it
but the crumbling process, not expected, perhaps, by the
thoughtless but seen and depreciated by those whose gaze
penetrated into the realities of a social order which—hid
its mortal weakness and its unbridled lust for gain and
power? That which in peacetime lay coiled up, broke loose
at the outbreak of war in a sad succession of acts at variance
with the human and Christian sense. International agreements to make war less inhuman by confining it to the
combatants to regulate the procedure of occupation and im-
prisonment of the conquered remained in various places a
dead letter. And who can see the end of this progressive
demoralization of the people, who can wish to watch help-
lessly this disastrous progress? Should they not rather, over

the ruins of a social order which has given such tragic proof of its ineptitude as a factor for the good of the people, gather together the hearts of all those who are magnanimous and upright, in the solemn vow not to rest until in all peoples and all nations of the earth a vast legion shall be formed of those handfuls of men who, bent on bringing back society to its center of gravity, which is the law of God, aspire to the service of the human person and of his common life ennobled in God.

Mankind owes that vow to the countless dead who lie buried on the field of battle: The sacrifice of their lives in the fulfillment of their duty is a holocaust offered for a new and better social order. Mankind owes that vow to the innumerable sorrowing host of mothers, widows and orphans who have seen the light, the solace and the support of their lives wrenched from them. Mankind owes that vow to those numberless exiles whom the hurricane of war has torn from their native land and scattered in the land of the stranger; who can make their own the lament of the Prophet: "Our inheritance is turned to aliens; our house to strangers." Mankind owes that vow to the hundreds of thousands of persons who, without any fault on their part, sometimes only because of their nationality or race, have been consigned to death or to a slow decline. Mankind owes that vow to the many thousands of non-combatants, women, children, sick and aged, from whom aerial warfare—whose horrors we have from the beginning frequently denounced—has without discrimination or through inadequate precautions, taken life, goods, health, home, charitable refuge, or house of prayer. Mankind owes that vow to the flood of tears and bitterness, to the accumulation of sorrow and suffering, emanating from the murderous ruin of the dreadful conflict and crying to Heaven to send down the Holy Spirit to liberate the world from the inundation of violence and terror. . . .

PEACE AND THE FUNCTION OF FORCE*

Once again, for the fifth time, beloved sons and daughters throughout the world, the great Christian family is preparing to celebrate the magnificent feast of peace and love, which in a sombre atmosphere of death and hate, redeems us and makes us all brothers. . . .

Unfortunately, the world, as it looks around, must still behold with horror the reality of strife and destruction which, growing daily wider and more cruel, dashes its hopes and, with the city blast of harsh experience, destroys and cuts short its most sanguine impulses. We see, indeed, only a conflict which degenerates into that form of warfare that excludes all restriction and restraint, as if it were the apocalyptic expression of a civilization in which ever-growing technical progress is accompanied by an ever greater decline in the realm of the soul and of morality.

Past History Pales

It is a form of war which proceeds without intermission on its horrible way and piles up slaughter of such a kind that the most blood-stained and horrible pages of past history pale in comparison with it. The peoples have had to witness a new and incalculable perfection of the means and arts of destruction, while at the same time they see an interior decadence which, starting from the weakening and deviation of the moral sense, is hurtling ever downward toward the state where every human sentiment is being crushed and the light of reason is eclipsed, so that the words of wisdom are fulfilled: "They were all bound together with one chain of darkness" (Wisdom 17:17). . . .

* Christmas message, 1943. As delivered on Vatican Radio.

To the Disillusioned

It is tragically sad, dear children, to think that countless men, while in their search for a happiness that will satisfy them on this earth, feel the bitterness of deceptive illusions and painful disillusionment and have closed the door to all hope; and living, as they do, far from the Christian Faith, they cannot retrace their steps towards the crib and towards that consolation in which the names of the Heroes of the Faith abound in joy in all their tribulations.

They see dashed to pieces the structure of those beliefs in which they humanly trusted and set up their ideal. But they never achieved that one true faith which would have given them comfort and renewed spirit. In this intellectual and moral trial they are seized by a depressing uncertainty and live in a state of inertia which weighs down their souls. It is a state which can be deeply understood and commiserated only by those who enjoy the delight of living in the clear, warm atmosphere of a supernatural faith which ascends above the storms of temporal contingency to dwell with the eternal.

In the ranks of these straying disillusioned souls it is not hard to find those who placed all their faith in a world expansion of economic life, thinking that this alone would suffice to draw the peoples together in a spirit of brotherhood, and promising themselves from its grandiose organization, perfected and refined to an ever greater degree, unheard of an unsuspected increase of prosperity for human society.

With that complacency and pride did they not contemplate the growth of commerce, the interchange, even between continents, of all goods and all inventions and products, the triumphal march of widely-diffused modern technical perfection, overcoming all limits of time and space!

Today, what is the reality that they behold! They see now that this economic life with all its gigantic contacts and wide ramifications, with its superabundant division and multiplication of labor, contributed in a thousand ways to generalize and accentuate the crisis of mankind, while, not having the corrective of any moral control, or any guiding light from beyond this world, it could not but end in the unworthy and humiliating exploitation of the nature and

personality of man, in a sad and terrifying want on one side
contrasting with a proud and provoking opulence on the
other, in a torturing, implacable divergence between the privileged and those who have nothing—ill-omened effects which
are not the last link in a chain of causes which led to the
immense tragedy of today. . . .

Those Who Put Their Faith in Godless Science

In the same way acted and thought in the past those
other deluded ones, who placed happiness and prosperity
exclusively in a form of science and culture which was averse
to the recognizing the Creator of the universe. These were
the exponents and followers not of the true science (which
is a wonderful reflection of the Light of God), but of an
arrogant science, which did not allow place for a personal
God, Who is untrammeled by any limitations and is superior
to all things earthly and boasted that it could explain the
happenings of the world exclusively by the rigid and blind
application of fixed laws of nature.

Such a science cannot give happiness or prosperity. The
apostacy from the Divine Word, by Whom all things were
made, has led man on to apostacy from the spirit and has
thus made it difficult for him to reach ideals and aims of a
high intellectual or moral order. In this way the science
which has apostatized from the life of the spirit, while it
deluded itself into thinking that it has acquired full
liberty and autonomy in denying God finds itself today punished by a servitude more humiliating than ever before. For
it has become the slave and the almost blind follower of
policies and orders which take no account of the rights of
truth or of the human person. What to this science seemed
liberty was in fact a humiliating and degrading fetter; and,
dethroned as it is it will not resume its primitive dignity
unless by a return to the Divine Word, the source of wisdom
so foolishly abandoned and forgotten. To such a return in
fact, the Son of God, Who is the Way, the Truth and the
Life invites us. He is the Way of happiness, the Truth which
exalts, the Life which gives man eternity. . . .

To Those Afflicted Without Hope

Besides those who go through life profoundly disconcerted because of the bankruptcy of social and intellectual trends largely followed by political leaders and scientists stands the not less numerous class of those who are in great distress and sorrow because of the collapse of their own personal and private ideal of life.

This class comprises the immense number of those for whom labor was the end of life, and for whom the goal of their fatigue was a comfortable material existence, but who, in the struggle to attain this end, had put far from them religious consideration, and had neglected to give their life a healthy moral orientation. The war has torn them from this customary congenial activity which was the delight and support of their life. It has dragged them from their professions and their tasks, so that they feel within themselves a dreadful void.

And if some can still continue their usual activities, the war has imposed conditions of work in which all personal initiative has been eliminated, orderly family life is made difficult or impossible, and that satisfaction of soul is no longer found, which can only be had from work as it was ennobled and ordained by God. . . .

Principles for Peace Program

And, now do you all, who have responsibility, all of you who by the disposition and permission of God hold in your hand the destiny of your own and other peoples, hear the suppliant *"Erudimini"* (be ye enlightened) which resounds in your ears from out the abysmal ruins of this terrible war. It is a duty and a warning for all, a trumpet call anticipating the coming judgment which will decree the condemnation and punishment of those who were deaf to the voice of humanity—which is also the voice of God. In the consciousness of your power your war aims may well have embraced entire peoples and continents. The question of guilty re-

sponsibility for the present war and the demand for repara-
tions may also lead you to raise your voice.

But today the devastation which the world war has produced in every walk of life, material and spiritual, has already reached such unprecedented gravity and extent, and
the dreaded danger that, as the war goes on, the destruction
will be increased by frightful horrors for both sides, and
for those who, against their will, have been drawn into it,
appears to Us so gloomy and threatening that We, anxious
for the welfare and even for the very existence of each and
every people, address this appeal to you.

Rise above yourselves, above every narrow calculating
judgment, above every beast of military superiority, above
every one-sided affirmation of right and justice. Take cognizance also of the unpleasant truths and teach your peoples
to look them in the face with gravity and fortitude. A true
peace is not the mathematical result of a proportion of
forces, but in its last and deepest meaning is a moral and
juridical process. It is not, in fact, achieved without the
employment of force, and its very existence needs the support of a normal measure of power.

But the real function of this force, if it is to be morally
correct, should consist in protecting and defending, and not
in lessening or suppressing rights. An hour like the present—
so full of possibilities for vast beneficent progress no less
than for fatal defects and blunders—has perhaps never been
seen in the history of mankind.

This hour demands, with insistent voice, that the aims
and programs for peace be inspired by the highest moral
sense. They should have as their supreme purpose nothing
less than the task of securing agreement and concord between the warring nations—an achievement which may
leave with every nation, in the consciousness of its duty to
unite with the rest of the family of State, the possibility of
cooperating with dignity, without renouncing or destroying
itself, in the great future task of recuperation and reconstruction.

Naturally, the achievement of such a peace would not
imply in any way the abandonment of necessary guarantees
and sanctions in the event of any attempt to use force
against right. Do not ask from any member of the family of
peoples, however small or weak, for that renunciation of
substantial rights or vital necessities, which you yourselves,
if it were demanded from your people, would deem·im-

practicable. Give mankind, thirsting for it, a peace that shall reinstate the human race in its own esteem and in that of history—a peace over whose cradle the vengeful lightning of hate and the instincts of unchecked desire for vengeance do not flash, but rather the resplendent dawn of a new spirit of world union which, sustained by the indispensable, supernatural help of the Christian faith, will alone be able to preserve humanity, after this unhappy war, from the unspeakable catastrophe of a peace built on wrong foundations and therefore ephemeral and illusory.

ELECTIONS AND VOTING*

It is a right and a duty to draw the attention of the faithful to the extraordinary importance of elections and the moral responsibility which rests on everyone who has the right to vote. Without any doubt, the Church intends to remain outside and above political parties, but how can she remain indifferent to the composition of a Parliament, when the Constitution gives it power to pass laws which so directly affect the highest religious interests and even the condition of life of the Church herself? Then there are also other arduous questions, above all the problems and economic struggles which closely touch the well-being of the people. In so far as they are of a temporal order (though in reality they also affect the moral order) Churchmen leave to others the care of pondering and treating technically with them for the common welfare of the nation. From all this it follows that:

It is a strict duty for all who have the right, men or women, to take part in the elections. Whoever abstains, especially out of cowardice, commits a grave sin, a mortal fault.

Everyone has to vote according to the dictates of his own conscience. Now, it is evident that the voice of this conscience imposes upon every sincere Catholic the duty of

* From an address to the Delegates of the International Conference on Emigration, October 17, 1951. Official version.

giving his or her vote to those candidates, or those lists of candidates, who really offer sufficient assurances for safeguarding the rights of God and the souls of men, for the real good of individuals, families, and society, according to the law of God and moral Christian doctrine.

FOOD FOR THE WORLD'S PEOPLES*

For several years We have followed the activities of the United Nations Food and Agricultural Organization with lively interest. We are therefore happy to welcome you, gentlemen, during the proceedings of your seventh session.

It is a fact, in spite of recent improvements, that the problem of food remains a crucial one for a large part of mankind. As you state in your reports, the present situation of the world, from an agricultural point of view, is characterized by a marked imbalance between developed areas and countries which are still insufficiently developed. In the first case production is increasing rapidly, the level of consumption is rising again and exports are mounting; in the other—particularly in the Far East—production remains inadequate, food insufficient and imports limited. The possibility of famine, with its frightful consequences, unceasingly haunts millions of men, a period of drought being enough to bring about that terrible calamity. Moreover, it is necessary to take account of the continuous growth of the population, which demands, at the risk of making the evil worse, a parallel increase in the goods to be consumed.

Effort to Abolish Suffering

Your organization has given itself the task of meeting this difficult situation and of engaging in a decisive world-wide

* From an address to delegates attending the seventh session of the U.N. Food and Agricultural Organization, December 6, 1953. From *The Catholic Mind*, March, 1954, pp. 187–188.

struggle to abolish suffering and the dangers which even today still threaten so many unfortunate people. What courage is necessary to dare to envisage tranquilly an undertaking which can be described without exaggeration as gigantic, and to devote oneself to it enthusiastically when it seems to become larger and more complicated the more one works at it. But, animated with indefatigable zeal, you have already succeeded in providing an indispensable basis for your work by obtaining the necessary information on the agricultural production and marketing conditions of the different countries. In many cases, in order to get precise information, you had to train experts and teach them modern statistical methods. Thus you have collected valuable materials which will be of great service to economists.

The essential part of your work consists of acting effectively in the field of agriculture and also of exploiting the fishing and forestry industries. You will undoubtedly be preoccupied with directing toward underfed peoples, who make up seventy per cent of the world's population, the surplus production of the more favored nations, thereby assuring the latter of stable markets. But it is much more urgent to provide for increased production in the very places where scarcity makes itself felt. In order to do this you desire first to reduce the often considerable losses due to the inexperience of farmers and to epidemics. Then you want to increase production through improvement of cultivation methods, the use of fertilizer and the selection of plant species. Finally, you look forward to putting into use lands that are still uncultivated, especially by means of irrigation.

In all of this the phases of achievement are necessarily preceded by inquiries and detailed studies designed to weigh the possibilities of improvement and to prevent the consequences of serious error. Let Us also mention as a significant example of the cultural aspects of your work the plan put into effect to raise paper production, which the U. N. Economic and Social Council has entrusted to you.

Uncommon Problems

This plan, so broad and varied, unquestionably raises uncommon problems. The most delicate perhaps, as you have clearly seen, will consist of creating social conditions in which the workers to whom you are going to give aid and advice will develop a taste for their work, interest themselves in it and exploit to the maximum the resources procured for them. In fact, it is useless to send out experts to teach new methods and improve mechanical equipment when the human conditions in which a man lives keep him from drawing from his efforts the profit he has a right to expect.

To stimulate interest and personal initiative, to show that the good of the community will not be achieved at the expense of the welfare of individuals, but to their profit, and to see to it that this is really the case are certainly elements of primary importance for your success. Thus to your economic task is added a no less decisive social one, whose value We should like to emphasize. That is why, eager to show you Our support and to collaborate with you in your undertaking, We were happy recently to make Our contribution to the program of extending technical assistance to various countries, especially in the poorest regions.

Despite the still limited means of your organization, you have not been afraid to interest in it all peoples who are eager, not only to improve themselves and obtain economic advantages, but also to help the less fortunate. Action of this sort, as We remarked in a speech given under similar circumstances on February 21, 1948, obliges nations to consider themselves both the beneficiaries and the benefactors of one another.

Victims of Hunger

The civilized world always looks with great sadness at the pitiful picture of hunger victims at a time when the earth is capable of feeding all men. To abolish such an evil once and for all is certainly worth sacrifices and justifies great devotion. Was not Christ careful to satisfy the hunger of the crowds which followed Him? Did He not teach His disciples a prayer that asks for daily bread? In pursuing the goal which you have set for yourselves, you are undoubtedly seeking an end dear to Him Who consecrated Himself to the salvation of humanity. That is why We want you to go on with your work without faltering. It is without question only at its beginning, but you have already learned a great deal from experience. The tools with which you work are being improved and your prestige is increasing among governments, which appreciate more and more the usefulness and the fruits of your activities. If the final goal is not yet in sight, you can at least hope that a greater understanding and a more active cooperation will come to reinforce and multiply the results already obtained and to guarantee more rapid progress in the future.

We desire this for you with all Our heart and ask for you, your families and all who share your work the most abundant blessings of Heaven.

MEDICAL ETHICS*

You have informed Us of the goals of the World Medical Association and of the results it has obtained in the seven years of its existence. It is with great interest that We have taken cognizance of that information and of the great number of tasks to which you have dedicated your attention and your efforts: the contacting and grouping of national medical associations, the mutual exchange of experiences, the examination of current problems of different countries, the formal agreements made with a series of related organizations, the creation of a general secretariat in New York and the founding of your own magazine, *World Medical Journal*.

Besides these accomplishments of a more or less administrative nature, there were the establishment and evaluation of some important points concerning the medical profession and its conditions, the defense of the reputation and honor of the corps of doctors, the preparation of an international code of medical ethics, that has already been accepted by forty-two nations, the acceptance of a new version of the Oath of Hippocrates (Oath of Geneva) and the official condemnation of euthanasia. And among many other questions, those concerning the transformation and development of

* An address to the Eighth Congress of the World Medical Association, September 30, 1954. From *The Catholic Mind*, April, 1955, pp. 242–252.

university instruction for the training of young doctors and for medical research were dealt with. We have here recalled only a few points. To the program of the present 8th congress you have added, for example, the duties of a doctor in time of war, of bacteriological war in particular, the position of the doctor in regard to chemical and atomic warfare and of experimentation on man.

The medical, as well as the technical and administrative, aspect of such questions is within your competence; but in those things which concern their moral and juridical aspect, We should like to call your attention to certain points. A series of the problems which are occupying you have occupied Us, too. These problems were the subject of special discourses. Thus, on September 14, 1952, to participants in the First International Congress on the Histopathology of the Nervous System We spoke, at their request, on the moral limits of modern methods of research and treatment. We linked up Our discussion to the examination of the three principles from which medicine derives the justification of its methods of research and treatment: the scientific interests of medicine, the interests of the patient and the interests of the community or, as they say, of the common good, the "bonum commune." [1]

In an address on October 19, 1953, to the members of the 16th International Congress of Military Medicine, We spoke on the essential principles of medical morality and medical law, their origin, their content and their application. [2] The 26th congress of the Italian Association of Urology put to Us the debatable question: is it morally permissible to destroy a sound organ in order to stop the progress of an illness that threatens life? We answered it in the discourse of October 8 of last year. Finally, We touched on the problems that are occupying your attention during the present congress—those of a moral appraisal of modern war and its conduct—in an address on October 3, 1953, to participants in the 6th International Congress on Penal Law. [3]

If today We do no more than recall briefly some of these points, notwithstanding their importance and scope, We hope that all the explanations We have given previously will serve

[1] *Catholic Mind*, LI, 305–313 (May, 1953).

[2] *Ibid.*, LII, 46–54 (Jan., 1954).

[3] *Ibid.*, LII, 107–118 (Feb., 1954).

as a complement. In order not to prolong this address too much, We shall cite them fully in footnotes each time (We refer to them).

A. War and Peace

That the doctor has a role during war, and a privileged role, is obvious. At no other time are there so many to be cared for and cured among soldiers and civilians, friends and enemies. It is necessary to concede to the doctor, without restrictions, the natural right to intervene where his help is needed and also to guarantee this to him by means of international conventions. It would be an aberration of the judgment and the heart to want to deny medical aid to the enemy and let him die.

Has not the doctor also a role to play in producing, perfecting and increasing the methods of modern warfare, in particular the methods of ABC warfare? One cannot answer this question without having first resolved this other one: is modern "total war," especially ABC warfare, permissible in principle? There can be no doubt, particularly in view of the horrors and immense sufferings caused by modern warfare, that to unleash it without a just cause (that is to say, without its being forced upon one by an obvious, extremely serious and otherwise unavoidable injustice) constitutes a "crime" worthy of the most severe national and international sanctions.

One cannot even in principle pose the question of the lawfulness of atomic, bacteriological and chemical warfare except in the case where it must be judged as indispensable in order to defend oneself under the circumstances pointed out above. Even then, however, one must strive to avoid it by all possible means through international understandings or to impose limits on its use that are so clear and rigorous that its effects remain restricted to the strict demands of defense. When, moreover, putting this method to use involves such an extension of the evil that it entirely escapes from the control of man, its use must be rejected as immoral. Here there would no longer be a question of "defense" against injustice or a necessary "safeguarding" of legitimate possessions, but the pure and simple annihilation of all human life within the radius of action. This is not permitted for any reason whatsoever.

Let us return to the doctor. If ever, within the compass of the limits already indicated, a modern (ABC) war can be justified, the question of the morally lawful collaboration of the doctor can then be raised. But you will be in agreement with Us: one prefers not to see the doctor occupied with a task of this sort. It is in too great a contrast to his basic duty: to give aid and cure, not to do injury or kill.

This will make understandable to you the meaning and justification of Our previous explanations, of what We have said on the condemnation of war in general and on the position and role of the military doctor (Notes 1 and 2).

B. Experimentation on Man

According to information coming to Us from you, you have added to the original program of your present congress the question of experimentation on living men.

The postwar trials of doctors have shown what proportions such experimentation can assume and to what abuses it can lead.

We permit Ourselves in regard to this subject to refer to a passage in one of Our previous discourses (Note 3).

That medical research and practice could not dispense with all experimentation on living men is easily understood. But there is the question of knowing what the necessary presuppositions of experimentation are, along with its limits, its obstacles and its decisive basic principles. In desperate cases, when a sick person is lost unless someone intervenes and when there exists a medication, a treatment or an operation which, without excluding all danger, still has a certain chance of succeeding, then an honest and reflecting mind immediately admits that the doctor may, with the explicit or tacit consent of the patient, proceed with the application of such a treatment. Research, life and practice, however, are not limited to such cases. They exceed them and go further. Even among serious and conscientious doctors the idea is expressed that if risks are not taken with new procedures, if new methods are not tried, progress is slowed down, when it is not altogether paralyzed. In the field of surgery especially it is pointed out that numerous operations which today do not entail any particular risk have behind them a long past and period of trial—the time necessary for the doctor to study and practice—and that a more or less large number of fatal cases marked the beginnings of these procedures.

It is within your professional competence to answer questions about the medical assumptions and information concerning experimentation on living men. The difficulty of a moral and juridical examination, however, makes a few suggestions appear necessary.

In Our address to military doctors We briefly formulated the essential directives on this subject (Note 4).

In order to treat and solve these problems recourse is had, as can be seen in the text We have cited, to a series of moral principles of the most fundamental importance: the questions of the relationship between the individual and the community, of the content and the limits of the right to use the property of others, of the assumptions and extension of the principle of integrity, of the relationship between the individual and social ends of man and other matters of a similar nature. Although these matters do not pertain specifically to the field of medicine, nevertheless medicine, just as any other human activity, must take them into consideration.

What goes for the doctor in regard to his patient, goes also for the doctor in regard to himself. He is subject to the same great moral and juridical principles. He cannot, therefore, submit himself to scientific experiments or practices that entail serious harm or that threaten his health. Still less is he authorized to attempt an experiment which, according to authoritative information, may involve mutilation or suicide. The same must be said, furthermore, of male and female nurses and of anyone who may be disposed to give himself to therapeutic research. They cannot submit themselves to such experiments.

This basic prohibition does not concern the personal motive of the person who offers himself, sacrifices himself and renounces himself on behalf of a sick person or because of a desire to collaborate in the advancement of an important science which he wants to assist and serve. If such were the case, an affirmative answer would be automatically given. In every profession, and particularly in medicine and nursing, there is no lack of persons who are ready to consecrate themselves completely to others and to the common good. But in this matter it is not a question of such a motive or such a personal sacrifice. In this matter it is a question, in the final analysis, of disposing of a non-personal good which one has no right to dispose of. Man only enjoys the use of, but is not the independent owner and proprietor of, his body, his life and all that the Creator has given him to make use of—to make use of in conformity with the purposes of nature. The basic principle, "Only he who has the right of disposition is competent to make use of it, and then only within the limits that have been established," is one of the ultimate and most universal norms of action to which spontaneous and sound judgment firmly adheres and without which the juridical order and the common life of man in society is impossible.

Concerning the removal of parts of the body of a dead person for therapeutic purposes, the doctor cannot be permitted to treat a corpse as he pleases. It is up to public authority to establish suitable rules. But neither can public authority proceed arbitrarily. There are some provisions of law against which it is possible to raise serious objections. A norm, such as that which permits a doctor in a sanatorium to remove parts of the body for therapeutic purposes, all intention of seeking a profit being excluded, is not yet admissible because of the possibility of interpreting it too freely. There must also be taken into consideration the rights and duties of those upon whom responsibility for the body of the deceased falls. Finally, respect must be had for the demands of natural morality, which forbids one to consider and to treat the corpse of a man simply as a thing or as that of an animal.

C. Medical Morality and Law

You will understand that, in going through the list of results that you have already obtained in the course of seven years of existence, the preparation of an international code of medical morality, already accepted by forty-two countries, has particularly aroused Our interest.

It might be thought that it was easy to create a world-wide medical morality and a uniform world medical code. Doubtless human nature is the same throughout the world in its basic laws and aspects. The goal of medical science, and hence of the serious doctor, is also everywhere the same:

to help, to cure and to prevent (disease), not to do injury or to kill. Granted this, there are certain things that no doctor does, that no doctor upholds or justifies, but that all doctors condemn. Likewise there are certain things that no doctor omits to do but which, on the contrary, every doctor demands and carries out. This is, if you will, the doctor's code of honor and of his duties.

In reality, nevertheless, present-day medical morality is actually still quite far from constituting a uniform and complete world morality. There are relatively few principles accepted everywhere. But this relatively small number is still worthy of consideration and merits high and positive appreciation as the point of departure for further development.

Regarding medical morality, We should like to propose for your consideration the following three basic ideas:

1. *Medical morality must be based on being and nature.* This is so because it must correspond to the essence of human nature and to its laws and immanent relations. All moral norms, even those of medicine, necessarily proceed from corresponding ontological principles. Whence comes the maxim: "Be what you are." That is why a purely positivist medical morality denies itself.

2. *Medical morality must conform to reason and finality and be oriented in accordance with values.* Medical morality does not live in things, but in men—in persons, in doctors, in their judgment, their personality and in their conception and realization of values. In a doctor medical morality is a question of personal conscience: "What does this norm of action impose? What is its justification?" That is to say, "What ends does it pursue and has it set up for itself?" "What values does it express in itself, in its personal relations and in its social structure?" In other words, "Of what does it treat?" "Why? For what purpose? What is it worth?" Moral men cannot be superficial and, if they are, cannot remain so.

3. *Medical morality must be rooted in the transcendental.* What, in the final analysis, has been established by man can, in the final analysis, be suppressed by man and man, if it is necessary or it pleases him, can get rid of it. This is in contradiction to the constancy of human nature, to the constancy of its destiny and of its purpose and to the absolute and imprescriptible character of its essential demands. In effect, these do not say: "If, as a doctor, you want to judge well and act well, do this." But they make themselves known

in the very depths of personal conscience in an altogether different form: "You must act well at all costs! Hence you must act in this way and not otherwise!" This absolute character of moral demands remains, whether a man heed them or not.

Moral duty does not depend on the pleasure of man! Only moral action is his affair. The phenomenon, which is noticed at all times, of the absolute character of the moral order obliges one to recognize that, in the last analysis, medical morality possesses a transcendental basis and rule. In our address to the Congress on Military Medicine, We developed these considerations and talked about the authority controlling medical morality (Note 5).

Let Us add a word on medical law, which We have in the past treated in more detail.

The life of men in a community demands determined and clearly defined norms, not, however, in greater number than the common good requires. Moral norms, on the contrary, extend much further, are much more numerous and, in many ways, are less clearly defined in order to permit their necessary adaptation to the justified demands of particular cases.

The doctor penetrates deeply into the life of the individual and the community by virtue of the profession he exercises. Within society he has need of broad juridical support and also of a special security for his person and his medical activities. On the other hand, society wants a guarantee of the ability and competence of those who present themselves and act as doctors. All this goes to show the necessity for a national and, as far as possible, an international medical code. But not in the sense of detailed regulations fixed by law. Let the state, on the contrary, entrust as far as possible the drafting of such regulations to associations of doctors, national and international, by giving them the necessary powers and sanctions. Let the state reserve to itself a higher supervision, the ultimate sanctions and the integration of the order and associations of doctors in the general structure of national life.

Medical law in its content must express medical morality, at least it should contain nothing that is opposed to morality. That it will succeed in proposing all that it should in order to satisfy the demands of natural ethics is, according to the experience we have had, a desire whose realization is still very remote.

In conclusion, medical morality is, fundamentally, based

on being, on reason and on God. Medical law, in addition, depends on man.

We have taken up three points of the broad program of your congress and We have said a word about war and peace, experimentation on man and the efforts to establish a world-wide medical morality and a world-wide medical law. We have wished in this way to stimulate and orientate your personal judgment and to contribute, on Our part, to the fruitful advancement and the deepening of your work.

Notes

1. In the first place, there is the crime of making a modern war which is not required by absolute necessity of self-defense, and which brings with it, as We can assert without hesitation, unthinkable ruin, sufferings and horrors. The community of nations must reckon with unprincipled criminals who, in order to realize their ambitious plans, are not afraid to unleash total war. This is the reason why other countries, if they wish to preserve their very existence and their most precious possessions, and unless they are prepared to accord free action to international criminals, have no alternative but to get ready for the day when they must defend themselves. This right to be prepared for self-defense cannot be denied, even in these days, to any state. That, however, does not in any way alter the fact that unjust war is to be accounted as one of the very gravest crimes which international penal law must proscribe, must punish with the heaviest penalties, and the authors of which are in every case guilty and liable to the punishment that has been agreed on (Address to delegates to the 6th International Congress on Penal Law).

THE DOCTOR AND WAR

2. This point is decisive for the position of the doctor in regard to war in general and to modern war in particular. The doctor is the enemy of war and the promoter of peace. As he is ready to heal the wounds of war, once they already exist, so should he do all he can to prevent them.

Mutual good will always allow states to avoid war as the final means of settling differences between themselves. Several days ago We again expressed Our desire that any war be punished at the international level which is not absolutely necessary for the self-defense of a community very seriously threatened by an injustice that cannot be prevented in any other way. Even such a war, however, must be waged at the risk of giving a free hand in international affairs to brute violence and lack of conscience. It is not enough, therefore, to have to defend oneself against just any injustice in order to justify resorting to the violent means of war. When the damages caused by war are not comparable to those of "tolerated injustice," one may have a duty to "suffer the injustice."

What We have just discussed applies especially to ABC warfare—atomic, biological and chemical. As to the question of knowing whether it (ABC warfare) can become clearly necessary in self-defense against ABC warfare, let it suffice for Us to have posed it there. The answer can be deduced from the same principles which are today decisive for permitting war in general. In any case, another question arises first: is it not possible through international understandings to proscribe and avert ABC warfare?

After the horrors of two world conflicts We do not have to remind you that any apotheosis of war is to be condemned as an aberration of mind and heart. Certainly, spiritual strength and bravery, even to the point of giving one's life when duty demands it, are great virtues; but to want to start a war because it is the school of great virtues and the occasion for practising them must be characterized as a crime and madness.

What We have said shows the direction in which one will find the answer to that other question: may the doctor put his knowledge and activity at the service of ABC warfare? "Injustice" he can never support, even in the service of his own country, and when that type of war constitutes an injustice, the doctor may not take part in it (Address to delegates to 16th International Congress on Military Medicine).

MORAL LIMIT ON COMMUNITY'S POWER

3. Nevertheless, for the third time We come back to the question: Is there any moral limit to the "medical interests of the community" in content or extension? Are there "full powers" over the living man in every serious medical case? Does it raise barriers that are still valid in the interests of

science or of the individual? Or, stated differently, can public authority, on which rests responsibility for the common good, give the doctor the power to experiment on the individual in the interests of science and the community in order to discover and try out new methods and procedures when these experiments transgress the right of the individual to dispose of himself? In the interests of the community can public authority really limit or even suppress the right of the individual over his body and life, his bodily and psychic integrity?

To forestall an objection We assume that there is question of serious research, of honest efforts to promote the theory and practice of medicine, not of a maneuver serving as a scientific pretext to mask other ends and achieve them with impunity.

In regard to these questions many people have been of the opinion, and are still of the opinion today, that the answer must be in the affirmative. To give weight to their contention they cite the fact that the individual is subordinated to the community, that the good of the individual must give way to the common good and be sacrificed to it. They add that the sacrifice of an individual for the purposes of research and scientific investigation profits the individual in the long run.

The great postwar trials brought to light a terrifying number of documents testifying to the sacrifice of the individual in the "medical interests of the community." In the minutes of these trials one finds testimony and reports showing how, with the consent, and at times even under the formal order, of public authority, certain research centers systematically demanded to be furnished with persons from concentration camps for their medical experiments. One finds how they were delivered to such centers, so many men, so many women, so many for one experiment, so many for another. There are reports on the conduct and the results of such experiments, of the subjective and objective symptoms observed during the different phases of the experiments. One cannot read these reports without feeling a profound compassion for the victims, many of whom went to their deaths, and without being frightened by such an aberration of the human mind and heart. But We can also add that those responsible for these atrocious deeds did no more than to reply in the affirmative to the question We have asked and to accept the practical consequences of their affirmation.

At this point, is the interest of the individual subordinated to the community's medical interests, or is there here a transgression, perhaps in good faith, against the most elementary demands of the natural law, a transgression that permits no medical research?

One would have to shut one's eyes to reality to believe that at the present time on could find no one in the medical world to hold and defend the ideas that gave rise to the facts We have cited. It is enough to follow for a short time the reports on medical efforts and experiments to convince oneself of the contrary. Involuntarily one asks oneself what has authorized, and what could ever authorize, any doctor's daring to try such an experiment. The experiment is described in all its stages and effects with calm objectivity. What is verified and what is not is noted. But there is not a word on its moral liceity. Nevertheless, this question exists, and one cannot suppress it by passing it over in silence.

INDIVIDUAL AND COMMUNITY

In the above-mentioned cases, insofar as the moral justification of the experiments rests on the mandate of public authority, and therefore on the subordination of the individual to the community, of the individual's welfare to the common welfare, it is based on an erroneous explanation of this principle. It must be noted that, in his personal being, man is not finally ordered to usefulness to society. On the contrary, the community exists for man.

The community is the great means intended by nature and God to regulate the exchange of mutual needs and to aid each man to develop his personality fully according to his individual and social abilities. Considered as a whole, the community is not a physical unity subsisting in itself, and its individual members are not integral parts of it. Considered as a whole, the physical organism of living beings, of plants, animals or man, has a unity subsisting in itself. Each of the members, for example, the hand, the foot, the heart, the eye, is an integral part destined by all its being to be inserted in the whole organism. Outside the organism it has not, by its very nature, any sense, any finality. It is wholly absorbed by the totality of the organism to which it is attached.

In the moral community and in every organism of a purely moral character, it is an entirely different story. Here the

whole has no unity subsisting in itself, but a simple unity of
finality and action. In the community, individuals are not
merely collaborators and instruments for the realization of
the common end.

What results as far as the physical organism is concerned?
The master and user of this organism, which possesses a
subsisting unity, can dispose directly and immediately of integral parts, members and organs within the scope of their
natural finality. He can also intervene, as often as and to
the extent that the good of the whole demands, to paralyze,
destroy, mutilate and separate the members. But, on the
contrary, when the whole has only a unity of finality and
action, its head—in the present case, the public authority—
doubtless holds direct authority and the right to make demands upon the activities of the parts, but in no case can it
dispose of its physical being. Indeed, every direct attempt
upon its essence constitutes an abuse of the power of authority (Address to delegates to the First International Congress
on the Histopathology of the Nervous System).

RIGHTS OF DOCTOR AND PATIENT

4. . . . the doctor justifies his decisions by the interests of
science, those of the patient and those of the common welfare. The question of the interests of science has already
been dealt with. As to those of the patient, the doctor has
no more rights in treatment than those the patient concedes
to him. The patient, on the other hand, the individual himself, does not have the right to dispose of his life, of the
integrity of his body, of particular organs or of their capacity
to function except insofar as the good of his whole body requires it.

This gives the key to the answer to the question with
which you were concerned: may a doctor apply a dangerous
remedy, undertake a probably or certainly fatal treatment,
only because the patient wants it or consents to it? It does
the same to the question which understandably concerns the
doctor working just behind the front lines or in a military
hospital: may he, in incurable cases, in cases of insupport-
able suffering or of horrible wounds, administer at the express request of the patient injections which are equivalent to
euthanasia?

In regard to the interests of the community, public authority has in general no direct right to dispose of the life or

bodily integrity of innocent persons. (The question of corporal and capital punishment We shall not examine here since We are speaking of the doctor, not the executioner. Since the state does not hold this direct right of disposal, it cannot, therefore, give it to the doctor for any motive or purpose whatsoever. The political community is not a physical being like the organism of the body, but a whole which possesses only the unity of finality and action. Man does not exist for the state, but the state for man. When it is a question of nonrational beings—plants or animals—man is free to dispose of their existence and life (which does not dispense him from the obligation he has to God and his own dignity to avoid senseless brutality and cruelty), but not of the life of other men or subordinates.

The military doctor draws from this a sure direction which, without taking away his responsibility for his decisions, is able to guard him from errors in judgment and furnish him with a clear and objective norm (Address to delegates to 16th International Congress on Military Medicine)

5. The final and highest authority is the Creator Himself God. We should not be doing justice to the fundamental principles of your program and to the consequences derived from them were We to characterize them as only the demands of humanity, only humanitarian goals. These they are, too, but they are essentially something more. The ultimate source from which they derive their force and dignity is the Creator of human nature. If it were a matter of principles formulated by the will of man only, then their binding force would have only the strength of men. They could be applied today and deposed tomorrow; one country could accept them and another country refuse them. The case is quite the opposite if the authority of the Creator intervenes. The basic principles of medical ethics are part of the divine law. This, then, is the motive which authorizes the doctor to put unconditional confidence in these basic principles of medical ethics (Ibid.).

ON INTERNATIONALISM*

Gathered from the corners of the earth at the center of Christianity to celebrate the 11th Plenary Assembly of the International Movement of Catholic Intellectuals, you have come together here, Dear Sons, to pay your respects first to the universal Father and to obtain his encouragement and benediction for your work. We welcome your request willingly and cordially. It is a source of happiness for Us to receive you here during this season of radiant Easter joy. The many delegations representing 64 organizations affiliated to the oldest branch of *Pax Romana*—a magnificent international élite of all professions—are accompanied by the executive committee of the students' division. This is at once the oldest and youngest group because it gave birth in 1947 to the movement which today celebrates so brilliantly its 10th anniversary. To all We give a cordial welcome.

In order to sum up and crown the various themes taken up in previous assemblies, you have decided this year to turn your thoughts to a vast and timely subject—the place and the role of the Catholic intellectual in the emerging world community. The principal aspects of the question will be presented by eminent speakers during your meetings. Nevertheless, you have asked of Us a few words by way of introduction. This is why, in response to your filial request, We propose to take, with you, a brief look at the emerging world community. We want to remind you of what it ought to be in the eyes of reason and faith. We wish also to reveal clearly what ought to be your attitude toward it.

Development of International Organizations

For some years now men and women have witnessed, in wonder and even anguish, the accelerated development of

* An address to the members of *Pax Romana*, Rome, April 27, 1957. From *The Catholic Mind*, Sept.–Oct., 1957, pp. 449–453.

international organizations. They are delighted by the wonderful progress of human relations in material, intellectual
and social fields. At the same time they cannot help but
fear that the unification toward which the world is rapidly
moving may be accomplished with violence. They fear that
the more powerful may attempt to impose their leadership
and their concept of the universe on all humanity. This
apprehension is all the greater because, in the event of a
world conflict, modern armaments are capable of causing a
frightful disaster. Some wonder whether the precipitate evolution of the world is not leading the entire human family
toward catastrophe or tyranny. There are others who, like
you, perceive by faith the great eternal tragedy of the salvation of souls. They feel a deeper need for light and certitude.

How could the Vicar of Christ fail to heed this appeal
and bring again the comfort of Catholic truth to an anxious
world?

In this matter of defining the role that certain persons
are called upon to play in the developing world community, we must first remind ourselves of the highest goal
—the one to which all others are subordinated. For a Christian the will of Christ is the ultimate reason for his choices
and his decisions. The Saviour was made man and gave
His life "to gather into one the children of God who were
scattered abroad" (John xi,52). He wished "to be lifted up
from the earth" (John xii,32) on the cross in order "to draw
all men to Him" and to unite them under His leadership
in "one fold and one shepherd" (John x,16; I Cor. xv,15-28).

The Christian and the World

The Christian therefore cannot remain indifferent to the
evolution of the world. If he sees now in rough outline a
development, under the pressure of events, of a constantly
narrowing international community, he knows that this unification, willed by the Creator, ought to culminate in a
union of minds and hearts which is held together by a
common faith and a common love. Not only can he, but
he must, work for the achievement of this community still
in the process of formation. The example and the plan of
the Divine Master are, for him, a beacon and an incom-

parable source of strength. All men are his brothers, not only in virtue of their common origin and their participation in the same nature but also, in a more pressing way, in virtue of their common calling to the supernatural life. Sustained by this certitude, the Christian is in a position to gauge to what extent God "wishes all men to be saved and to come to the knowledge of the truth; for there is one God and one Mediator between God and men, Himself man, Christ Jesus, who gave Himself a ransom for all" (I Tim. ii,4-6).

The revealed truth involved in this scriptural text has been confided to the infallible teaching power of the Church. But it also forms the patrimony of the Christian community which takes its nourishment from it and also lives by it. It furnishes to each of the faithful an attitude of thought. It gives him a norm by which he can judge men and events. This Catholic point of view is yours, Dear Sons. You should make it your business to penetrate it still more, to plumb its grandeur and its beauty in order to appreciate its value and its depth. May it truly be a light to your intellects, a source of strength for your actions and a comfort for your souls.

But you are not isolated seekers after truth. You are not autonomous thinkers. You are Catholic intellectuals. This means you are charged with a universal social responsibility toward everything which concerns the spread of Christian truth. Your culture and the competence you have acquired in your profession have conferred upon you an authority which, in your milieu, constitutes you both a question and an answer. By the grace of your vocation you are a light which attracts and which cannot be rejected by anyone without implicitly condemning himself, provided the light you bear is truly the light of Christ. Nevertheless, this rejection, which human imperfection always justifies under some pretext or other, limits the responsibility of Catholic intellectuals in the confusion of a society in which the essential questions are often left aside, whether they concern current affairs or decisions of universal import involving the political, social and cultural orientation of countries or continents.

Catholic Cooperation in the World Community

Does this mean that one cannot collaborate in the service of the world community with those institutions where God is not expressly recognized as the author and legislator of the universe? It is important to distinguish here the different levels of cooperation. Without ever forgetting that his ultimate goal is to contribute to the eternal salvation of his brothers, the Christian will be mindful that the coming of the Kingdom of God in hearts and institutions most often requires a minimum of human enlightenment, a simple appeal to reason with which every man normally concurs, even if he has not the grace of faith.

The Christian will therefore be ready to work for the relief of all material miseries, for the universal development of a basic training in social attitudes—in a word, toward all enterprises which have as their purpose the better lot of the poor and the disenfranchised. In that way the Christian will fulfill his obligation of collective charity. He will pave the way for a greater number of men to enter into a personal life worthy of the name. He will promote the spontaneous cooperation of men in all efforts which lead them to a better state of life. For thus are men permitted to look higher, to receive the light and to adhere to the sole truth which makes men free (John viii,32).

Those who are constantly in the public eye and, for that reason, able to influence public opinion, should feel themselves charged with a more serious task. Truth does not tolerate in itself either admixture or impurity. Their participation in doubtful enterprises could seem to put the stamp of approval on political or social systems which are inadmissible. Nevertheless, even here a vast area exists in which minds free of prejudice and passion can act in harmony and cooperate for a genuine and worthwhile common good. Sound reason is enough to establish the basis for human rights, to recognize the inviolable character of the individual, the dignity of the family and the prerogatives and limits of public authority.

For this reason the cooperation of Catholics is desirable in all institutions which, in theory and practice, respect the provisions of the natural law. They will seek to maintain them in their essential purity and, by their active participation in them, play the beneficent role which the Divine Master compared to that of the salt and the leaven. They will find in these organizations, which propose for themselves a universal and humanitarian goal, generous souls and superior minds susceptible of rising above material preoccupations. They will find men capable of understanding that the truly collective destiny of humanity presupposes the absolute value of each of the individuals who constitute it; of recognizing the establishment outside of time of the true society of which the earthly community can only be a reflection and a rough outline.

The Need for Mutual Sacrifice

Let us develop one essential component of this developing social mentality—greater abnegation. Some Christians will not be surprised to hear Us make this statement. Besides it is a fact of experience and a logical necessity that a real community impose mutual sacrifices on its members. You recall how the Son of God made man, He who "did not come to be served but to serve and to give His life as a ransom for many" (Matt. 20:28), taught men the conditions of unity. By these words He Himself wished to illustrate the necessity and fruitfulness of sacrifice in achieving a kind of superior life to which all men are called by virtue of a supernatural vocation—to form the union of the Sons of God.

In conclusion, need I invoke the joy and victory of Easter? Yes, truly, Dear Sons, you have a beautiful mission to fulfill. Amid a restless world may you bring hope and the peace of fraternal devotion on a universal scale. Be the salt without which everything risks degeneration and corruption. Be the leaven which raises the stolid mass. Make out of the shapeless dough the loaf of human solidarity. May everyone understand, thanks to you, that "it is better to give than to receive," more noble to serve than to be served, more joyful to give one's life for his brothers than to keep it for oneself.

This is the wish We formulate for all of you and the favor We implore of the Risen Saviour for each of your associations and for the whole movement. As a pledge of this We grant you with the warmth of Our paternal heart the most ample and affectionate apostolic blessing.

MORALITY AND APPLIED PSYCHOLOGY*

Having come from all over the world to attend the 13th Congress of the International Association of Applied Psychology, you have wished, gentlemen, to take this occasion to visit Us. We are happy to receive you here and We wholeheartedly welcome each one of you.

The subject which interests you and from which the present Congress derives its name is applied psychology. Not limiting your research only to practical applications you also take into sizeable consideration questions relating to theoretical psychology. This appears from the abundant documentation which you have submitted to Us on the four sections into which your work is divided: psychology applied to labor and professional orientation, medical psychology, scholastic psychology and criminal and penitentiary psychology. Each part deals on many occasions with questions of deontology involved in these matters. You have also observed that in this respect there exist certain differences of opinion between psychologists and theologians which give rise to regrettable uncertainties in ideas and actions. You have requested Us to give clarification in so far as possible.

Two points especially have been brought to Our notice: the widespread use of certain tests by which one goes so far as to delve unscrupulously into the intimate depths of the soul, and the related, but larger, problem of the moral responsibility of the psychologist, that of the extent and limitations of his rights and of his duties in the use of scientific methods, whether in theoretical research or in practical application.

We will deal with these two points in our survey, by embodying them within the framework of a greater synthesis: the religious and moral aspects of the human personality and the object of psychology. We will take the following points into consideration:

* An address to the Congress of the International Association of Applied Psychology, Rome, April 10, 1958. From *The Catholic Mind*, July–August, 1958, pp. 353–367.

1. The definition of human personality from the psychological and moral point of view;

2. The moral obligations of the psychologist in relation to the human personality;

3. The fundamental moral principles related to the human personality and to psychology.

I. The Definition of the Human Personality from the Psychological and Moral Point of View

1. The expression "personality" is found today almost everywhere but with different meanings. It is, in fact, sufficient to glance through the abundant bibliography on the subject to realize that many of the concepts regarding the psychic structure of man are expressed in technical terms which in every case preserve the same fundamental meaning. Yet several elements of human psyche are still badly described and have not yet been given an adequate definition. The terminology "personality" is one of them in scientific psychology as in applied psychology.

It is therefore important that We should specify Our interpretation of it. Though We take into account above all the moral and religious aspects and you stop principally at the psychological one, We do not believe that these different points of view should engender opposition or contradiction, as long as they remain objective and endeavor to keep to the facts.

We define personality as "the psychosomatic unity of man in so far as it is determined and governed by the soul."

2. This definition refers first of all to the personality as a "unity" because it is considered as a whole, of which the parts, though preserving their specific characteristics, are not separated but are organically linked between themselves. This is why psychology can take equally into consideration the psychic faculties and their functions separately from the point of view of their individual structure and their immanent laws, as well as from the point of view of their organic whole.

The definition then describes that unity as "psychosomatic." The opinions of the theologian and of the psychologist meet here on many points. In fact the technical works on psychology examine in detail the influence of the body over the mind to which it brings continued energies through its vital processes. A study is also made of the influence of the mind over the body. These studies endeavor to determine scientifically the modalities of the control of psychic tendencies by the spiritual soul and to draw from them practical applications.

The definition then asserts that the psychosomatic unity of man is "determined and governed by the soul." The individual, in so far as he is a unity and indivisible totality, constitutes a unique and universal center of being and of action, an "I" which has self-control and is the master of itself. This "I" is the same in all psychic functions and remains the same despite the passage of time.

The universality of the "I" in extent and duration applies particularly to the causal bond which links it to its spiritual activities. This universal and permanent "I," under the influence of internal or external causes consciously perceived or implicitly accepted, but always by free choice, acquires a definite attitude, and a permanent character, both in its interior being and in its external behavior.

Since this specific character of the personality is ultimately derived from the spiritual soul, one describes it as being "determined by the soul." Since it is not the case of an occasional process but of a continuous process, one adds "governed by the soul."

It can happen that certain traits of character acquire greater prominence. This is described by the word "personality." But it is not necessary that these predominant characteristics exist to be able to speak of a personality in the terms of the definition.

Personality can be considered either as a simple fact or in the light of moral values which must govern it. It is a fact that there are worthwhile personalities and others which are insignificant. Some are confused, vicious or depraved, others are open, forthright and honest. But both have these characteristics because they have adopted by free decision this or that spiritual orientation. Neither psychology nor morals will disregard this fact, even though both prefer to take into account the ideal to which the personality tends.

3. Since the moral and religious aspects coincide to a great extent with the former, it will be sufficient for Us to add a few indications. Metaphysics considers man in his ultimate end. It studies him as a living being, gifted with intelligence and freedom, in which the body and the soul

are united in one single nature with an independent existence. Technically one would refer to *"rationalis naturae
individua substantia"* (cfr. S.Th., I, Q. 29, a.l.). In this
respect, man is always a person, an "individual" distinct
from all others, an "I" from the very first to the very
last second of his life, even when he is not conscious of
it. There is, therefore, a certain difference between this point
of view and the utterances of psychology, but, nevertheless,
there are no unsolvable contradictions.

TRAITS OF PERSONALITY

The most important traits of the personality from the
moral and religious points of view are the following:

1. Man is entirely the work of the Creator. Even though
psychology does not take this into account in its researches,
in its experiments and clinical applications, it always labors
on the work of the Creator. This consideration is essential from the religious and moral point of view. But, as
long as the theologian and the psychologist remain objective,
no conflict need be feared. Both can proceed in their own
fields according to the principles of their science.

When one considers man as the work of God, one dis-
covers in him two important characteristics for the development and the value of the Christian personality: his re-
semblance to God, derived from the act of creation, and
his divine sonship in Christ made manifest by revelation.

In fact, Christian personality becomes incomprehensible
if one neglects these points. Psychology, especially applied
psychology, also lays itself open to misunderstandings and
errors if it disregards them. For these facts are not imagined
or assumed, but real. That they are known through revelation does not in any way detract from their authenticity,
because revelation calls upon man to exceed the boundaries
of limited intelligence and to let himself be drawn by God's
infinite intelligence.

2. The question of finality is equally essential from the
religious and moral point of view. Man has the possibility
and duty to perfect his nature, not as he himself understands it but according to the divine plan. In order that
he may achieve the image of God in his personality, he
must not follow his instincts but the objective norms, such
as those of medical deontology which assert themselves on

his intelligence and on his will and which are dictated by his conscience and by revelation.

Conscience will in fact be enlightened by consulting the opinion of others and the traditional wisdom of humanity. A few years ago a code of medical deontology called "Ethical Standards for Psychologists," and based on the answers of 7,500 members of the "American Psychological Association" (Washington, D.C.), was compiled in America. Though this code may contain certain questionable assertions, one must approve the idea which inspires it—namely the recourse to serious and competent people to formulate and discover moral norms. Whoever neglects or scorns the norms of a moral objective order will only acquire a deformed and imperfect personality.

3. On the other hand, to say that man is committed to observe certain rules of morality is tantamount to holding him responsible, to believe that he has the objective and subjective possibility to act according to these rules.

AGREEMENT ON PRINCIPLES DESIRABLE

This affirmation of responsibility and liberty is also essential to personality. One cannot, therefore, despite certain opinions defended by a few psychologists, abandon the following principles. It would be desirable that an agreement as broad as possible on these principles be achieved between psychologists and theologians.

1. Any man must be considered normal until there is proof to the contrary.

2. The normal man does not have a theoretical freedom alone but enjoys the real use of it.

3. When the normal man puts to proper use the spiritual energies at his disposal, he is capable of surmounting the difficulties which hinder his observation of moral law.

4. Abnormal psychological tendencies are not always constraining and do not always deprive the subject of all possibilities of acting freely.

5. Even the dynamisms of the unconscious and of the subconscious are not irresistible; there are still great possibilities for mastering them, particularly for the normal subject.

6. The normal man is therefore ordinarily responsible for the decisions he makes.

Finally, in order to understand the personality one cannot disregard the eschatological aspect. As long as man lives on earth he can wish either good or evil, but once the soul has been separated from the body by death, it remains fixed in the dispositions acquired during life.

From the moral and religious point of view, the decisive element in the structure of personality is precisely the attitude which it adopts with regard to God and the ultimate end set for it by its very nature. If it has been oriented toward Him, it remains so; if, on the contrary, it has departed from this road, it will retain the disposition which it voluntarily acquired. For psychology, this last stage of the psychic future can be but of secondary consideration. But, since psychology is concerned with psychical structures and with the resulting acts which contribute to the final development of the personality, it should not be totally indifferent to the destiny of the personality.

These are the points We wished to develop regarding the subject of personality, viewed from the moral and the religious point of view. Let Us add a few brief observations.

The works of your specialty also deal with predominances in the structure of the personality, that is to say, with the tendencies which determine the aspects of its psyche. You thus divide men into groups, according to whether their predominant traits are the senses, the instincts, the emotions and the affections, sentiment, will, intelligence. Even from the religious and moral point of view, this classification is not without importance, because the reactions of the various groups to moral and religious motives are often different.

Your publications also often deal with the question of character. The distinction and the meaning of the concepts of the "character" and of the "personality" are not uniform everywhere. One sometimes even goes so far as to consider them synonymous. Certain persons claim that the principal element of the character is the attitude which man adopts with regard to his responsibility; for others, it is his attitude toward values.

The personality of the normal man is necessarily confronted with the values and norms of moral life which, as We have said, also include medical deontology; these values are not simple indications but compulsory directives. One must adopt an attitude in regard to them and accept them or refute them. This explains how a psychologist defines the character as "the relative coefficient of the personal search for appreciation and acceptance of values." Many works of your Congress allude to this definition and even comment on it widely.

One last fact which attracts the common interest of the psychologist and of the theologian is the existence of certain personalities the only constant of which is, one might say, inconstancy. Their superficiality seems invincible. They admit as values only thoughtlessness or indifference. For the psychologist and for the theologian this does not constitute grounds for discouragement, but rather a stimulant to work and an invitation to a fruitful collaboration toward the formation of authentic personalities and of strong characters for the welfare of individuals and communities.

II. The Moral Obligations of the Psychologist Regarding the Human Personality

We now reach the questions of medical deontology, of which you have asked Us the solution—first, concerning the licitness of certain techniques and the manner of applying certain psychological tests, then regarding the principles of a religious and moral order which are fundamental for the psychologist and the patient. We will in this respect observe that the questions of deontology dealt with here also concern anyone who has the faculty of reasoning and, in a general way, anyone capable of making a conscious psychic act.

Tests and other psychological methods of investigation have contributed enormously to the knowledge of the human personality and have been of considerable service to it. One might then think that there does not exist in this domain any particular problem of medical morals and that everything can be approved without reservation. No one will in fact deny that modern psychology in general deserves approval from the religious and moral point of view.

But, if one takes into consideration the specific objectives of psychology and the means it uses to achieve them, one will be led to make a distinction. Its objectives, that is to say the scientific study of human psychology and the healing of psychic diseases, only deserve praise; but the means used sometimes give grounds for justifiable reservations, such as We mentioned previously concerning the publication in

America of the work "Ethical Standards for Psychologists." [1]

Limitations of Psychology

The best psychologists are aware of the fact that the most clever use of existing methods does not succeed in penetrating the area of the psyche which constitutes, one might say, the center of the personality and which always remains a mystery. At this point the psychologist cannot but acknowledge with modesty his limitations and respect the individuality of the man on whom he must pass judgment; he should strive to perceive the divine plan in every man and help develop it in so far as it is possible. Human personality with its specific characteristics is in fact the most noble and wondrous work of creation.

Now, to anyone who takes cognizance of your works, it would appear that certain moral problems arise here. You reveal, in fact, several times the objections raised against the intrusion of the psychologist into the intimacy of the personalities of other beings. Thus, for instance, the use of narcosynthesis, already questioned in psychotherapy, is considered illicit in legal proceedings. So too is the use of the instrument for the detection of lies, known as "lie-detector" or "polygraph." [2] One author will denounce the harmful consequences of violent emotive tensions, provoked in a subject for experimental reasons, but he will also affirm that preference should be given to the interest of scientific progress over that of the individual person who serves as

[1] The test is described as an experiment of diagnosis which aims at revealing, as objectively and accurately as possible, the distinctive characteristics of the psyche of a personality, or even only a few of its particulars.

[2] Narcosynthesis is a more or less special form of interrogation under the action of a hypnotic substance (sodium-pentothal commonly known as "truth serum") which, administered in measured doses by intravenous injections, favors the revelation of attitudes or thoughts which the subject, when in a state of clear consciousness, intentionally or unconsciously conceals. The "lie-detector" or "polygraph" is an apparatus which permits the simultaneous recording of different somatic manifestations—and of their nature, uncontrolled by the subject—which accompany emotive attitudes produced under certain conditions at the same time as conscious lies, of which these somatic manifestations thus become indirect indications, outside any free participation of the subject under examination (cf. Prof. Leandro Canestrelli, *Liberta e Responsabilita nella Ricerca Psychologica*. Rome, 1955, pages 8–9).

subject for the experiment. Some in psychiatric research and treatment intrude without the previous consent of the patient, or without the patient being aware of their exact bearing. And the revelation of the real elements of their personality can, in the case of some people, provoke serious traumatisms.

In short, it can be said that one must sometimes deplore the unjustified intrusion of the psychologist into the depths of the personality and the serious psychic harm resulting therefrom to the patient and even to third parties. It sometimes happens that the complete consent of the interested person is not secured, and that in order to justify disputable proceedings the priority of science over moral values and over the interests of the individuals (in other words the priority of the common good over the individual good) is alleged.

We are, therefore, going to examine the value of the principles which even good psychologists invoke to justify certain disputable proceedings.

I. The Interest of Science and the Importance of the Psychologist

Moral law teaches that scientific demands do not by themselves alone justify the indiscriminate use of psychological techniques and methods, even by serious psychologists and for useful objectives.

The reason for this is that people concerned with the processes of psychological investigation must take into account not only scientific laws, but also transcendent norms. In fact, the primary question is not psychology itself and its possible progress but the human person who applies it and who obeys high social, moral and religious norms.

The same also holds true for the other branches of science; mathematics, for instance, or physics are in themselves alien to morals and therefore do not come under these norms, but the person who dedicates himself to their study and applies their laws is never removed from the moral field, because at no time does his free action cease to prepare his transcendent destiny.

Psychology as a science can only make its demands prevail in so far as the echelon of values and higher norms to which We have referred and which includes right, justice, equity, respect of human dignity, and well-ordered charity for oneself and for others, is respected. There is nothing mysterious in these norms. They are clear for any honest conscience and are formulated by natural reasoning and by revelation. Inasmuch as they are observed, there is nothing to prevent the just demands of the science of psychology in favor of modern methods of investigation from being asserted.

II. THE CONSENT OF THE SUBJECT

The second principle under discussion is that of the rights of the person who lends himself to psychological experiments or treatments. In itself, the content of the psyche is the exclusive property of the person himself (here regarding experiments and treatments) and is known only to him. But he already reveals something of it by his behavior.

When the psychologist concerns himself with what has been thus revealed, he does not violate the intimate psyche of the patient. He can also act with complete freedom when the patient consciously expresses a part of it and thereby indicates that he attaches no importance to the secret. But there is a considerable part of his interior world that a person reveals only to a few confidants and which he defends against the intrusion of others.

Certain matters will be kept secret at all cost from everyone, no matter whom. And then there are other matters which he could not bring himself to consider.

Psychology also shows that there exists a region of the intimate psyche—particularly tendencies and dispositions—concealed to such an extent that the individual will never know of them or even suspect their existence. And in the same way as it is illicit to take what belongs to others or to make an attempt against a person's corporal integrity without his consent, neither is one allowed to enter his interior domain without his permission, whatever may be the techniques or methods used.

But one can also ask whether the consent of the patient is sufficient to give the psychologist unlimited access to his psyche. If the consent is unfairly extorted, all action on the part of the psychologist will be illicit; if it is impaired by lack of freedom (due to ignorance, to error or to deception) all attempts to penetrate the depths of the soul will be immoral. But if consent is given freely, the psychologist can in the majority of cases, but not always, act according to the principles of his science without contravening any moral norms. One must ascertain whether the interested person has not overstepped the limits of his competence and capacity in giving a valid consent. Man, in fact, does not have an unlimited power over himself. Often in your works one quotes (without, however, giving the formula) the juridical principle: *"volenti non fit injuria"*—there is no injustice done to the person who consents.

Let us first of all observe that the intervention of the psychologist might well injure the rights of a third party, for instance through the revelation of secrets (of state, of office, of family or of confession), or simply the rights of individuals or communities to their reputations. It does not suffice that the psychologist himself or his assistants are sworn to secrecy, or that secrets can be entrusted sometimes to a cautious person for serious reasons. Because, as We already pointed out in Our address of April 13, 1953, on psychotherapy and psychology, there are certain secrets which absolutely cannot be revealed, not even to one cautious person.

As for the principle *"volenti non fit injuria,"* it puts only one obstacle in the way of the psychologist, namely, the right of the person to protect his interior world. But there may be other obstacles which continue to exist by virtue of moral obligations and which the subject involved cannot suppress at his pleasure—religiousness, self-respect, chastity and decency for instance. In this case, though he does not violate any right, the psychologist is wanting morally. One must therefore examine with regard to each specific case whether one of these reasons of moral order is not opposed to his intervention and their bearing must be accurately estimated.

III. HEROIC ALTRUISM

What must one think of the motive of heroic altruism, invoked to justify the unconditional application of psychological techniques or exploration and treatment? The moral value of human action depends in the first place on its object. If this is immoral the action is also immoral; it is of no use to invoke the motive behind it or the aim pursued. If the object is indifferent to good, one can then question the motives or the end which confer new moral values on the action. But however noble a motive may be, it can never render an evil action good.

Thus, any psychological intervention must be examined from the point of view of its object in the light of the given indications. If this object is not in line with right and morals, the motive of heroic altruism does not make it acceptable: if the object is licit, a higher moral value, in addition to the motive invoked, can be attributed to the action.

People who, urged by this motive, offer themselves for the most painful experiments so as to help others and be useful to them deserve admiration and should be imitated. But one must be wary of confusing the motive or the aim of the action with its object and of transferring to the latter a moral value which it does not deserve.

IV. THE GENERAL INTEREST AND THE INTERVENTION OF THE PUBLIC AUTHORITIES

Can the general interest and the intervention of the public authorities authorize the psychologist to use just any method?

No one can deny that the public authorities can, with regard to individuals and for just motives, put to advantage the proven acquisitions and methods of psychology. But here the question reverts to the choice of certain techniques and methods.

A characteristic trait of the totalitarian states is to give no thought to the means employed but to use indiscriminately all that serves the aim pursued without any regard for the exigencies of moral law. We already have denounced in Our speech of October 3, 1953, to the Sixth International Congress of Criminal Law the aberrations still sadly displayed by the 20th Century in its acceptance of torture and violence in judiciary proceedings.

The fact that immoral procedures are imposed by the public authorities does not in any way make them legal. Therefore, when the public authorities create experimental or consulting offices, the principles which We have described apply to all the steps of a psychological order that they may have to take. In so far as the free researches and initiatives of these offices are concerned, the principles applicable to free research and individual initiatives and to the use of theoretical and applied psychology in general will be enforced.

As regards the competence of the public authority to impose psychological examinations, the general principles concerning the limitations of the competence of the public authority will be applied. In Our speeches of September 13, 1952, on the moral limitations of medical research and treatment (*Discourses and Radio Messages*, Vol. XIV, pp. 320-325) and of September 30, 1954, to the *"Sodalitas Medicorum Universalis"* (*Discourses and Radio Messages* Vol. XVI, pp. 174-176), We enunciated the principles which regulate the relations between the doctor and his patients and the public authorities, and examined particularly the possibility for the public authorities to grant rights to certain doctors and psychologists which exceed the usual ones of a doctor concerning his patients.

Decisions taken by the public authorities calling for children and youth to be submitted to certain examinations—assuming that the object of such examinations is licit—must take the educators into account if they are to be moral. These are the family and the Church who have a more immediate authority over the children and the youth than the state does.

Furthermore, neither the family nor the Church will oppose steps taken in the interest of the children; but they will not allow the state to act in this field without taking into account their own rights, as was declared by Our Predecessor Pius XI in the Encyclical *Divini Illius Magistri* of December 31, 1929, and as We Ourselves have stressed on several occasions.

III. The Fundamental Moral Principles Concerning the Human Personality in Psychology

The answers which We have given up to the present still call for a survey of the basic principles from which they are derived and on the basis of which, in each specific case, you will be able to form a fully justified personal judgment.

We will only refer to the principles of a moral order which concern both the personality of the person who practices psychology and that of the patient, to the extent that the latter intervenes through a free and responsible step.

Certain actions are contrary to morals because they only violate the norms of a positive law; others are in themselves of an immoral character; among these—the only ones which

We will deal with—some will never be moral; others will become immoral because of determined circumstances.

Thus, for example, it is immoral to penetrate into the conscience of someone; but this act becomes moral if the person involved gives his valid consent. It can also happen that certain actions lay a person open to the dangers of violating a moral law. Thus, for instance, the use of tests can in certain cases engender immoral impressions, but the action becomes moral when proportionate motives justify the danger incurred.

THREE KINDS OF IMMORAL ACTIONS

One can therefore establish three kinds of immoral actions, which can be judged as such by referring to the three basic principles: whether they are immoral either in themselves, or because the person who enacts them lacks the right to do so, or because of the dangers they provoke without sufficient motive.

Immoral actions in themselves are those where the constitutive elements are incompatible with moral order, that is to say, with healthy reasoning; where conscious and free action is contrary either to the essential principles of human nature or to the essential relations which it has with the Creator and with other men, or to the rules governing the use of material things, in the sense that man must never become their slave but must remain their master.

It is therefore contrary to moral order that man should freely and consciously submit his rational faculties to inferior instincts. When the application of the tests, or of psychoanalysis or of any other method reaches this extreme, it becomes immoral and must be refuted without discussion. It is naturally up to your conscience to determine, in the individual cases, the lines of conduct to be rejected.

Actions which are immoral because the person who enacts them has no right to do so, do not in themselves contain any essential immoral element but, if they are to be licit, they must suppose the existence of an explicit or implicit right, as will be the case in the majority of instances for the doctor and the psychologist. Since a right cannot be taken for granted, it must first of all be established through positive proof by the person who assumes it and based on a juridical reason.

As long as the right has not been obtained, the action is

immoral. But if, at a specific time, an action appears to be immoral, it does not still follow that it will always remain such, because it can happen that the right shown to be lacking is acquired later.

Nevertheless, the right in question can never be taken for granted. As We said previously, again in this instance, it is up to you to decide in concrete cases, many examples of which are quoted in the publications of your specialization, whether this principle is applicable to such or such an action.

Certain actions are immoral because of the danger incurred without a proportionate motive. We naturally refer to moral danger for the individual or the community, either regarding the personal property of the body, of life, of reputation, of customs or with respect to material assets.

It is obviously impossible to avoid danger completely and such a demand would paralyze all enterprise and seriously harm everyone's interests; hence, moral law permits this risk to be taken on the condition that it is justified by a motive proportionate to the importance of the assets at stake and to the proximity of the danger which threatens them.

NEED FOR A MORAL SENSE

You refer several times in your works to the danger engendered by certain techniques, by certain procedures used in applied psychology. The principle which We have laid before you will help you solve in each case the difficulties that may arise.

The norms which We have formulated are above all of a moral order. When psychology discusses a method or the effectiveness of a technique on the theoretical plane, it only considers their aptitude to achieve the specific aim psychology pursues and does not deal with the moral aspect. In the practical application one must also take into account the spiritual values involved both in the psychologist and the patient and add to the scientific and medical point of view that of the human personality in general.

These fundamental norms are obligatory because they are engendered by the nature of things and belong to the essential order of human action, the supreme and immediately evident principle of which is that one must do good and avoid evil.

At the beginning of this address, We described personality as the "psychosomatic unity of man in so far as determined and governed by the soul" and We have specified the meaning of this definition. Then, We endeavored to answer your questions on the use of certain psychological methods and on the general principles which determine the moral responsibility of the psychologist.

One does not expect the psychologist to have only a theoretical knowledge of abstract norms, but also a deep moral and pondered sense formed by constant loyalty to his conscience. The psychologist who really wishes to seek only the welfare of his patient will be all the more careful to respect the limitations placed upon his actions by morals, since one can say that he holds in his hands the psychic faculties of a man, his capacity of acting freely, of attaining the highest values of his personal destiny and of his social vocation.

Chapter 5

✠

John XXIII (1959-1963)

Angelo Rancalli was born on 25 November 1881 to a peasant family. He was ordained on 10 August 1904, and became secretary to the Bishop of Bergamo. He interrupted his studies for two years in World War I to do his military service. In 1935 he was appointed apostolic delegate to Bulgaria, and on 19 March 1925 he was raised to the rank of archbishop. He was appointed apostolic delegate to Turkey and Greece in 1935, and papal nuncio to France in December 1944. He was made a cardinal in 1953, and Patriarch of Venice in January 1953. He became Pope in 1958, and summoned the second Vatican Council, which met in St. Peter's in October, 1962. He died on June 3, 1963.

AD PETRI CATHEDRAM
On Peace, Truth, and Unity*

May 29, 1959

Since the time when despite our utter unworthiness, we were elevated to the Chair of Peter, we have been considering anew not without a suggestion of consolation the things which we saw and heard as almost everyone from every nation and every persuasion mourned the death of our im-

---

* Official translation. The Vatican Polyglot Press.

mediate Predecessor. Later, when we were called to the
dignity of the Supreme Pontificate, although the world was
disturbed and unsettled by other events and circumstances
of serious import, literally multitudes turned their minds and
hearts toward us and looked to us with hope and expectation.
This openly demonstrates that the Catholic Church flourishes
with an everlasting youth, and is, as it were, "a standard
lifted up among the nations." [1] From it is poured forth a
light that pierces the darkness and a gentle love that reaches
out to all the people.

Furthermore, when we announced that we intended to
hold an Ecumenical Council and Roman Synod and that
we intended to prepare a Code of Canon Law adapted to
modern needs and to publish a new Code of the same type
for the Eastern Churches, it was a source of great pleasure
to us to have found so many in agreement with our plans.
We were delighted to have fed the common hope that the
minds of men be stirred with pleasure to a better and more
thorough knowledge of the truth, to a profitable renewal
of the Christian way of life, and to the restoration of unity,
harmony, and peace.

At present, then, in this Encyclical Letter, the first we are
issuing to the Universal Church, we are going to discuss
these three topics, truth, unity and peace together with the
necessity of acquiring and promoting them under the inspiration of love. The obligations of the Apostolic Office
which we hold seem to demand this in a very particular
way. May the guiding light of the Holy Spirit from on high
be at our hand as we write and in your hearts as you read
and may the grace of God which shapes the soul move all
toward the acquisition of these things. They are actually the
expression of a common desire despite the fact that prejudiced opinions, many difficulties and many obstacles stand
in the way of their realization.

I: Truth

KNOWLEDGE OF TRUTH, ESPECIALLY REVELATION

Of all the evils which corrupt individuals, society and
even whole nations and which upset the minds of many, the

[1] Isais. xi, 12.

ause, or a better word might be, the root is this: the ignorance of truth or more correctly, not only an ignorance of
t, but even at times, a contempt for and a rash betrayal of
t. From this source, all kinds of errors spring, errors which
ake an evil disease penetrate into the deepest recesses of
he soul and enter the blood stream of human society. They
knock all values out of kilter and result in incalculable losses
o the individual and the whole social structure. . . .

PRESS AND OBLIGATION TO TRUTH

In this regard, then, those who willingly and rashly impugn
he known truth and who employ the weapon of the lie in
heir writing, speaking or acting to attract and win over to
hemselves the unlearned poor people, and who strive in this
vay to mold the inexperienced and pliable minds of youth
nd to shape them to their way of thinking, are without a
doubt abusing the guilelessness of the innocent and are engaged in a work worthy of the deepest scorn. Consequently,
ve cannot help but appeal to those who, through books,
magazines and the daily paper (today their name is legion),
olay so large a part in teaching and forming the minds of
heir fellow men. Particularly in the case of the young, they
are influential in forming opinions and in controlling the
one of moral life. We beg them to handle the truth with
care, caution and prudence. They are bound under a very
serious obligation not to publicize the lie, the half-truth and
he moral evil of society. On the contrary, they should emphasize truth and especially those things which lead to
lives of solid virtue rather than to lives of vice.

With sadness of heart, we see that our Predecessor of immortal memory, Leo XIII used to complain of "the imper-
ceptible but bold entrance of the lie through the ponderous
tome or the slender pamphlet, through the ephemeral pages
of the newspaper and the deliberate allurements of the
theater." [2] We note that he also refers to "the books and
magazines published for the sole purpose of making sport of
virtue and of glorifying crime." [3]

RADIO, MOTION PICTURES AND TELEVISION

In our modern age . . . there have been added to these the
radio program, the motion picture and most especially, tele-

[2] Letter *Saepenumero Considerantes* A.L. Vol. III, 1883, p. 262.
[3] Letter *Exeunte iam anno* A.L., Vol. VIII, 1888, p. 398.

vision. The last of these invades the very family circle. Ye
from all of these, if they are devoted to the good and th
true, attractive inducements to good living, even Christia
living, can get their start. But, alas, they can all too fre
quently stir the minds, particularly of the young, to loos
morals, to the seamy side of life, to the deceit of error an
to the ever dangerous allurements of pleasure. For this rea
son, we must don the armor of goodness and truth to with
stand these weapons of destruction so that the force of thes
evils so great, evils which grow almost imperceptibly stronge
every day, might by our watchfulness and care be kept ir
check. To counteract the evil and deceitful writings, it be
comes a matter of necessity to provide books that are morally
sound. As an antidote to the type of radio program, motior
picture and television show that makes error attractive and
vice enticing, we should present those things which safe
guard truth and which strive to preserve the blameless whole
someness of sound moral living. This we must do that these
new arts which can be such powerful allies of the forces of
evil might be harnessed for the benefit and salvation of
mankind without subtracting one bit from their entertain
ment value. Thus the remedy itself will be found in the
very source from which the evil poisons flow in abundance.

RELIGIOUS INDIFFERENCE

In addition, there is a certain group who, though they do
not deliberately attack the truth, yet by their want of respect
for it war against it just as though God did not give us the
faculty to seek after and discover it. Acting in this fashion
leads to the untenable position that since there is no distinction between the true and the false, all religions are
basically true. "This kind of reasoning," in the words of our
Predecessor quoted above, "is pointed toward the destruction
of all religion, and in particular of the Catholic Faith since,
of all religions, this alone is true, and cannot be equated with
others without serious injustice." [4] We would go even farther and state that a failure to distinguish between con-
traries has only this fatal outcome: an unwillingness to accept or practice any religion. For how can God who is truth
have any patience with the carelessness, negligence or lazi-
ness of those who completely disregard their obligation of
searching for and finding these essential truths, though such

[4] Encyclical Letter *Humanum genus* A.L., Vol. IV, 1884, p. 53.

an obligation is concerned with the eternal salvation of all of us, and who in the end refuse to render to God the lawful worship due to Him alone.

If so much effort and industry are spent in adding to the store of human knowledge and to pushing back the horizons of natural science so that this, our age rejoices, and justly so, in the remarkable progress that has been made in scientific and philosophical knowledge, why should we not show the same ingenuity and assiduity, nay even greater, in acquiring in a safe and certain manner that knowledge that is concerned not with the passing things of this world but with the heavenly goal that is to come. Only when we accept that truth which flows from the pages of the Gospels and which should overflow into our daily actions, then only, we say, will our spirit rest in that peace and that joy which far exceeds in measure the pride in accomplishment from the findings of modern science and from the marvelous inventions which we enjoy today and which are extolled to the heavens in daily press notices.

II: Unity, Harmony, Peace

TRUTH ADVANCES THE CAUSE OF PEACE

From the wholehearted acceptance of full and complete truth, there should bubble forth a unity which will permeate our minds, our hearts, and all our actions. For all discord, all disagreements and all dissension flow as from a primal spring from this one source, from a failure to recognize truth or, what is worse, from a rejection of it even though it has been studied and understood, be this for the sake of the conveniences and benefits that are often expected to come from false hypotheses or because of that willful blindness which men are all too prone to use as an excuse for vice and evil.

It is imperative, then, that everyone, the private citizen as well as those who handle the affairs of state, cherish the truth in their hearts if they wish to find that peace and harmony from which the well-being of the individual as well as of society can spring.

To this harmony and peace, we expressly exhort those who are active in political life. We who are placed above the disagreements between nations, we who embrace all people with equal affection, we who are not motivated by earthly benefits nor by desire of political ascendency, nor by any desires in this present life, seem to be able to be judged with fairness, heard with equanimity by all regardless of national background when we speak on matters of such importance.

MEN CREATED AS BROTHERS

God created men to be brothers, not enemies. He gave them the earth to be cultivated in the sweat of their brow that everyone might share in its fruits and take from it the necessities of daily existence. The various nations are nothing other than societies of men, that is, of brothers who ought to strive not only for their own individual prosperity, but, bound together in a bond of brotherly love, for the good of all human society.

Furthermore, this earthly life is not to be considered as an end in itself or even in the light of the pleasures it gives. The end of life is not complete destruction at death but rather an immortal life and a homeland that will endure forever. If this teaching, this hope so full of consolation is stripped from the lives of men, then the whole reason for existence collapses. There is left no check-rein strong enough to bridle the greed, dissension and discord that try to burst from our very souls. In place of the olive branch of peace shining forth in our hearts, the firebrands of discord will burst into flames. In short, our plight becomes synonymous with that of the beast who is devoid of reason. As a matter of fact, our lot is worse for, since we have been endowed with reason, we can sink to lower depths by the abuse of it. Alas, as rather often happens, we can collapse into utter ruin and just like Cain, can stain the earth with the serious crime of spilling a brother's blood.

Our first task is then, to realign our thinking in accordance with right principles of action if we wish, as we ought, that our actions be firmly placed on the path of justice. For why if we are brothers in name and in fact, if we are sharers in a common destiny both in this life and in that to come, why, we repeat, can we act as adversaries, rivals and bitter foes toward each other? Why envy others? Why stir up hatred and prepare death-dealing weapons against our brothers? Alas, there is already enough strife among men! Already too many of our young men have poured out their

blood in the flower of their youth! Already too many ceme-
teries, gorged with the victims of war, dot the earth and in
solemn tones admonish all of us to return at long last to
harmony, unity and a just peace! Let us therefore, occupy
our minds not with those thoughts that divide and sever
one man from the other, but rather with those things by
which men can be united in a mutual and equable respect
for himself, his possessions and his goals.

UNION AND AGREEMENT AMONG NATIONS

If all, as they should be, are eager for peace and not for
war, if they look forward with sincerity of heart toward the
peace of brotherhood, then only can governments and the
affairs of state be seen in their proper perspective and properly regulated. Herein lies the only possibility of a search
for and the adoption of that co-operative planning from
which will flow out to the whole family of mankind that
unity so universally desired. In the enjoyment of this harmony, individual nations will then discover the proper limits
of their freedom and will strive not to destroy others by
stepping out of their prescribed limits. This is a unity which
is foreign to the minds of those who try to oppress others or
who strive to deprive them of their freedom. In accord with
this is the opinion of our most wise Predecessor of happy
memory, Leo XIII: "There is nothing better adapted to
checking ambition, to curbing greed for another's goods, or
to bridling envy, all of which are the firebrands of war, than
Christian virtue and most especially justice." [5]

If, on the other hand, the people of the world do not seek
this brotherly unity which ought to rest on the demands of
justice and be fed by the fire of love, conditions will remain
in a state of crisis. Because of this, prudent men everywhere
sorrow and are sad that the uncertainty persists as to
whether they are steering in the direction of a peace sound,
sincere and true, or are rapidly slipping into a new and
terrifying flare-up of war through their utter blindness. We
repeat "utter blindness"; for if, and may God spare us this,
a new war breaks out, the potential destructive power of the
arms that have graced our age promises and holds out to all,
the victor as well as the vanquished, nothing other than im-
measurable destruction and complete ruin. . . .

[5] Letter *Praeclara gratulationis* A.L., Vol. XIV, 1894, p. 210.

SIGNS OF LESSENING TENSIONS

In regard to this point, we must confess—and indeed this bears the hope of better things—that rather recently in some areas, the necessary relationships between classes are becoming less bitter and less strained. Our most recent Predecessor called attention to this in his words to the Catholics of Germany: "The extremely terrifying destruction of the last war which inflicted so much damage on you brought with it at least this advantage that among many classes of your people with the laying aside of prejudice and the love of personal advantage, conflicting class interest came closer to peaceful settlement. Adversity borne in common is a teacher of salutary albeit bitter lessons." [6]

In reality, class distinctions are today less pronounced than formerly for they cannot be limited to that between capital and labor but have become so numerous that they embrace all citizens. Then, too, those who are particularly industrious or skillful have an opportunity of climbing to a higher step in the ladder of social standing. In relation to the day-laborer, it is consoling to see all the recent advances made to provide a more human environment in the factories and other places where they ply their trades. As a result, these workmen have not only an economic value but one more in keeping with human dignity.

LABOR PROBLEMS

Yet, there still remains much to be done. Since there still remains too great a difference in the distribution of wealth, there are still too many causes for disagreement among the classes. This springs mainly from the concept of the right of private property, which is at times defective and downright unjust, held by those who are interested only in their own personal benefit and convenience. Added to this are those despicable lay-offs from work which affect so many and work such hardship upon them. Today, particularly, they work even greater hardships, for the human worker is so often replaced by some kind of supposedly more perfect machine. . . .

Consequently, we earnestly exhort all those who hold responsible positions in the field of labor and those into whose

[6] "Radio Message to the 73rd Congress of German Catholics," *op. cit.*, Vol. XI, p. 189.

hands falls the fate, and at times the very existence, of the workingman not only to weigh carefully the wages given for their hire, not only to see that their rights in this regard are protected but also that they regard them as fellow men or more specifically as brothers. They should see to it that the workman shares more and more in the fruits of his labor and that he be made aware that he is, as it were, an integral part of the entire enterprise. We offer these suggestions that the rights and obligations of the employer and employee be placed on a more equal basis and that the proper recognition be given them. Then, the various professional organizations in the field of industry "may seem to be not a weapon for inflicting or warding off wrongdoing which stirs up the resolute will and stubbornness of others, not as a dam bursting forth from its broken retaining wall, but rather as a bridge joining together the opposite banks of a river." [7]

Oh! let it never happen and for this we earnestly beseech God that this oneness so desirable, so agreeable, so necessary be ever shattered. If the sacrosanct customs of the family hearth are destroyed, if the teachings of the Divine Redeemer on this matter are passed over and allowed to collapse, then the immediate result will be the weakening of the very foundations of the public weal and the ultimate collapse of civil society with the consequent loss and damage to the individual.

III: The Unity of the Church

MOTIVES FOR HOPE

Now we want to speak of that unity which is closest to our heart and with which this pastoral office entrusted to us by God is most particularly concerned. We refer to the Unity of the Church.

It is a matter of record that our Divine Redeemer founded a society which was of such a nature that it alone would exist until the end of the world. This He promised in the words "Behold, I am with you all days even to the consummation of the world" [8] and for this he prayed ever so

---

[7] "Toward a Sound Social Order." Discourses and Radio Addresses of His Holiness Pope Pius XII, Vol. VII, p. 35.

[8] Matthew xxviii, 20.

ardently to His heavenly Father. This prayer of Jesus, "Tha all may be one, even as thou, Father, in me and I in thee that they also may be one in us" [9] was without a doub accepted and heeded because of its deep reverence.[10] B this, we are given the most gratifying hope and assuranc that, at some time, all the sheep that are not of this fol will earnestly desire to return to it. Thus, in accordanc with the sentiment expressed by our Divine Redeemer, "ther shall be one fold and one shepherd." [11]

The promise of this hope has already stirred us deeply to the action of announcing our intention of convening a Ecumenical Council to which Bishops from every corner of the globe will come to consider the serious problems confronting religion. Its special concerns will be the growth o the Catholic Church, the renewal of the spirit of the Gospe in the hearts of people everywhere and the adjustment of Christian discipline to the exigencies of modern day living This will surely be a particularly remarkable display of truth, unity and love, a display which those who are cut off from this Apostolic See will observe. We sincerely hope that they will receive it as a gentle invitation to seek and acquire that unity which Jesus Christ prayed for so ardently to His heavenly Father.

DESIRES FOR UNITY BY NON-CATHOLICS

In regard to this, we are aware, and this is a consolation to us, that the faith and teachings of the Catholic Church have struck a responsive chord in the souls of many among several communities separated from the Chair of Peter. Then, too, considerable respect toward this Apostolic See has arisen and has grown daily as the desire for truth has meant the downfall of prejudice. In addition, we have noticed that almost all those who are called Christians, even though they are separated from us, have again and again held congresses for finding a bond of unity among themselves and have established Councils for this purpose. What further proof do we need that they are experiencing a desire of coming to at least a basic unity?

UNITY OF THE CHURCH

Without a doubt, Our Divine Redeemer established His Church endowed with and buttressed by a very solid unity.

9 See Hebr. V, 7.
10 John xvii, 21.
11 John x, 16.

If, on the other hand, He had not done so (and here we speak foolishly), He would have established something transitory and eventually at least self-contradictory in much the same way as almost all philosophical systems, springing from the ebb and flow of human opinion, are born one from the other, are transformed and finally disappear. Surely there is no one who cannot see that this is diametrically opposed to the Divine Teaching of Jesus Christ, "the Way, the Truth and the Life." [12]

This unity, Venerable Brethren and Beloved Children, as we have said, by its very nature can be nothing frail, wavering or transitory but on the contrary, solid strong and safe.[13] Though it may be lacking to other Christian communities, all who give it a moment's serious consideration can see that it is part of the warp and woof of the Catholic Church. It is a unity distinguished and embellished by one faith, one government, one worship. It is so immediately apparent to the eyes of all that they can recognize and follow it. It is, in short, patterned after the will of our Divine Founder, Himself, in that all the sheep are really gathered together in one fold under the leadership of one shepherd. It is so fashioned that all children are called to the one paternal home which rests on the corner stone of Peter, and, thus, strive to unite all men by a bond of brotherly love into one kingdom of God. In this kingdom, all the members are joined together among themselves in unity of mind and affection with the hope of some day enjoying eternal happiness in heaven.

UNITY OF DOCTRINE

In relation to doctrine, the Catholic Church expressly teaches that all the truths that have been divinely revealed must be believed faithfully and firmly. This includes all that is contained in Sacred Scripture and in oral or written tradition and all that from apostolic times down through the centuries has had the stamp of approval or the definition of either the Supreme Pontiff or of the lawfully constituted Ecumenical Councils. As often as anyone has strayed from this path, the Church in its motherly solicitude has never ceased to call him back to the path of truth. She knows indeed that there is only one truth and that "truth" opposed

12 John xiv, 6.
13 See Enc. Letter, Pius XI *Mortalium animos* "On Embracing the Unity of the True Religion." A.A.S., Vol. XX, 1928, p. 5 ffg.

to it cannot be held. She clearly asserts and bears witness to the statement of the Apostle of the Gentiles as though it were her own: "We can do nothing against the truth but only for the truth." [14]

There are a few things that the Catholic Church leaves open to the discussion of theologians inasmuch as they are not completely certain. Besides, controversies of this type, as that bright light of the English Church, John Henry Cardinal Newman, has pointed out, do not destroy unity but rather add quite a bit to the deeper and better understanding of dogma. Such controversies throw new light on old truths and by the mere airing of opinions level the paths and straighten the way to a better unity.[15] It is well to keep in mind and give your approval to that old axiom attributed to many authors and even expressed at different times in different words "In essentials, unity; in doubt, freedom; in all things, charity."

UNITY OF GOVERNMENT

Besides this unity of faith, it is perfectly obvious to everyone that there is a unity of government in the Catholic Church. For indeed, just as the faithful are subject to their priests and their priests to their bishops, whom "the Holy Spirit has placed . . . to rule the Church of God" [16] so each and every bishop must be subject to the Roman Pontiff. He must be considered the successor of St. Peter whom Christ the Lord placed as the rock and foundation stone of His Church [17] and to whom He gave in a very particular way the full power of binding and loosing upon earth,[18] of strengthening his brethren [19] and of feeding the entire flock.[20]

UNITY OF WORSHIP

Finally, there is a unity of worship. No one can deny that the Catholic Church from its first beginnings down to the

[14] II Cor. xiii, 8.

[15] See Newman, J.H., *Difficulties of Anglicans*, Vol. I, Lecture X, p. 261 ffg.

[16] Acts xx, 28.

[17] See Matthew xvi, 18.

[18] See Matthew xvi, 19.

[19] See Luke xxii, 32.

[20] See John xxi, 15–17.

present has had seven sacraments, no more, no less. These were received as a sacred heritage from Jesus Christ Himself and from birth to death, contribute unceasingly to the nourishing and fostering of the supernatural life of the faithful. Who can deny that there is only one sacrifice, that of the Eucharist? In this sacrifice, in an unbloody manner Christ Himself, our Salvation and our Redeemer, is really and truly immolated for us just as He once hung from a cross in the place called Calvary. In this way, He pours forth upon us in His mercy the vast riches of His grace. St. Cyprian rightly and meritoriously comments on this point in these words: "There can be no other priesthood and no other altar save the one altar and the one priesthood." [21] This does not, however, rule out the existence and the approval of different rites within the Church. In this way, this great sacrifice shines forth more beautifully, when like the daughter of the king of kings, it is seen dressed in various robes.[22]

That all might attain to this true and harmonious unity, the catholic priest in his celebration of Mass offers a spotless host to the most clement God with a prayer for "Your holy Catholic Church that You might deign to give her peace and protection, to unite and guide her the world over, together with Your servant our Pope, and all true believers who cherish the catholic and apostolic faith." [23]

FATHERLY INVITATION TO UNITY

We direct a plea to all you who are separated from this Apostolic See. May this wondrous manifestation of unity by which the Catholic Church shines forth for all to see, and may her prayers from the heart by which she begs this unity from God for all of you, move you in a deep and salutary way.

Do not object if we give in to the desire of our heart and call you brothers and children. Do not object if in the loving way of a father, we nourish the hope of your return. We long to address you with the same zeal with which Theophilus, the Bishop of Alexandria, addressed his brothers

---

[21] Epist. xliii, 5 Corp. Vind. III, 2, 594; see Epist. XL, apud Migne PL IV, 345.

[22] See Psalm xliv, 15.

[23] Canon Missae.

when faced with an unfortunate schism which rent the seam less robe of the Church. "Let us, beloved and heirs of heavenly heritage, imitate for our mutual good the Leader and Accomplisher of our salvation, Jesus. Let us embrace the humility of soul which lifts us up, the love that joins us to God, the sincere faith toward the divine mysteries. Flee schism, avoid discord, embrace each other in mutual love. Heed the word of Christ as He says: 'By this shall all men know that you are my disciples, if you have love one for another.' " [24]

Please note that when we call you tenderly to the unity of the true Church, we are not inviting you to a strange home, but to your very own, the common home of our Father. In our longing, permit us to exhort all of you "in the heart of Jesus Christ" [25] to call to mind your fathers "who spoke to you the word of God. Consider how they ended their lives and imitate their faith." [26] The illustrious cohort of saints which every one of your nations has sent before you into heaven, and in particular, those who in their writ ings have handed down true and lucid explanations of the teachings of Jesus Christ, seem to invite you by the example of their lives toward that unity with this Apostolic See to which every Christian community was, for so many years so strongly connected.

Again we address all of you who are separated from us as brothers on the strength of these words of St. Augustine: "Whether they wish it or not, they are our brothers. They will only cease to be our brothers if they cease to say 'Our Father.' " [27] "Let us love the Lord our God, let us love the Church; let us love Him as father, her as mother; the former as the Master, the latter as the maidservant for we are all children of that maidservant. This marriage is joined by bonds of great love; no one can offend the one and expect the approval of the other. What advantage is it to you not to have offended a Father who will not leave unrevenged an offended mother? Therefore, with one mind, regard God as a father, the Church as a mother." [28] . . .

[24] See Hom. in mysticam caenam, p. 6, LXXVII, 1027.

[25] Philippians i, 8.

[26] Hebrews xiii, 7.

[27] St. Augustine In Ps. 32, Enarr. II, 29 Migne, PL XXXVI, 299.

[28] St. Augustine In Ps. 82, Enarr. II, 14 Migne. PL XXXVII, 1140.

MATER ET MAGISTRA
Christianity and Social Progress*

May 15, 1961

THE Catholic Church has been established by Jesus Christ as MOTHER AND TEACHER of nations, so that all who in the course of centuries come to her loving embrace, may find salvation as well as the fullness of a more excellent life. To this Church, "the pillar and mainstay of the truth," [1] her most holy Founder has entrusted the double task of begetting sons unto herself, and of educating and governing those whom she begets, guiding with maternal providence the life both of individuals and of peoples. The lofty dignity of this life, she has always held in the highest respect and guarded with watchful care.

2. For the teaching of Christ joins, as it were, earth with heaven, in that it embraces the whole man, namely his soul and body, intellect and will, and bids him to lift up his mind from the changing conditions of human existence to that heavenly country where he will one day enjoy unending happiness and peace.

3. Hence, although Holy Church has the special task of sanctifying souls and of making them sharers of heavenly blessings, she is also solicitous for the requirements of men in their daily lives, not merely those relating to food and sustenance, but also to their comfort and advancement in various kinds of goods and in varying circumstances of time.

4. Realizing all this, Holy Church implements the commands of her Founder, Christ, who refers primarily to man's

* Trans. by William J. Gibbons, S.J. Reprinted with the permission of The Paulist Press, 401 West 59 Street, New York 19, N.Y., copyright 1961, 1962, by The Missionary Society of St. Paul the Apostle in the State of New York.

[1] Cf. 1 Tim. 3, 15.

eternal salvation when He says, "I am the Way, and the Truth, and the Life"[2] and elsewhere "I am the Light of the World."[3] On other occasions, however, seeing the hungry crowd, He was moved to exclaim sorrowfully, "I have compassion on the crowd,"[4] thereby indicating that He was also concerned about the earthly needs of mankind. The divine Redeemer shows this care not only by His words but also by the actions of His life, as when, to alleviate the hunger of the crowds, He more than once miraculously multiplied bread.

5. By this bread, given for the nourishment of the body, He wished to foreshadow that heavenly food of the soul which He was to give to men on *the day before He suffered*.

6. It is no wonder, then, that the Catholic Church, instructed by Christ and fulfilling His commands, has for two thousand years, from the ministry of the early deacons to the present time, tenaciously held aloft the torch of charity not only by her teaching but also by her widespread example— that charity which, by combining in a fitting manner the precepts and the practice of mutual love, puts into effect in a wonderful way this twofold commandment of *giving*, wherein is contained the full social teaching and action of the Church.

7. By far the most notable evidence of this social teaching and action, which the Church has set forth through the centuries, undoubtedly is the very distinguished Encyclical Letter *Rerum Novarum*,[5] issued seventy years ago by our predecessor of immortal memory, Leo XIII. Therein he put forward teachings whereby the question of the workers' condition would be resolved in conformity with Christian principles.

8. Seldom have the admonitions of a Pontiff been received with such universal approbation, as was that Encyclical of Leo XIII, rivaled by few in the depth and scope of its reasoning and in the forcefulness of its expression. Indeed, the norms and recommendations contained therein were so momentous that their memory will never fall into oblivion. As a result, the action of the Catholic Church became more widely known. For its Supreme Pastor, making his own the problems of weak and harassed men, their complaints and aspira-

---

[2] John 14, 6.
[3] John 8, 12.
[4] Mark 8, 2.
[5] *Acta Leonis* XIII, XI (1891), pp. 97–144.

tions, had devoted himself especially to the defense and restoration of their rights.

9. Even today, in spite of the long lapse of time since the Letter was published, much of its effectiveness is still evident. It is indeed evident in the documents of the Popes who succeeded Leo XIII, and who, when they discussed economic and social affairs, have always borrowed something from it, either to clarify its application or to stimulate further activity on the part of Catholics. The efficacy of the document also is evident in the laws and institutions of many nations. Thus does it become abundantly clear that the solidly grounded principles, the norms of action, and the paternal admonitions found in the masterly Letter of our predecessor, even today retain their original worth. Moreover, from it can be drawn new and vital criteria, whereby men may judge the nature and extent of the social question, and determine what their responsibilities are in this regard. . . .

RADIO BROADCAST OF PENTECOST, 1941

41. In specifying social rights and obligations, our predecessor of immortal memory, Pius XII, made a significant contribution, when on the feast of Pentecost, June 1, 1941, he broadcast to the world community a message: "in order to call to the attention of the Catholic world the memory of an event worthy of being written in letters of gold on the Calendar of the Church: namely, the fiftieth anniversary of the publication of the epoch-making Encyclical of Leo XIII, *Rerum Novarum*." [6] He broadcast this message, moreover, "to render special thanks to Almighty God that His Vicar on earth, in a Letter such as this, gave to the Church so great a gift, and also to render praise to the eternal Spirit that through this same Letter, He enkindled a fire calculated to rouse the whole human race to new and better effort." [7]

42. In the message, the great Pontiff claimed for the Church "the indisputable competence" to "decide whether the bases of a given social system are in accord with the unchangeable order which God our Creator and Redeemer has fixed both in the natural law and revelation." [8] He noted that the Letter of Leo XIII is of permanent value and has rich and abiding usefulness. He takes the occasion "to explain in greater

[6] Cf. *Acta Apostolicae Sedis*, XXXIII (1941), p. 196.
[7] Cf. *Ibid.*, p. 197.
[8] Cf. *Ibid.*, p. 196.

detail what the Catholic Church teaches regarding the three principal issues of social life in economic affairs, which are mutually related and connected one with the other, and thus interdependent: namely, the use of material goods, labor, and the family." [9]

43. Concerning the use of material goods, our predecessor declared that the right of every man to use them for his own sustenance is prior to all other rights in economic life, and hence is prior even to the right of private ownership. It is certain, however, as our predecessor noted, that the right of private property is from the natural law itself. Nevertheless, it is the will of God the Creator that this right to own property should in no wise obstruct the flow of "material goods created by God to meet the needs of all men, to all equitably, as justice and charity require." [10]

44. As regards labor, Pius XII repeating what appeared in Leo XIII's Letter, declared it to be both a duty and a right of every human being. Consequently, it is in the first place the responsibility of men themselves to regulate mutual labor relations. Only in the event that the interested parties are unwilling or unable to fulfill their functions, does it "devolve upon the State to intervene and to assign labor equitably, safeguarding the standards and aims that the common good properly understood demands." [11]

45. Turning to the family, the Supreme Pontiff stresses that private ownership of material goods helps to safeguard and develop family life. Such goods are an apt means "to secure for the father of a family the healthy liberty he needs in order to fulfill the duties assigned him by the Creator, regarding the physical, spiritual, and religious welfare of the family." [12] From this arises the right of the family to migrate. Accordingly, our predecessor reminds governments, both those permitting emigration and those accepting immigrants, that "they never permit anything whereby mutual and sincere understanding between States is diminished or destroyed." [13] If this be mutually accomplished, it will come to pass that benefits are equalized and diffused widely among peoples, as the supply of goods and the arts and crafts are increased and fostered.

[9] Cf. *Ibid.*, p. 198f.
[10] Cf. *Ibid.*, p. 199.
[11] Cf. *Ibid.*, p. 201.
[12] Cf. *Ibid.*, p. 202.
[13] Cf. *Ibid.*, p. 203.

FURTHER CHANGES

46. But just as contemporary circumstances seemed to Pius XII quite dissimilar from those of the earlier period, so they have changed greatly over the past twenty years. This can be seen not only in the internal situation of each individual country, but also in the mutual relations of countries.

47. In the fields of science, technology, and economics, these developments are especially worthy of note: the discovery of atomic energy, employed first for military purposes and later increasingly for peaceful ends; the almost limitless possibilities opened up by chemistry in synthetic products; the growth of automation in the sectors of industry and services; the modernization of agriculture; the nearly complete conquest, especially through radio and television, of the distance separating peoples; the greatly increased speed of all manner of transportation; the initial conquests of outer space.

48. Turning to the social field, the following contemporary trends are evident: development of systems for social insurance; the introduction of social security systems in some more affluent countries; greater awareness among workers, as members of unions, of the principal issues in economic and social life; a progressive improvement of basic education; wider diffusion among the citizenry of the conveniences of life; increased social mobility and a resulting decline in divisions among the classes: greater interest than heretofore in world affairs on the part of those with average education. Meanwhile, if one considers the social and economic advances made in a growing number of countries, he will quickly discern increasingly pronounced imbalances: first, between agriculture on the one hand and industry and the services on the other; between the more and the less developed regions within countries; and, finally, on a worldwide scale, between countries with differing economic resources and development.

49. Turning now to political affairs, it is evident that there, too, a number of innovations have occurred. Today, in many communities, citizens from almost all social strata participate in public life. Public authorities intervene more and more in economic and social affairs. The peoples of Asia and Africa, having set aside colonial systems, now govern themselves according to their own laws and institutions. As the mutual relationships of peoples increase, they become daily

more dependent one upon the other. Throughout the world, assemblies and councils have become more common, which, being supranational in character, take into account the interests of all peoples. Such bodies are concerned with economic life, or with social affairs, or with culture and education, or, finally, with the mutual relationships of peoples.

REASONS FOR THE NEW ENCYCLICAL

50. Now, reflecting on all these things, we feel it our duty to keep alive the torch lighted by our great predecessors and to exhort all to draw from their writings light and inspiration, if they wish to resolve the social question in ways more in accord with the needs of the present time. Therefore, we are issuing this present Letter not merely to commemorate appropriately the Encyclical Letter of Leo XIII, but also, in the light of changed conditions, both to confirm and explain more fully what our predecessors taught, and to set forth the Church's teaching regarding the new and serious problems of our day.

Part II: Explanation and Development of the Teachings of "Rerum Novarum"

PRIVATE INITIATIVE AND STATE INTERVENTION IN ECONOMIC LIFE

51. At the outset it should be affirmed that in economic affairs first place is to be given to the private initiative of individual men who, either working by themselves, or with others in one fashion or another, pursue their common interests.

52. But in this matter, for reasons pointed out by our predecessors, it is necessary that public authorities take active interest, the better to increase output of goods and to further social progress for the benefit of all citizens.

53. This intervention of public authorities that encourages, stimulates, regulates, supplements, and complements, is based on the *principle of subsidiarity* [14] as set forth by Pius XI in his Encyclical *Quadragesimo Anno:* "It is a fundamental

[14] *Acta Apostolicae Sedis,* XXIII (1931), p. 203.

principle of social philosophy, fixed and unchangeable, that one should not withdraw from individuals and commit to the community what they can accomplish by their own enterprise and industry. So, too, it is an injustice and at the same time a grave evil and a disturbance of right order, to transfer to the larger and higher collectivity functions which can be performed and provided for by lesser and subordinate bodies. Inasmuch as every social activity should, by its very nature, prove a help to members of the body social, it should never destroy or absorb them." [15]

54. Indeed, as is easily perceived, recent developments of science and technology provide additional reasons why, to a greater extent than heretofore, it is within the power of public authorities to reduce imbalances, whether these be between various sectors of economic life, or between different regions of the same nation, or even between different peoples of the world as a whole. These same developments make it possible to keep fluctuations in the economy within bounds, and to provide effective measures for avoiding mass unemployment. Consequently, it is requested again and again of public authorities responsible for the common good, that they intervene in a wide variety of economic affairs, and that, in a more extensive and organized way than heretofore, they adapt institutions, tasks, means, and procedures to this end.

55. Nevertheless, it remains true that precautionary activities of public authorities in the economic field, although widespread and penetrating, should be such that they not only avoid restricting the freedom of private citizens, but also increase it, so long as the basic rights of each individual person are preserved inviolate. Included among these is the right and duty of each individual normally to provide the necessities of life for himself and his dependents. This implies that whatever be the economic system, it allow and facilitate for every individual the opportunity to engage in productive activity.

56. Furthermore, the course of events thus far makes it clear that there cannot be a prosperous and well-ordered society unless both private citizens and public authorities work together in economic affairs. Their activity should be characterized by mutual and amicable efforts, so that the roles assigned to each fit in with requirements of the common good, as changing times and customs suggest.

[15] *Ibid.*, p. 203.

57. Experience, in fact, shows that where private initiative of individuals is lacking, political tyranny prevails. Moreover, much stagnation occurs in various sectors of the economy, and hence all sorts of consumer goods and services, closely connected with needs of the body and more especially of the spirit, are in short supply. Beyond doubt, the attainment of such goods and services provides remarkable opportunity and stimulus for individuals to exercise initiative and industry.

58. Where, on the other hand, appropriate activity of the State is lacking or defective, commonwealths are apt to experience incurable disorders, and there occurs exploitation of the weak by the unscrupulous strong, who flourish, unfortunately, like cockle among the wheat, in all times and places.

COMPLEXITY OF SOCIAL STRUCTURE

DIRECTION OF THE TREND

59. One of the principal characteristics of our time is the multiplication of social relationships, that is, a daily more complex interdependence of citizens, introducing into their lives and activities many and varied forms of association, recognized for the most part in private and even in public law. This tendency seemingly stems from a number of factors operative in the present era, among which are technical and scientific progress, greater productive efficiency, and a higher standard of living among citizens.

60. These developments in social living are at once both a symptom and a cause of the growing intervention of public authorities in matters which, since they pertain to the more intimate aspects of personal life, are of serious moment and not without danger. Such, for example, are the care of health, the instruction and education of youth, the choice of a personal career, the ways and means of rehabilitating or assisting those handicapped mentally or physically. But this trend also indicates and in part follows from that human and natural inclination, scarcely resistible, whereby men are impelled voluntarily to enter into association in order to attain objectives which each one desires, but which exceed the capacity of single individuals. This tendency has given rise, especially in recent years, to organizations and institutes on both national and international levels, which relate to eco-

nomic and social goals, to cultural and recreational activities, to athletics, to various professions, and to political affairs.

EVALUATION

61. Such an advance in social relationships definitely brings numerous services and advantages. It makes possible, in fact, the satisfaction of many personal rights, especially those of economic and social life; these relate, for example, to the minimum necessities of human life, to health services, to the broadening and deepening of elementary education, to a more fitting training in skills, to housing, to labor, to suitable leisure and recreation. In addition, through the ever more perfect organization of modern means for the diffusion of thought—press, cinema, radio, television—individuals are enabled to take part in human events on a world-wide scale.

62. But as these various forms of association are multiplied and daily extended, it also happens that in many areas of activity, rules and laws controlling and determining relationships of citizens are multiplied. As a consequence, opportunity for free action by individuals is restricted within narrower limits. Methods are often used, procedures are adopted, and such an atmosphere develops wherein it becomes difficult for one to make decisions independently of outside influences, to do anything on his own initiative, to carry out in a fitting way his rights and duties, and to fully develop and perfect his personality. Will men perhaps, then, become automatons, and cease to be personally responsible, as these social relationships multiply more and more? It is a question which must be answered negatively.

63. Actually, increased complexity of social life by no means results from a blind drive of natural forces. Indeed, as stated above, it is the creation of free men who are so disposed to act by nature as to be responsible for what they do. They must, of course, recognize the laws of human progress and the development of economic life and take these into account. Furthermore, men are not altogether free of their milieu.

64. Accordingly, advances in social organization can and should be so brought about that maximum advantages accrue to citizens while at the same time disadvantages are averted or at least minimized.

65. That these desired objectives be more readily obtained, it is necessary that public authorities have a correct understanding of the common good. This embraces the

sum total of those conditions of social living, whereby men are enabled more fully and more readily to achieve their own perfection. Hence, we regard it as necessary that the various intermediary bodies and the numerous social undertakings wherein an expanded social structure primarily finds expression, be ruled by their own laws, and as the common good itself progresses, pursue this objective in a spirit of sincere concord among themselves. Nor is it less necessary that the above mentioned groups present the form and substance of a true community. This they will do, only if individual members are considered and treated as persons, and are encouraged to participate in the affairs of the group.

66. Accordingly, as relationships multiply between men, binding them more closely together, commonwealths will more readily and appropriately order their affairs to the extent these two factors are kept in balance: (1) the freedom of individual citizens and groups of citizens to act autonomously, while cooperating one with the other; (2) the activity of the State whereby the undertakings of private individuals and groups are suitably regulated and fostered.

67. Now if social systems are organized in accordance with the above norms and moral laws, their extension does not necessarily mean that individual citizens will be gravely discriminated against or excessively burdened. Rather, we can hope that this will enable man not only to develop and perfect his natural talents, but also will lead to an appropriate structuring of the human community. Such a structure, as our predecessor of happy memory, Pius XI, warned in his Encyclical Letter *Quadragesimo Anno*,[16] is absolutely necessary for the adequate fulfillment of the rights and duties of social life.

REMUNERATION FOR WORK

STANDARDS OF JUSTICE AND EQUITY

68. Our heart is filled with profound sadness when we observe, as it were, with our own eyes a wretched spectacle indeed—great masses of workers who, in not a few nations, and even in whole continents, receive too small a return from their labor. Hence, they and their families must live in conditions completely out of accord with human dignity. This can be traced, for example, to the fact that in these

16 Cf. *Ibid.*, p. 222f.

regions, modern industrial techniques either have only recently been introduced or have made less than satisfactory progress.

69. It happens in some of these nations that, as compared with the extreme need of the majority, the wealth and conspicuous consumption of a few stand out, and are in open and bold contrast with the lot of the needy. It happens in other places that excessive burdens are placed upon men in order that the commonwealth may achieve within a brief span, an increase of wealth such as can by no means be achieved without violating the laws of justice and equity. Finally, it happens elsewhere that a disproportionate share of the revenue goes toward the building up of national prestige, and that large sums of money are devoted to armaments.

70. Moreover, in the economically developed countries, it frequently happens that great, or sometimes very great, remuneration is had for the performance of some task of lesser importance or doubtful utility. Meanwhile, the diligent and profitable work that whole classes of decent and hard-working citizens perform, receives too low a payment and one insufficient for the necessities of life, or else, one that does not correspond to the contribution made to the community, or to the revenues of the undertakings in which they are engaged, or to the national income.

71. Wherefore, we judge it to be our duty to reaffirm once again that just as remuneration for work cannot be left entirely to unregulated competition, neither may it be decided arbitrarily at the will of the more powerful. Rather, in this matter, the norms of justice and equity should be strictly observed. This requires that workers receive a wage sufficient to lead a life worthy of man and to fulfill family responsibilities properly. But in determining what constitutes an appropriate wage, the following must necessarily be taken into account: first of all, the contribution of individuals to the economic effort; the economic state of the enterprises within which they work; the requirements of each community, especially as regards over-all employment; finally, what concerns the common good of all peoples, namely, of the various States associated among themselves, but differing in character and extent.

72. It is clear that the standards of judgment set forth above are binding always and everywhere. However, the measure in which they are to be applied in concrete cases cannot be established unless account is taken of the resources at hand. These resources can and in fact do vary in

quantity and quality among different peoples, and may even change within the same country with the passing of time.

BALANCING ECONOMIC DEVELOPMENTS AND SOCIAL PROGRESS

73. Whereas in our era the economics of various countries are evolving very rapidly, more especially since the last great war, we take this opportunity to draw the attention of all to a strict demand of social justice, which explicitly requires that, with the growth of the economy, there occur a corresponding social development. Thus, all classes of citizens will benefit equitably from an increase in national wealth. Toward this end vigilance should be exercised and effective steps taken that class differences arising from disparity of wealth not be increased, but lessened so far as possible.

74. "National wealth"—as our predecessor of happy memory, Pius XII, rightfully observed—"inasmuch as it is produced by the common efforts of the citizenry, has no other purpose than to secure without interruption those material conditions in which individuals are enabled to lead a full and perfect life. Where this is consistently the case, then such a people is to be judged truly rich. For the system whereby both the common prosperity is achieved and individuals exercise their right to use material goods, conforms fully to norms laid down by God the Creator." [17] From this it follows that the economic prosperity of any people is to be assessed not so much from the sum total of goods and wealth possessed as from the distribution of goods according to norms of justice, so that everyone in the community can develop and perfect himself. For this, after all, is the end toward which all economic activity of a community is by nature ordered.

75. We must here call attention to the fact that in many countries today, the economic system is such that large and medium size productive enterprises achieve rapid growth precisely because they finance replacement and plant expansion from their own revenues. Where this is the case, we believe that such companies should grant to workers some share in the enterprise, especially where they are paid no more than the minimum wage.

76. In this matter, the principle laid down by our predecessor of happy memory, Pius XI, in the Encyclical Letter *Quadragesimo Anno*, should be borne in mind: "It is totally

[17] Cf. *Acta Apostolicae Sedis*, XXXIII (1941), p. 200.

false to ascribe to a single factor of production what is in fact produced by joint activity; and it is completely unjust for one factor to arrogate to itself what is produced, ignoring what has been contributed by other factors." [18]

77. The demands of justice referred to, can be met in various ways, as experience shows. Not to mention other ways, it is very desirable that workers gradually acquire some share in the enterprise by such methods as seem more appropriate. For today, more than in the times of our predecessor, "every effort should be made that at least in the future, only an equitable share of the fruits of production accumulate in the hands of the wealthy, and a sufficient and ample portion go to the workingmen." [19]

78. But we should remember that adjustments between remuneration for work and revenues are to be brought about in conformity with the requirements of the common good, both of one's own community and of the entire human family.

79. Considering the common good on the national level, the following points are relevant and should not be overlooked: to provide employment for as many workers as possible; to take care lest privileged groups arise even among the workers themselves; to maintain a balance between wages and prices; to make accessible the goods and services for a better life to as many persons as possible; either to eliminate or to keep within bounds the inequalities that exist between different sectors of the economy—that is, between agriculture, industry and services; to balance properly any increases in output with advances in services provided to citizens, especially by public authority; to adjust, as far as possible, the means of production to the progress of science and technology; finally, to ensure that the advantages of a more humane way of existence not merely subserve the present generation but have regard for future generations as well.

80. As regards the common good of human society as a whole, the following conditions should be fulfilled: that the competitive striving of peoples to increase output be free of bad faith; that harmony in economic affairs and a friendly and beneficial cooperation be fostered; and, finally, that effective aid be given in developing the economically underdeveloped nations.

81. It is evident from what has been said that these de-

[18] *Acta Apostolicae Sedis*, XXIII (1931), p. 195.
[19] *Ibid.*, p. 198.

mands of the common good, on both the national and world levels, should be borne in mind, when there is question of determining the share of earnings assigned to those responsible for directing the productive enterprise, or as interest and dividends to those who have invested capital.

DEMANDS OF JUSTICE AS REGARDS PRODUCTIVE INSTITUTIONS

INSTITUTIONS CONFORMING TO THE DIGNITY OF MAN

82. Justice is to be observed not merely in the distribution of wealth, but also in regard to the conditions under which men engage in productive activity. There is, in fact, an innate need of human nature requiring that men engaged in productive activity have an opportunity to assume responsibility and to perfect themselves by their efforts.

83. Consequently, if the organization and structure of economic life be such that the human dignity of workers is compromised, or their sense of responsibility is weakened, or their freedom of action is removed, then we judge such an economic order to be unjust, even though it produces a vast amount of goods, whose distribution conforms to the norms of justice and equity.

REAFFIRMATION OF A DIRECTIVE

84. Nor is it possible in economic affairs to determine in one formula all the measures that are more conformable to the dignity of man, or are more suitable in developing in him a sense of responsibility. Nevertheless, our predecessor of happy memory, Pius XII, appropriately laid down certain norms of action: "Small and medium-sized holdings in agriculture, in the arts and crafts, in commerce and industry, should be safeguarded and fostered. Such enterprises should join together in mutual-aid societies in order that the services and benefits of large-scale enterprises will be available to them. So far as these larger enterprises are concerned, work agreements should in some way be modified by partnership arrangements." [20]

ARTISAN ENTERPRISES AND COOPERATIVE ASSOCIATIONS

85. Wherefore, conformably to requirements of the common good and the state of technology, artisan and farm en-

[20] Radio Broadcast, September 1, 1944; cf. *A.A.S.*, XXXVI (1944), p. 254.

terprises of family type should be safeguarded and fostered, as should also cooperatives that aim to complement and perfect such enterprises.

86. We shall return shortly to the subject of farm enterprises. Here, we think it appropriate to say something about artisan enterprises and cooperative associations.

87. Above all, it must be emphasized that enterprises and bodies of this sort, in order that they may survive and flourish, should be continuously adapted—both in their productive structure and in their operating methods—to new conditions of the times. These new conditions constantly arise from advances in science and technology, or from changing consumer needs and preferences. It is especially appropriate that all this be done by the craftsmen themselves and by the associates in the cooperatives.

88. Hence, it is most fitting not only that both these groups be suitably formed in technical and in spiritual and intellectual matters, but also that they be joined together professionally. Nor is it less fitting that the State make special provision for them in regard to instruction, taxes, credit facilities, social security and insurance.

89. Moreover, the measures taken by the State on behalf of the craftsmen and members of cooperatives are also justified by the fact that these two categories of citizens are producers of genuine wealth, and contribute to the advance of civilization.

90. Accordingly, we paternally exhort our beloved sons, craftsmen and members of cooperatives throughout the world, that they fully realize the dignity of their role in society, since, by their work, the sense of responsibility and spirit of mutual aid can be daily more intensified among the citizenry, and the desire to work with dedication and originality be kept alive.

PARTICIPATION OF WORKERS IN MEDIUM-SIZE AND LARGE ENTERPRISES

91. Furthermore, as did our predecessors, we regard as justifiable the desire of employees to be partners in enterprises with which they are associated and wherein they work. We do not think it possible, however, to decide with certain and explicit norms the manner and degree of such partnerships, since this must be determined according to the state of the individual productive enterprises. For the situation is not everywhere the same, and, in fact, it can change suddenly within one and the same enterprise. Nevertheless,

we do not doubt that employees should have an active part in the affairs of the enterprise wherein they work, whether these be private or public. But it is of the utmost importance that productive enterprises assume the character of a true human fellowship whose spirit suffuses the dealings, activities, and standing of all its members.

92. This requires that mutual relations between employers and directors on the one hand and the employees of the enterprise on the other, be marked by mutual respect, esteem, and good will. It also demands that all collaborate sincerely and harmoniously in their joint undertaking, and that they perform their work not merely with the objective of deriving an income, but also of carrying out the role assigned them and of performing a service that results in benefit to others. This means that the workers may have a say in, and may make a contribution toward, the efficient running and development of the enterprise. Thus, our predecessor of happy memory, Pius XII, clearly indicated: "The economic and social functions which everyone aspires to fulfill, require that efforts of individuals be not wholly subjected to the will of others." [21] Beyond doubt, an enterprise truly in accord with human dignity should safeguard the necessary and efficient unity of administration. But it by no means follows that those who work daily in such an enterprise are to be considered merely as servants, whose sole function is to execute orders silently, and who are not allowed to interject their desires and interests, but must conduct themselves as idle stand-bys when it comes to assignment and direction of their tasks.

93. Finally, attention is drawn to the fact that the greater amount of responsibility desired today by workers in productive enterprises, not merely accords with the nature of man, but also is in conformity with historical developments in the economic, social, and political fields.

94. Unfortunately, in our day, there occur in economic and social affairs many imbalances that militate against justice and humanity. Meanwhile, throughout all of economic life, errors are spread that seriously impair its operation, purposes, organization, and the fulfillment of responsibilities. Nevertheless, it is an undeniable fact that the more recent productive systems, thanks to the impulse deriving from advances in technology and science, are becoming more mod-

ern and efficient, and are expanding at a faster rate than in the past. This demands of workers greater abilities and professional qualifications. Accordingly, workers should be provided with additional aids and time to achieve a suitable and more rounded formation, and to carry out more fittingly their duties as regards studies, morals, and religion.

95. Thus it happens that in our day youths can be allotted additional years to acquire a basic education and necessary skills.

96. Now if these things be done, a situation will emerge wherein workers are enabled to assume greater responsibilities even within their own enterprises. As regards the commonwealth as such, it is of great importance that all ranks of citizens feel themselves daily more obligated to safeguard the common good.

PARTICIPATION OF WORKERS AT ALL LEVELS

97. Now, as is evident to all, in our day associations of workers have become widespread, and for the most part have been given legal status within individual countries and even across national boundaries. These bodies no longer recruit workers for purposes of strife, but rather for pursuing a common aim. And this is achieved especially by collective bargaining between associations of workers and those of management. But it should be emphasized how necessary, or at least very appropriate, it is to give workers an opportunity to exert influence outside the limits of the individual productive unit, and indeed within all ranks of the commonwealth.

98. The reason is that individual productive units, whatever their size, efficiency, or importance within the commonwealth, are closely connected with the over-all economic and social situation in each country, whereon their own prosperity ultimately depends.

99. Nevertheless, to decide what is more helpful to the over-all economic situation is not the prerogative of individual productive enterprises, but pertains to the public authorities and to those institutions which, established either nationally or among a number of countries, function in various sectors of economic life. From this is evident the propriety or necessity of ensuring that not only managers or agents of management are represented before such authorities and institutions, but also workers or those who have the responsibility of safeguarding the rights, needs, and aspirations of workers.

100. It is fitting, therefore, that our thoughts and paternal affection be directed toward the various professional groups and associations of workers which, in accord with principles of Christian teaching, carry on their activities on several continents. We are aware of the many and great difficulties experienced by these beloved sons of ours, as they effectively worked in the past and continue to strive, both within their national boundaries and throughout the world, to vindicate the rights of workingmen and to improve their lot and conduct.

101. Furthermore, we wish to give deserved praise to the work of these our sons. Their accomplishments are not always immediately evident, but nevertheless permeate practically the entire field of labor, spreading correct norms of action and thought, and the beneficial influence of the Christian religion.

102. And we wish also to praise paternally those dear sons of ours who, imbued with Christian principles, give their special attention to other labor associations and those groups of workingmen that follow the laws of nature and respect the religious and moral liberty of individuals.

103. Nor can we at this point neglect to congratulate and to express our esteem for the International Labor Organization —variously signified popularly by the letters O.I.L. or I.L.O. or O.I.T.—which, for many years, has done effective and valuable work in adapting the economic and social order everywhere to the norms of justice and humanity. In such an order, the legitimate rights of workers are recognized and preserved.

PRIVATE PROPERTY

CHANGED CONDITIONS

104. In recent years, as we are well aware, the role played by the owners of capital in very large productive enterprises has been separated more and more from the role of management. This has occasioned great difficulties for governments, whose duty it is to make certain that directors of the principal enterprises, especially those of greatest influence in the economic life of the entire country, do not depart from the requirements of the common good. These difficulties, as we know from experience, are by no means less, whether it be private citizens or public bodies that make the capital investments requisite for larger-scale enterprises.

105. It is also quite clear that today the number of persons is increasing who, because of recent advances in insurance programs and various systems of social security, are able to look to the future with tranquillity. This sort of tranquillity once was rooted in the ownership of property, albeit modest.

106. It sometimes happens in our day that men are more inclined to seek some professional skill than possession of goods. Moreover, such men have greater esteem for income from labor or rights arising from labor, than for that deriving from capital investment or rights associated therewith.

107. This clearly accords with the inherent characteristics of labor, inasmuch as it proceeds directly from the human person, and hence is to be thought more of than wealth in external goods. These later, by their very nature, must be regarded as instruments. This trend indicates an advance in civilization.

108. Economic conditions of this kind have occasioned popular doubt as to whether, under present circumstances, a principle of economic and social life, firmly enunciated and defended by our predecessors, has lost its force or is to be regarded as of lesser moment: namely, the principle whereby it is established that men have from nature a right of privately owning goods, including those of a productive kind.

CONFIRMATION OF THE RIGHT OF
PRIVATE PROPERTY

109. Such a doubt has no foundation. For the right of private property, including that pertaining to goods devoted to productive enterprises, is permanently valid. Indeed, it is rooted in the very nature of things, whereby we learn that individual men are prior to civil society, and hence, that civil society is to be directed toward man as its end. Indeed, the right of private individuals to act freely in economic affairs is recognized in vain, unless they are at the same time given an opportunity of freely selecting and using things necessary for the exercise of this right. Moreover, experience and history testify that where political regimes do not allow to private individuals the possession also of productive goods, the exercise of human liberty is violated or completely destroyed in matters of primary importance. Thus it becomes clear that in the right of property, the exercise of liberty finds both a safeguard and a stimulus.

110. This explains the fact that socio-political groups and associations which endeavor to reconcile freedom with jus-

tice within society, and which until recently did not uphold
the right of private property in productive goods, have now
enlightened by the course of social events, modified their
views and are disposed actually to approve this right.

111. Accordingly, we make our own the insistence of our
predecessor of happy memory, Pius XII: "In defending the
right of private property, the Church has in mind a very
important ethical aim in social matters. She does not, of
course, strive to uphold the present state of affairs as if it
were an expression of the divine will. And even less does
she accept the patronage of the affluent and wealthy, while
neglecting the rights of the poor and needy. . . . The Church
rather does intend that the institution of private property be
such as is required by the plan of divine wisdom and the
law of nature." [22] Private ownership should safeguard the
rights of the human person, and at the same time make its
necessary contribution to the establishment of right order in
society.

112. While recent developments in economic life progress
rapidly in a number of countries, as we have noted, and produce goods ever more efficiently, justice and equity require
that remuneration for work also be increased within limits
allowed by the common good. This enables workers to save
more readily and hence to achieve some property status of
their own. Wherefore, it is indeed surprising that some reject
the natural role of private ownership. For it is a right which
continually draws its force and vigor from the fruitfulness
of labor, and which, accordingly, is an effective aid in safeguarding the dignity of the human person and the free exercise of responsibility in all fields of endeavor. Finally, it
strengthens the stability and tranquillity of family life, thus
contributing to the peace and prosperity of the commonwealth.

EFFECTIVE DISTRIBUTION

113. It is nót enough, then, to assert that man has from
nature the right of privately possessing goods as his own,
including those of productive character, unless, at the same
time, a continuing effort is made to spread the use of this
right through all ranks of the citizenry.

114. Our predecessor of happy memory, Pius XII, clearly
reminded us that on the one hand the dignity of the human

[22] Radio Broadcast, September 1, 1944; cf. *A.A.S.*, XXXVI (1944),
p. 253.

erson necessarily "requires the right of using external goods
1 order to live according to the right norm of nature. And
) this right corresponds a most serious obligation, which
equires that, so far as possible, there be given to all an
pportunity of possessing private property." [23] On the other
and, the nobility inherent in work, besides other require-
nents, demands "the conservation and perfection of a social
rder that makes possible a secure, although modest, property
) all classes of people." [24]

115. It is especially appropriate that today, more than
eretofore, widespread private ownership should prevail,
ince, as noted above, the number of nations increases
vherein the economic systems experience daily growth.
Therefore, by prudent use of various devices already proven
ffective, it will not be difficult for the body politic to modify
conomic and social life so that the way is made easier for
videspread private possession of such things as durable
goods, homes, gardens, tools requisite for artisan enterprises
nd family-type farms, investments in enterprises of medium
or large size. All of this has occurred satisfactorily in some
ations with developed social and economic systems.

PUBLIC PROPERTY

116. Obviously, what we have said above does not preclude
wnership of goods pertaining to production of wealth by
States and public agencies, especially "if these carry with
hem power too great to be left in private hands, without
njury to the community at large." [25]

117. It seems characteristic of our times to vest more and
nore ownership of goods in the State and in other public
oodies. This is partially explained by the fact that the com-
non good requires public authorities to exercise ever
greater responsibilities. However, in this matter, the *principle
of subsidiarity*, already mentioned above, is to be strictly
observed. For it is lawful for States and public corporations
o expand their domain of ownership only when manifest and
genuine requirements of the common good so require, and
hen with safeguards, lest the possession of private citizens
oe diminished beyond measure, or, what is worse, destroyed.

23 Radio Broadcast, December 24, 1942; cf. *A.A.S.*, XXXV (1943),
p. 17.

24 Cf. *Ibid.*, p. 20

25 Encyclical Letter *Quadragesimo Anno; A.A.S.*, XXIII (1931),
p. 214.

118. Finally, we cannot pass over in silence the fact that economic enterprises undertaken by the State or by public corporations should be entrusted to citizens outstanding in skill and integrity, who will carry out their responsibilities to the commonwealth with a deep sense of devotion. Moreover the activity of these men should be subjected to careful and continuing supervision, lest, in the administration of the State itself, there develop an economic imperialism in the hands of a few. For such a development is in conflict with the highest good of the commonwealth.

SOCIAL FUNCTION OF PROPERTY

119. Our predecessors have always taught that in the right of private property there is rooted a social responsibility. Indeed, in the wisdom of God the Creator, the over-all supply of goods is assigned, first of all, that all men may lead a decent life. As our predecessor of happy memory, Leo XIII, clearly reminded us in the Encyclical Letter *Rerum Novarum*, "This is the heart of the matter: whoever has received from the divine bounty a larger share of blessings, whether these be corporal or external or gifts of the mind, has received them to use for his own perfection, and, at the same time, as the minister of God's providence, for the benefit of others. 'He who has a talent' [says St. Gregory the Great], 'let him take care that he hides it not; he who has abundance, let him arouse himself to mercy and generosity; he who has skill in managing affairs, let him make special effort to share the use and utility thereof with his neighbor.' " [26]

120. Although in our day, the role assigned the State and public bodies has increased more and more, it by no means follows that the social function of private ownership is obsolescent, as some seem to think. For social responsibility in this matter derives its force from the very right of private property. Furthermore, it is quite clear that there always will be a wide range of difficult situations, as well as hidden and grave needs, which the manifold providence of the State leaves untouched, and of which it can in no way take account. Wherefore, there is always wide scope for humane action by private citizens and for Christian charity. Finally, it is evident that in stimulating efforts relating to spiritual welfare, the work done by individual men or by private

[26] *Acta Leonis* XIII, XI (1891), p. 114.

civic groups has more value than what is done by public authorities.

121. Moreover, it is well to recall here that the right of private ownership is clearly evident in the Gospels, which reveal Jesus Christ ordering the rich to share their goods with the poor so as to turn them into spiritual possessions: "Do not lay up for yourselves treasures on earth, where rust and moth consume, and where thieves break in and steal; but lay up for yourselves treasures in heaven, where neither rust nor moth consumes nor thieves break in and steal." [27] And the divine Master states that whatever is done for the poor is done for Him: "Amen I say to you, as long as you did it for one of these, the least of My brethren, you did it for Me." [28]

Part III: New Aspects of the Social Question

122. The progress of events and of time have made it increasingly evident that the relationships between workers and management in productive enterprises must be readjusted according to norms of justice and charity. But the same is also true of the systems whereby various types of economic activity and the differently endowed regions within a country ought to be linked together. Meanwhile, within the over-all human community, many nations with varied endowments have not made identical progress in their economic and social affairs.

JUST REQUIREMENTS IN THE MATTER OF INTERRELATED PRODUCTIVE SECTORS

AGRICULTURE: A DEPRESSED SECTOR

123. First of all, to lay down some norms in regard to agriculture, we would note that the over-all number of rural dwellers seemingly has not diminished. Beyond doubt, however, many farmers have abandoned their rural birthplace, and seek out either the more populous centers or the cities themselves. Now since this is the case in almost all countries,

[27] Matt. 6, 19-20.
[28] Matt. 25, 40.

and since it affects large numbers of human beings, problems concerning life and dignity of citizens arise, which are indeed difficult to overcome.

124. Thus, as economic life progresses and expands, the percentage of rural dwellers diminishes, while the great number of industrial and service workers increases. Yet, we feel that those who transfer from rural activities to other productive enterprises often are motivated by reasons arising from the very evolution of economic affairs. Very often, however, they are caught up by various enticements of which the following are noteworthy: a desire to escape from a confined environment offering no prospect of a more comfortable life; the wish, so common in our age, to undertake new activities and to acquire new experiences; the attraction of quickly acquired goods and fortunes; a longing after a freer life, with the advantages that larger towns and cities usually provide. But there is no doubt about this point: rural dwellers leave the fields because nearly everywhere they see their affairs in a state of depression, both as regards labor productivity and the level of living of farm populations.

125. Accordingly, in this grave matter, about which enquiries are made in nearly all countries, we should first of all ask what is to be done to prevent so great imbalances between agriculture, industry, and the services in the matter of productive efficiency? Likewise, what can be done to minimize differences between the rural standard of living and that of city dwellers whose money income is derived from industry or some service or other? Finally, how can it be brought about that those engaged in agricultural pursuits no longer regard themselves as inferior to others? Indeed, rural dwellers should be convinced not only that they can strengthen and develop their personalities by their toil, but also that they can look forward to the future vicissitudes with confidence.

126. Accordingly, we judge it opportune in this connection to lay down some norms of permanent validity; although, as is evident, these must be adapted as various circumstances of time and place permit, or suggest, or absolutely require.

PROVISION FOR ESSENTIAL PUBLIC SERVICES

127. First, it is necessary that everyone, and especially public authorities, strive to effect improvements in rural areas as regards the principal services needed by all. Such are, for example: highway construction; transport services; market-

ing facilities; pure drinking water; housing; medical services; elementary, trade, and professional schools; things requisite for religion and for recreation; finally, furnishings and equipment needed in the modern farm home. Where these requirements for a dignified farm life are lacking to rural dwellers, economic and social progress does not occur at all, or else very slowly. Under such conditions, nothing can be done to keep men from deserting the fields, nor can anyone readily estimate their number.

GRADUAL AND ORDERLY DEVELOPMENT
OF THE ECONOMIC SYSTEM

128. It is desirable, moreover, that economic development of commonwealths proceed in orderly fashion, meanwhile preserving appropriate balance between the various sectors of the economy. In particular, care must be had that within the agricultural sector innovations are introduced as regards productive technology, whether these relate to productive methods, or to cultivation of the fields, or to equipment for the rural enterprise, as far as the over-all economy allows or requires. And all this should be done as far as possible, in accordance with technical advances in industry and in the various services.

129. In this way, agriculture not only absorbs a larger share of industrial output, but also demands a higher quality of services. In its turn, agriculture offers to the industrial and service sectors of the economy, as well as to the community as a whole, those products which in kind and in quantity better meet consumer needs. Thus, agriculture contributes to stability of the purchasing power of money, a very positive factor for the orderly development of the entire economic system.

130. By proceeding in this manner, the following advantages, among others, arise: first of all, it is easier to know the origins and destinations of rural dwellers displaced by modernization of agriculture. Thereupon, they can be instructed in skills needed for other types of work. Finally, economic aids and helps will not be lacking for their intellectual and cultural development, so that they can fit into new social groups.

APPROPRIATE ECONOMIC POLICY

131. To achieve orderly progress in various sectors of economic life, it is absolutely necessary that as regards agri-

culture, public authorities give heed and take action in the following matters: taxes and duties, credit, insurance, prices, the fostering of requisite skills, and, finally, improved equipment for rural enterprises.

TAXATION

132. As regards taxation, assessment according to ability to pay is fundamental to a just and equitable system.

133. But in determining taxes for rural dwellers, the general welfare requires public authorities to bear in mind that income in a rural economy is both delayed and subject to greater risk. Moreover, there is difficulty in finding capital so as to increase returns.

CAPITAL AT SUITABLE INTEREST

134. Accordingly, those with money to invest are more inclined to invest it in enterprises other than in the rural economy. And for the same reason, rural dwellers cannot pay high rates of interest. Nor are they generally able to pay prevailing market rates for capital wherewith to carry on and expand their operations. Wherefore, the general welfare requires that public authorities not merely make special provision for agricultural financing, but also for establishment of banks that provide capital to farmers at reasonable rates of interest.

SOCIAL INSURANCE AND SOCIAL SECURITY

135. It also seems necessary to make provision for a two-fold insurance, one covering agricultural output, the other covering farmers and their families. Because, as experience shows, the income of individual farmers is, on the average, less than that of workers in industry and the services, it does not seem to be fully in accord with the norms of social justice and equity to provide farmers with insurance or social security benefits that are inferior to those of other classes of citizens. For those insurance plans or provisions that are established generally should not differ markedly one from the other, whatever be the economic sector wherein the citizens work, or from which they derive their income.

136. Moreover, since social security and insurance can help appreciably in distributing national income among the citizens according to justice and equity, these systems can be regarded as means whereby imbalances among various classes of citizens are reduced.

PRICE PROTECTION

137. Since agricultural products have special characteristics, it is fitting that their price be protected by methods worked out by economic experts. In this matter, although it is quite helpful that those whose interest are involved take steps to safeguard themselves, setting up, as it were, appropriate goals, public authorities cannot stand entirely aloof from the stabilization procedure.

138. Nor should this be overlooked, that, generally speaking, the price of rural products is more a recompense for farmers' labor than for capital investment.

139. Thus, our predecessor of happy memory, Pius XI, touching on the welfare of the human community, appropriately notes in his Encyclical Letter *Quadragesimo Anno, that* "a reasonable relationship between different wages here enters into consideration." But he immediately adds, "Intimately connected with this is a reasonable relationship between the prices obtained for the products of the various economic groups: agrarian, industrial, and so forth." [29]

140. Inasmuch as agricultural products are destined especially to satisfy the basic needs of men, it is necessary that their price be such that all can afford to buy them. Nevertheless, there is manifest injustice in placing a whole group of citizens, namely, the farmers, in an inferior economic and social status, with less purchasing power than required for a decent livelihood. This, indeed, is clearly contrary to the common good of the country.

STRENGTHENING FARM INCOME

141. In rural areas it is fitting that industries be fostered and common services be developed that are useful in preserving, processing, and finally, in transporting farm products. There is need, moreover, to establish councils and activities relating to various sectors of economic and professional affairs. By such means, suitable opportunity is given farm families to supplement their incomes, and that within the milieu wherein they live and work.

APPROPRIATE ORGANIZATION OF FARMING ENTERPRISES

142. Finally, no one person can lay down a universal rule regarding the way in which rural affairs should be definitely organized, since in these matters there exists considerable

[29] Cf. *Acta Apostolicae Sedis,* XXIII (1931), p. 202.

variation within each country, and the difference is even greater when we consider the various regions of the world. However, those who hold man and the family in proper esteem, whether this be based upon nature alone, or also upon Christian principles, surely look toward some form of agricultural enterprise, and particularly of the family type, which is modeled upon the community of men wherein mutual relationships of members and the organization of the enterprise itself are conformed to norms of justice and Christian teaching. And these men strive mightily that such organization of rural life be realized as far as circumstances permit.

143. The family farm will be firm and stable only when it yields money income sufficient for decent and humane family living. To bring this about, it is very necessary that farmers generally receive instruction, be kept informed of new developments, and be technically assisted by trained men. It is also necessary that farmers form among themselves mutual-aid societies; that they establish professional associations; that they function efficiently in public life, that is, in various administrative bodies and in political affairs.

RURAL WORKERS: PARTICIPANTS IN IMPROVING CONDITIONS

144. We are of the opinion that in rural affairs, the principal agents and protagonists of economic improvement, of cultural betterment, or of social advance, should be the men personally involved, namely, the farmers themselves. To them it should be quite evident that their work is most noble, because it is undertaken, as it were, in the majestic temple of creation; because it often concerns the life of plants and animals, a life inexhaustible in its expression, inflexible in its laws, rich in allusions to God, Creator and Provider. Moreover, labor in the fields not only produces various foodstuffs wherewith humankind is nourished, but also furnishes an increasing supply of raw materials for industry.

145. Furthermore, this is a work endowed with a dignity of its own, for it bears a manifold relationship to the mechanical arts, chemistry, and biology: these must be continually adapted to the requirements of emerging situations because scientific and technological advance is of great importance in rural life. Work of this kind, moreover, possesses a special nobility because it requires farmers to understand well the course of the seasons and to adapt themselves to the same; that they

await patiently what the future will bring; that they appreciate the importance and seriousness of their duties; that they constantly remain alert and ready for new developments.

SOLIDARITY AND COOPERATION

146. Nor may it be overlooked that in rural areas, as indeed in every productive sector, farmers should join together in fellowships, especially when the family itself works the farm. Indeed, it is proper for rural workers to have a sense of solidarity. They should strive jointly to set up mutual-aid societies and professional associations. All these are very necessary either to keep rural dwellers abreast of scientific and technical progress, or to protect the prices of goods produced by their labor. Besides, acting in this manner, farmers are put on the same footing as other classes of workers who, for the most part, join together in such fellowships. Finally, by acting thus, farmers will achieve an importance and influence in public affairs proportionate to their own role. For today it is unquestionably true that the solitary voice speaks, as they say, to the winds.

RECOGNIZING DEMANDS OF THE COMMON GOOD

147. But when rural dwellers, just as other classes of workers, wish to make their influence and importance felt, they should never disregard moral duties or civil law. Rather they should strive to bring their rights and interests into line with the rights and needs of other classes, and to refer the same to the common good. In this connection, farmers who strive vigorously to improve the yield of their farm may rightly demand that their efforts be aided and complemented by public authorities, provided they themselves keep in mind the common needs of all and also relate their own efforts to the fulfillment of these needs.

148. Wherefore, we wish to honor appropriately those sons of ours who everywhere in the world, either by founding and fostering mutual-aid societies or some other type of association, watchfully strive that in all civic affairs farmers enjoy not merely economic prosperity but also a status in keeping with justice.

VOCATION AND MISSION

149. Since everything that makes for man's dignity, perfection, and development seems to be invoked in agricultural labor, it is proper that man regard such work as an assign-

ment from God with a sublime purpose. It is fitting, therefore, that man dedicate work of this kind to the most provident God who directs all events for the salvation of men. Finally, the farmer should take upon himself, in some measure, the task of educating himself and others for the advancement of civilization.

AID TO LESS DEVELOPED AREAS

150. It often happens that in one and the same country citizens enjoy different degrees of wealth and social advancement. This especially happens because they dwell in areas which, economically speaking, have grown at different rates. Where such is the case, justice and equity demand that the government make efforts either to remove or to minimize imbalances of this sort. Toward this end, efforts should be made, in areas where there has been less economic progress, to supply the principal public services, as indicated by circumstances of time and place and in accord with the general level of living. But in bringing this about, it is necessary to have very competent administration and organization to take careful account of the following: labor supply, internal migration, wages, taxes, interest rates, and investments in industries that foster other skills and developments—all of which will further not merely the useful employment of workers and the stimulation of initiative, but also the exploitation of resources locally available.

151. But it is precisely the measures for advancement of the general welfare which civil authorities must undertake. Hence, they should take steps, having regard for the needs of the whole community, that progress in agriculture, industry, and services be made at the same time and in a balanced manner so far as possible. They should have this goal in mind, that citizens in less developed countries—in giving attention to economic and social affairs, as well as to cultural matters—feel themselves to be the ones chiefly responsible for their own progress. For a citizen has a sense of his own dignity when he contributes the major share to progress in his own affairs.

152. Hence, those also who rely on their own resources and initiative should contribute as best they can to the equitable adjustment of economic life in their own community. Nay, more, those in authority should favor and help private enterprise in accordance with the *principle of sub-*

sidiarity, in order to allow private citizens themselves to accomplish as much as is feasible.

IMBALANCES BETWEEN LAND AND POPULATION

153. It is appropriate to recall at this point that in a number of nations there exists a discrepancy between available agricultural land and the number of rural dwellers. Some nations experience a shortage of citizens, but have rich land resources; others have many citizens but an insufficiency of agricultural land.

154. Nor are there lacking nations wherein, despite their great resource potential, farmers use such primitive and obsolete methods of cultivation that they are unable to produce what is needed for the entire population. On the other hand, in certain countries, agriculture has so adapted itself to recent advances that farmers produce surpluses which to some extent harm the economy of the entire nation.

155. It is evident that both the solidarity of the human race and the sense of brotherhood which accords with Christian principles, require that some peoples lend others energetic help in many ways. Not merely would this result in a freer movement of goods, of capital, and of men, but it also would lessen imbalances between nations. We shall treat of this point in more detail below.

156. Here, however, we cannot fail to express our approval of the efforts of the Institute known as F.A.O. which concerns itself with the feeding of peoples and the improvement of agriculture. This Institute has the special goal of promoting mutual accord among peoples, of bringing it about that rural life is modernized in less developed nations, and finally, that help is brought to people experiencing food shortages.

REQUIREMENTS OF JUSTICE AS BETWEEN NATIONS DIFFERING IN ECONOMIC DEVELOPMENT

PROBLEM OF THE MODERN WORLD

157. Perhaps the most pressing question of our day concerns the relationship between economically advanced commonwealths and those that are in process of development. The former enjoy the conveniences of life; the latter experience dire poverty. Yet, today men are so intimately

associated in all parts of the world that they feel, as i
were, as if they are members of one and the same household
Therefore, the nations that enjoy a sufficiency and abundance
of everything may not overlook the plight of other nation:
whose citizens experience such domestic problems that they
are all but overcome by poverty and hunger, and are no'
able to enjoy basic human rights. This is all the more so
inasmuch as countries each day seem to become more dependent on each other. Consequently, it is not easy for them
to keep the peace advantageously if excessive imbalances exist
in their economic and social conditions.

158. Mindful of our role of universal father, we think it
opportune to stress here what we have stated in another connection: "We all share responsibility for the fact that
populations are undernourished.[30] [Therefore], it is necessary to arouse a sense of responsibility in individuals and
generally, especially among those more blessed with this
world's goods." [31]

159. As can be readily deduced, and as the Church has
always seriously warned, it is proper that the duty of helping
the poor and unfortunate should especially stir Catholics,
since they are members of the Mystical Body of Christ. "In
this we have come to know the love of God," said John the
Apostle, "that He laid down His life for us; and we likewise
ought to lay down our life for the brethren. He who has the
goods of this world and sees his brother in need and closes
his heart to him, how does the love of God abide in him?" [32]

160. Wherefore, we note with pleasure that countries with
advanced productive systems are lending aid to less privileged
countries, so that these latter may the more readily improve
their condition.

EMERGENCY ASSISTANCE

161. It is clear to everyone that some nations have
surpluses in foodstuffs, particularly of farm products, while
elsewhere large masses of people experience want and hunger. Now justice and humanity require that these richer
countries come to the aid of those in need. Accordingly, to
destroy entirely or to waste goods necessary for the lives
of men, runs counter to our obligations in justice and
humanity.

[30] *Allocution.* May 3, 1960; cf. *A.A.S.*, LII (1960), p. 465.
[31] Cf. *Ibid.*
[32] 1 John 3, 16-17.

162. We are quite well aware that to produce surpluses, especially of farm products, in excess of the needs of a country, can occasion harm to various classes of citizens. Nevertheless, it does not therefore follow that nations with surpluses have no obligation to aid the poor and hungry where some particular emergency arises. Rather, diligent efforts should be made that inconveniences arising from surplus goods be minimized and borne by every citizen on a fair basis.

SCIENTIFIC, TECHNICAL, AND FINANCIAL COOPERATION

163. However, the underlying causes of poverty and hunger will not be removed in a number of countries by these means alone. For the most part, the causes are to be found in the primitive state of the economy. To effect a remedy, all available avenues should be explored with a view, on the one hand, to instruct citizens fully in necessary skills and in carrying out their responsibilities, and, on the other hand, to enable them to acquire the capital wherewith to promote economic growth by ways and means adapted to our times.

164. It has not escaped our attention that in recent years there has grown in many minds a deep awareness of their duty to aid poorer countries still lacking suitable economic development, in order that these may more readily make economic and social progress.

165. Toward this end, we look to councils, either of a number of nations, or within individual nations; we look to private enterprises and societies to exert daily more generous efforts on behalf of such countries, transmitting to them requisite productive skills. For the same reason help is given to as many youths as possible that they may study in the great universities of more developed countries, thus acquiring a knowledge of the arts and sciences in line with the standards of our time. Moreover, international banks, single nations, or private citizens often make loans to these countries that they may initiate various programs calculated to increase production. We gladly take this opportunity to give due praise to such generous activity. It is hoped that in the future the richer countries will make greater and greater efforts to provide developing countries with aid designed to promote sciences, technology, and economic life.

AVOIDANCE OF PAST ERRORS

166. In this matter we consider it our duty to offer some warnings.

167. First of all, it seems only prudent for nations which thus far have made little or no progress, to weigh well the principal factor in the advance of nations that enjoy abundance.

168. Prudent foresight and common need demand that not only more goods be produced, but that this be done more efficiently. Likewise, necessity and justice require that wealth produced be distributed equitably among all citizens of the commonwealth. Accordingly, efforts should be made to ensure that improved social conditions accompany economic advancement. And it is very important that such advances occur simultaneously in the agricultural, industrial, and various service sectors.

RESPECT FOR INDIVIDUAL CHARACTERISTICS OF COUNTRIES

169. It is indeed clear to all that countries in process of development often have their own individual characteristics, and that these arise from the nature of the locale, or from cultural tradition, or from some special trait of the citizens.

170. Now when economically developed countries assist the poorer ones, they not only should have regard for these characteristics and respect them, but also should take special care lest, in aiding these nations, they seek to impose their own way of life upon them.

DISINTERESTED AID

171. Moreover, economically developed countries should take particular care lest, in giving aid to poorer countries, they endeavor to turn the prevailing political situation to their own advantage, and seek to dominate them.

172. Should perchance such attempts be made, this clearly would be but another form of colonialism, which, although disguised in name, merely reflects their earlier but outdated dominion, now abandoned by many countries. When international relations are thus obstructed, the orderly progress of all peoples is endangered.

173. Genuine necessity, as well as justice, require that whenever countries give attention to the fostering of skills or commerce, they should aid the less developed nations without thought of domination, so that these latter eventually

will be in a position to progress economically and socially on their own initiative.

174. If this be done, it will help much toward shaping a community of all nations, wherein each one, aware of its rights and duties, will have regard for the prosperity of all.

RESPECT FOR A HIERARCHY OF VALUES

175. There is no doubt that when a nation makes progress in science, technology, economic life, and the prosperity of its citizens, a great contribution is made to civilization. But all should realize that these things are not the highest goods, but only instruments for pursuing such goods.

176. Accordingly, we note with sorrow that in some nations economic life indeed progresses, but that not a few men are there to be found, who have no concern at all for the just ordering of goods. No doubt, these men either completely ignore spiritual values, or put these out of their mind, or else deny they exist. Nevertheless, while they pursue progress in science, technology, and economic life, they make so much of external benefits that for the most part they regard these as the highest goods of life. Accordingly, there are not lacking grave dangers in the help provided by more affluent nations for development of the poorer ones. For among the citizens of these latter nations, there is operative a general awareness of the higher values on which moral teaching rests—an awareness derived from ancient traditional custom which provides them with motivation.

177. Thus, those who seek to undermine in some measure the right instincts of these peoples, assuredly do something immoral. Rather, those attitudes, besides being held in honor, should be perfected and refined, since upon them true civilization depends.

CONTRIBUTION OF THE CHURCH

178. Moreover, the Church by divine right pertains to all nations. This is confirmed by the fact that she already is everywhere on earth and strives to embrace all peoples.

179. Now, those peoples whom the Church has joined to Christ have always reaped some benefits, whether in economic affairs or in social organization, as history and contemporary events clearly record. For everyone who professes Christianity promises and gives assurance that he will contribute as far as he can to the advancement of civil institutions. He must also strive with all his might not only that human

dignity suffer no dishonor, but also, by the removal of every
kind of obstacle, that all those forces be promoted which
are conducive to moral living and contribute to it.

180. Moreover, when the Church infuses her energy into
the life of a people, she neither is, nor feels herself to be, an
alien institution imposed upon that people from without.
This follows from the fact that wherever the Church is present, there individual men are reborn or resurrected in Christ.
Those who are thus reborn or who have risen again in Christ
feel themselves oppressed by no external force. Rather, realizing they have achieved perfect liberty, they freely move
toward God. Hence, whatever is seen by them as good and
morally right, that they approve and put into effect.

181. "The Church of Jesus Christ," as our predecessor
Pius XII clearly stated, "is the faithful guardian of God's
gracious wisdom. Hence, she makes no effort to discourage or
belittle those characteristics and traits which are proper to
particular nations, and which peoples religiously and tenaciously guard, quite justly, as a sacred heritage. She aims
indeed at a unity which is profound and in conformity with
that heavenly love whereby all are moved in their innermost
being. She does not seek a uniformity which is merely external in its effects and calculated to weaken the fibre of the
peoples concerned. And all careful rules that contribute to the
wise development and growth within bounds of these capacities and forces, which indeed have their deeply rooted
ethnic traits, have the Church's approval and maternal
prayers, provided they are not in opposition to those duties
which spring from the common origin and destiny of all
mortal men." [33]

182. We note with deep satisfaction that Catholic men, citizens of the less developed nations, are for the most part
second to no other citizens in furthering efforts of their
countries to make progress economically and socially according to their capacity.

183. Furthermore, we note that Catholic citizens of the
richer nations are making extensive efforts to ensure that aid
given by their own countries to needy countries is directed
increasingly toward economic and social progress. In this
connection, it seems specially praiseworthy that appreci-
able aid in various forms is provided increasingly each

[33] Encyclical Letter *Summi Pontificatus; A.A.S.,* XXXI (1939),
p. 428-29.

year to young people from Africa and Asia, so that they may pursue literary and professional studies in the great universities of Europe and America. The same applies to the great care that has been taken in training for every responsibility of their office men prepared to go to less developed areas, there to carry out their profession and duties.

184. To those sons of ours who, by promoting solicitously the progress of peoples and by spreading, as it were, a wholesome civilizing influence, everywhere demonstrate the perennial vitality of Holy Church and her effectiveness, we wish to express our paternal praise and gratitude.

POPULATION INCREASE
AND ECONOMIC DEVELOPMENT

185. More recently, the question often is raised how economic organization and the means of subsistence can be balanced with population increase, whether in the world as a whole or within the needy nations.

IMBALANCE BETWEEN POPULATION
AND MEANS OF SUBSISTENCE

186. As regards the world as a whole, some, consequent to statistical reasoning, observe that within a matter of decades mankind will become very numerous, whereas economic growth will proceed much more slowly. From this some conclude that unless procreation is kept within limits, there subsequently will develop an even greater imbalance between the number of inhabitants and the necessities of life.

187. It is clearly evident from statistical records of less developed countries that, because recent advances in public health and in medicine are there widely diffused, the citizens have a longer life expectancy consequent to lowered rates of infant mortality. The birth rate, where it has traditionally been high, tends to remain at such levels, at least for the immediate future. Thus the birth rate in a given year exceeds the death rate. Meanwhile the productive systems in such countries do not expand as rapidly as the number of inhabitants. Hence, in poorer countries of this sort, the standard of living does not advance and may even deteriorate. Wherefore, lest a serious crisis occur, some are of the opinion that the conception or birth of humans should be avoided or curbed by every possible means.

THE TERMS OF THE PROBLEM

188. Now to tell the truth, the interrelationships on a global scale between the number of births and available resources are such that we can infer grave difficulties in this matter do not arise at present, nor will in the immediate future. The arguments advanced in this connection are so inconclusive and controversial that nothing certain can be drawn from them.

189. Besides, God in His goodness and wisdom has, on the one hand, provided nature with almost inexhaustible productive capacity; and, on the other hand, has endowed man with such ingenuity that, by using suitable means, he can apply nature's resources to the needs and requirements of existence. Accordingly, that the question posed may be clearly resolved, a course of action is not indeed to be followed whereby, contrary to the moral law laid down by God, procreative function also is violated. Rather, man should, by the use of his skills and science of every kind, acquire an intimate knowledge of the forces of nature and control them ever more extensively. Moreover, the advances hitherto made in science and technology give almost limitless promise for the future in this matter.

190. When it comes to questions of this kind, we are not unaware that in certain locales and also in poorer countries, it is often argued that in such an economic and social order, difficulties arise because citizens, each year more numerous, are unable to acquire sufficient food or sustenance where they live, and peoples do not show amicable cooperation to the extent they should.

191. But whatever be the situation, we clearly affirm these problems should be posed and resolved in such a way that man does not have recourse to methods and means contrary to his dignity, which are proposed by those persons who think of man and his life solely in material terms.

192. We judge that this question can be resolved only if economic and social advances preserve and augment the genuine welfare of individual citizens and of human society as a whole. Indeed, in a matter of this kind, first place must be accorded everything that pertains to the dignity of man as such, or to the life of individual men, than which nothing can be more precious. Moreover, in this matter, international cooperation is necessary, so that conformably with the welfare of all, information, capital, and men themselves may move about among the peoples in orderly fashion.

RESPECT FOR THE LAWS OF LIFE

193. In this connection, we strongly affirm that human life is transmitted and propagated through the instrumentality of the family which rests on marriage, one and indissoluble, and, so far as Christians are concerned, elevated to the dignity of a sacrament. Because the life of man is passed on to other men deliberately and knowingly, it therefore follows that this should be done in accord with the most sacred, permanent, inviolate prescriptions of God. Everyone without exception is bound to recognize and observe these laws. Wherefore, in this matter, no one is permitted to use methods and procedures which may indeed be permissible to check the life of plants and animals.

194. Indeed, all must regard the life of man as sacred, since from its inception, it requires the action of God the Creator. Those who depart from this plan of God not only offend His divine majesty and dishonor themselves and the human race, but they also weaken the inner fibre of the commonwealth.

EDUCATION TOWARD A SENSE OF RESPONSIBILITY

195. In these matters it is of great importance that new offspring, in addition to being very carefully educated in human culture and in religion—which indeed is the right and duty of parents—should also show themselves very conscious of their duties in every action of life. This is especially true when it is a question of establishing a family and of procreating and educating children. Such children should be imbued not only with a firm confidence in the providence of God, but also with a strong and ready will to bear the labors and inconveniences which cannot be lawfully avoided by anyone who undertakes the worthy and serious obligation of associating his own activity with God in transmitting life and in educating offspring. In this most important matter certainly nothing is more relevant than the teachings and supernatural aids provided by the Church. We refer to the Church whose right of freely carrying out her function must be recognized also in this connection.

CREATION FOR MAN'S BENEFIT

196. When God, as we read in the book of Genesis, imparted human nature to our first parents, He assigned them two tasks, one of which complements the other. For He first

directed: "Be fruitful and multiply," [34] and then immediately added: "Fill the earth and subdue it." [35]

197. The second of these tasks, far from anticipating a destruction of goods, rather assigns them to the service of
human life.

198. Accordingly, with great sadness we note two conflicting trends: on the one hand, the scarcity of goods is
vaguely described as such that the life of men reportedly is
in danger of perishing from misery and hunger; on the other
hand, the recent discoveries of science, technical advances,
and economic productivity are transformed into means whereby the human race is led toward ruin and a horrible death.

199. Now the provident God has bestowed upon humanity
sufficient goods wherewith to bear with dignity the burdens
associated with procreation of children. But this task
will be difficult or even impossible if men, straying from the
right road and with a perverse outlook, use the means mentioned above in a manner contrary to human reason or to
their social nature, and hence, contrary to the directives of
God Himself.

INTERNATIONAL COOPERATION

WORLD DIMENSIONS OF
IMPORTANT HUMAN PROBLEMS

200. Since the relationships between countries today are
closer in every region of the world, by reason of science and
technology, it is proper that peoples become more and more
interdependent.

201. Accordingly, contemporary problems of moment—
whether in the fields of science and technology, or of
economic and social affairs, or of public or of cultural advancement—these, because they may exceed the capacities
of individual States, very often affect a number of nations
and at times all the nations of the earth.

202. As a result, individual countries, although advanced in culture and civilization, in number and industry
of citizens, in wealth, in geographical extent, are not able
by themselves to resolve satisfactorily their basic problems.
Accordingly, because States must on occasion complement

[34] Gen., 1, 28.
[35] Ibid.

or perfect one another, they really consult their own interests only when they take into account at the same time the interests of others. Hence, dire necessity warns commonwealths to cooperate among themselves and provide mutual assistance.

MUTUAL DISTRUST

203. Although this becomes more and more evident each day to individuals and even to all peoples, men, and especially those with high responsibility in public life, for the most part seem unable to accomplish the two things toward which peoples aspire. This does not happen because peoples lack scientific, technical, or economic means, but rather because they distrust one another. Indeed, men, and hence States, stand in fear of one another. One country fears lest another is contemplating aggression and lest the other seize an opportunity to put such plans into effect. Accordingly, countries customarily prepare defenses for their cities and homeland, namely, armaments designed to deter other countries from aggression.

204. Consequently, the energies of man and the resources of nature are very widely directed by peoples to destruction rather than to the advantage of the human family, and both individual men and entire peoples become so deeply solicitous that they are prevented from undertaking more important works.

FAILURE TO ACKNOWLEDGE THE MORAL ORDER

205. The cause of this state of affairs seems to be that men, more especially leaders of States, have differing philosophies of life. Some even dare to assert that there exists no law of truth and right which transcends external affairs and man himself, which of necessity pertains to everyone, and, finally, which is equitable for all men. Hence, men can agree fully and surely about nothing, since one and the same law of justice is not accepted by all.

206. Although the word *justice* and the related term *demands of justice* are on everyone's lips, such verbalizations do not have the same meaning for all. Indeed, the opposite frequently is the case. Hence, when leaders invoke *justice* or the *demands of justice*, not only do they disagree as to the meaning of the words, but frequently find in them an occasion of serious contention. And so they conclude that there is no way of achieving their rights or advantages, unless they resort to force, the root of very serious evils.

GOD, THE FOUNDATION OF THE MORAL ORDER

207. That mutual faith may develop among rulers and nations and may abide more deeply in their minds, the laws of truth and justice first must be acknowledged and preserved on all sides.

208. However, the guiding principles of morality and virtue can be based only on God; apart from Him, they necessarily collapse. For man is composed not merely of body, but of soul as well, and is endowed with reason and freedom. Now such a composite being absolutely requires a moral law rooted in religion, which, far better than any external force or advantage, can contribute to the resolution of problems affecting the lives of individual citizens or groups of citizens, or with a bearing upon single States or all States together.

209. Yet, there are today those who assert that, in view of the flourishing state of science and technology, men can achieve the highest civilization even apart from God and by their own unaided powers. Nevertheless, it is because of this very progress in science and technology that men often find themselves involved in difficulties which affect all peoples, and which can be overcome only if they duly recognize the authority of God, author and ruler of man and of all nature.

210. That this is true, the advances of science seem to indicate, opening up, as they do, almost limitless horizons. Thus, an opinion is implanted in many minds that inasmuch as mathematical sciences are unable to discern the innermost nature of things and their changes, or express them in suitable terms, they can scarcely draw inferences about them. And when terrified men see with their own eyes that the vast forces deriving from technology and machines can be used for destruction as well as for the advantage of peoples, they rightly conclude that things pertaining to the spirit and to moral life are to be preferred to all else, so that progress in science and technology does not result in destruction of the human race, but prove useful as instruments of civilization.

211. Meanwhile it comes to pass that in more affluent countries men, less and less satisfied with external goods, put out of their mind the deceptive image of a happy life to be lived here forever. Likewise, not only do men grow daily more conscious that they are fully endowed with all the rights of the human person, but they also strive mightily that relations among themselves become more equitable and more

conformed to human dignity. Consequently men are beginning to recognize that their own capacities are limited, and they seek spiritual things more intensively than heretofore. All of which seems to give some promise that not only individuals, but even peoples may come to an understanding for extensive and extremely useful collaboration.

Part IV: Reconstruction of Social Relationships in Truth, Justice and Love

INCOMPLETE AND ERRONEOUS PHILOSOPHIES OF LIFE

212. As in the past, so too in our day, advances in science and technology have greatly multiplied relationships between citizens; it seems necessary, therefore, that the relationships themselves, whether within a single country or between all countries, be brought into more humane balance.

213. In this connection many systems of thought have been developed and committed to writing: some of these already have been dissipated as mist by the sun; others remain basically unchanged today; still others now elicit less and less response from men. The reason for this is that these popularized fancies neither encompass man, whole and entire, nor do they affect his inner being. Moreover, they fail to take into account the weaknesses of human nature, such as sickness and suffering: weaknesses that no economic or social system, no matter how advanced, can completely eliminate. Besides, men everywhere are moved by a profound and unconquerable sense of religion, which no force can ever destroy nor shrewdness suppress.

214. In our day, a very false opinion is popularized which holds that the sense of religion implanted in men by nature is to be regarded as something adventitious or imaginary, and hence, is to be rooted completely from the mind as altogether inconsistent with the spirit of our age and the progress of civilization. Yet, this inward proclivity of man to religion confirms the fact that man himself was created by God, and irrevocably tends to Him. Thus we read in Augustine: "Thou hast made us for Thyself, O Lord, and our hearts are restless until they rest in Thee." [36]

215. Wherefore, whatever the progress in technology and

[36] *Confessions*, I, 1.

economic life, there can be neither justice nor peace in the world, so long as men fail to realize how great is their dignity; for they have been created by God and are His children. We speak of God, who must be regarded as the first and final cause of all things He has created. Separated from God, man becomes monstrous to himself and others. Consequently, mutual relationships between men absolutely require a right ordering of the human conscience in relation to God, the source of all truth, justice, and love.

216. It is well known and recognized by everyone that in a number of countries, some of ancient Christian culture, many of our very dear brothers and sons have been savagely persecuted for a number of years. Now this situation, since it reveals the great dignity of the persecuted, and the refined cruelty of their persecutors, leads many to reflect on the matter, though it has not yet healed the wounds of the persecuted.

217. However, no folly seems more characteristic of our time than the desire to establish a firm and meaningful temporal order, but without God, its necessary foundation. Likewise, some wish to proclaim the greatness of man, but with the source dried up from which such greatness flows and receives nourishment: that is, by impeding and, if it were possible, stopping the yearning of souls for God. But the turn of events in our times, whereby the hopes of many are shattered and not a few have come to grief, unquestionably confirm the words of Scripture: "Unless the Lord build the house, they labor in vain who built it." [37]

THE CHURCH'S TRADITIONAL TEACHING REGARDING MAN'S SOCIAL LIFE

218. What the Catholic Church teaches and declares regarding the social life and relationships of men is beyond question for all time valid.

219. The cardinal point of this teaching is that individual men are necessarily the foundation, cause, and end of all social institutions. We are referring to human beings, insofar as they are social by nature, and raised to an order of existence that transcends and subdues nature.

220. Beginning with this very basic principle whereby the dignity of the human person is affirmed and defended, Holy Church—especially during the last century and with

[37] Ps. 126, 1.

the assistance of learned priests and laymen, specialists in the field—has arrived at clear social teachings whereby the mutual relationships of men are ordered. Taking general norms into account, these principles are in accord with the nature of things and the changed conditions of man's social life, or with the special genius of our day. Moreover, these norms can be approved by all.

221. But today, more than ever, principles of this kind must not only be known and understood, but also applied to those systems and methods, which the various situations of time or place either suggest or require. This is indeed a difficult, though lofty, task. Toward its fulfillment we exhort not only our brothers and sons everywhere, but all men of good will.

STUDY OF SOCIAL MATTERS

222. Above all, we affirm that the social teaching proclaimed by the Catholic Church cannot be separated from her traditional teaching regarding man's life.

223. Wherefore, it is our earnest wish that more and more attention be given to this branch of learning. First of all, we urge that attention be given to such studies in Catholic schools on all levels, and especially in seminaries, although we are not unaware that in some of these latter institutions this is already being done admirably. Moreover, we desire that social study of this sort be included among the religious materials used to instruct and inspire the lay apostolate, either in parishes or in associations. Let this diffusion of knowledge be accomplished by every modern means: that is, in journals, whether daily or periodical; in doctrinal books, both for the learned and the general reader; and finally, by means of radio and television.

224. We judge that our sons among the laity have much to contribute through their work and effort, that this teaching of the Catholic Church regarding the social question be more and more widely diffused. This they can do, not merely by learning it themselves and governing their actions accordingly, but also by taking special care that others also come to know its relevance.

225. Let them be fully persuaded that in no better way can they know this teaching to be correct and effective, than by demonstrating that present day social difficulties will yield to its application. In this way they will win minds today antagonistic to the teaching because they do not know it. Per-

haps it will also happen that such men will find some enlightenment in the teaching.

APPLICATION OF SOCIAL TEACHING

226. But social norms of whatever kind are not only to be explained but also applied. This is especially true of the Church's teaching on social matters, which has truth as its guide, justice as its end, and love as its driving force.

227. We consider it, therefore, of the greatest importance that our sons, in addition to knowing these social norms, be reared according to them.

228. To be complete, the education of Christians must relate to the duties of every class. It is therefore necessary that Christians thus inspired conform their behavior in economic and social affairs to the teaching of the Church.

229. If it is indeed difficult to apply teaching of any sort to concrete situations, it is even more so when one tries to put into practice the teaching of the Catholic Church regarding social affairs. This is especially true for the following reasons: there is deeply rooted in each man an instinctive and immoderate love of his own interests; today there is widely diffused in society a materialistic philosophy of life; it is difficult at times to discern the demands of justice in a given situation.

230. Consequently, it is not enough for men to be instructed, according to the teachings of the Church, on their obligation to act in a Christian manner in economic and social affairs. They must also be shown ways in which they can properly fulfill their duty in this regard.

231. We do not regard such instructions as sufficient, unless there be added to the work of instruction that of the formation of man, and unless some action follow upon the teaching, by way of experience.

232. Just as, proverbially, no one really enjoys liberty unless he uses it, so no one really knows how to act according to Catholic teaching in the economic and social fields, unless he acts according to this teaching in the same area.

A TASK FOR LAY APOSTOLATE

233. Accordingly, in popular instruction of this kind, it seems proper that considerable attention be paid to groups promoting the lay apostolate, especially those whose aim is to ensure that efforts in our present concern draw their in-

spiration wholly from Christian law. Seeing that members of such groups can first train themselves by daily practice in these matters, they subsequently will be able the better to instruct young people in fulfilling obligations of this kind.

234. It is not inappropriate in this connection to remind all, the great no less than the lowly, that the will to preserve moderation and to bear difficulties, by God's grace, can in no wise be separated from the meaning of life handed down to us by Christian wisdom.

235. But today, unfortunately, very many souls are preoccupied with an inordinate desire for pleasure. Such persons see nothing more important in the whole of life than to seek pleasure, to quench the thirst for pleasure. Beyond doubt, grave ills to both soul and body proceed therefrom. Now in this matter, it must be admitted that one who judges even with the aid of human nature alone, concludes that it is the part of the wise and prudent man to preserve balance and moderation in everything, and to restrain the lower appetites. He who judges matters in the light of divine revelation, assuredly will not overlook the fact that the Gospel of Christ and the Catholic Church, as well as the ascetical tradition handed down to us, all demand that Christians steadfastly mortify themselves and bear the inconveniences of life with singular patience. These virtues, in addition to fostering a firm and moderate rule of mind over body, also present an opportunity of satisfying the punishment due to sin, from which, except for Jesus Christ and His Immaculate Mother, no one is exempt.

PRACTICAL SUGGESTIONS

236. The teachings in regard to social matters for the most part are put into effect in the following three stages: first, the actual situation is examined; then, the situation is evaluated carefully in relation to these teachings; then only is it decided what can and should be done in order that the traditional norms may be adapted to circumstances of time and place. These three steps are at times expressed by the three words: *observe, judge, act.*

237. Hence, it seems particularly fitting that youth not merely reflect upon this order of procedure, but also, in the present connection, follow it to the extent feasible, lest what they have learned be regarded merely as something to be thought about but not acted upon.

238. However, when it comes to reducing these teachings

to action, it sometimes happens that even sincere Catholic men have differing views. When this occurs they should take care to have and to show mutual esteem and regard, and to explore the extent to which they can work in cooperation among themselves. Thus they can in good time accomplish what necessity requires. Let them also take great care not to weaken their efforts in constant controversies. Nor should they, under pretext of seeking what they think best, meanwhile, fail to do what they can and hence should do.

239. But in the exercise of economic and social functions, Catholics often come in contact with men who do not share their view of life. On such occasions, those who profess Catholicism must take special care to be consistent and not compromise in matters wherein the integrity of religion or morals would suffer harm. Likewise, in their conduct they should weigh the opinions of others with fitting courtesy and not measure everything in the light of their own interests. They should be prepared to join sincerely in doing whatever is naturally good or conducive to good. If, indeed, it happens that in these matters sacred authorities have prescribed or decreed anything, it is evident that this judgment is to be obeyed promptly by Catholics. For it is the Church's right and duty not only to safeguard principles relating to the integrity of religion and morals, but also to pronounce authoritatively when it is a matter of putting these principles into effect.

MANIFOLD ACTION AND RESPONSIBILITY

240. But what we have said about the norms of instruction should indeed be put into practice. This has special relevance for those beloved sons of ours who are in the ranks of the laity inasmuch as their activity ordinarily centers around temporal affairs and making plans for the same.

241. To carry out this noble task, it is necessary that laymen not only should be qualified, each in his own profession, and direct their energies in accordance with rules suited to the objective aimed at, but also should conform their activity to the teachings and norms of the Church in social matters. Let them put sincere trust in her wisdom; let them accept her admonitions as sons. Let them reflect that, when in the conduct of life they do not carefully observe principles and norms laid down by the Church in social matters, and which we ourselves reaffirm, then they are negligent in their duty and often injure the rights of others. At times, matters can come to a point where confidence in this teaching is

diminished, as if it were indeed excellent but really lacks the force which the conduct of life requires.

A GRAVE DANGER

242. As we have already noted, in this present age men have searched widely and deeply into the laws of nature. Then they invented instruments whereby they can control the forces of nature; they have perfected and continue to perfect remarkable works worthy of deep admiration. Nevertheless, while they endeavor to master and transform the external world, they are also in danger, lest they become neglectful and weaken the powers of body and mind. This is what our predecessor of happy memory, Pius XI, noted with sorrow of spirit in his Encyclical Letter *Quadragesimo Anno*: "And so bodily labor, which was decreed by divine providence for the good of man's body and soul even after original sin, has too often been changed into an instrument of perversion: for dead matter leaves the factory ennobled and transformed whereas men are there corrupted and degraded." [38]

243. And our predecessor of happy memory, Pius XII, rightly asserted that our age is distinguished from others precisely by the fact that science and technology have made incalculable progress, while men themselves have departed correspondingly from a sense of dignity. It is a "monstrous masterpiece" of this age "to have transformed man, as it were, into a giant as regards the order of nature, yet in the order of the supernatural and the eternal, to have changed him into a pygmy." [39]

244. Too often in our day is verified the testimony of the Psalmist concerning worshipers of false gods, namely, human beings in their activity very frequently neglect themselves, but admire their own works as if these were gods: "Their idols are silver and gold; the handiwork of men." [40]

RESPECT FOR THE HIERARCHY OF VALUES

245. Wherefore, aroused by the pastoral zeal wherewith we embrace all men, we strongly urge our sons that, in fulfilling their duties and in pursuing their goals, they do not allow their consciousness of responsibilities to grow cool, nor neglect the order of the more important goods.

[38] *Acta Apostolicae Sedis*, XXIII (1931), p. 221f.
[39] Radio Broadcast, Christmas Eve, 1953; cf. *A.A.S.*, XLVI (1954), p. 10.
[40] Ps. 113, 4.

246. For it is indeed clear that the Church has always taught and continues to teach that advances in science and technology and the prosperity resulting therefrom, are truly to be counted as good things and regarded as signs of the progress of civilization. But the Church likewise teaches that goods of this kind are to be judged properly in accordance with their natures: they are always to be considered as instruments for man's use, the better to achieve his highest end: that he can the more easily improve himself, in both the natural and supernatural orders.

247. Wherefore, we ardently desire that our sons should at all times heed the words of the divine Master: "For what does it profit a man, if he gain the whole world, but suffer the loss of his own soul? Or what will a man give in exchange for his soul?" [41]

SANCTIFICATION OF HOLY DAYS

248. Not unrelated to the above admonitions is the one having to do with rest to be taken on feast days.

249. In order that the Church may defend the dignity with which man is endowed, because he is created by God and because God has breathed into him a soul to His own image, she has never failed to insist that the third commandment: "Remember to keep holy the Sabbath day," [42] be carefully observed by all. It is the right of God, and within His power, to order that man put aside a day each week for proper and due worship of the divinity. He should direct his mind to heavenly things, setting aside daily business. He should explore the depths of his conscience in order to know how necessary and inviolable are his relations with God.

250. In addition, it is right and necessary for man to cease for a time from labor, not merely to relax his body from daily hard work and likewise to refresh himself with decent recreation, but also to foster family unity, for this requires that all its members preserve a community of life and peaceful harmony.

251. Accordingly, religion, moral teaching, and care of health in turn require that relaxation be had at regular times. The Catholic Church has decreed for many centuries that Christians observe this day of rest on Sunday, and that they be present on the same day at the Eucharistic Sacrifice because it renews the memory of the divine Redemption and at the same time imparts its fruits to the souls of men.

41 Matt. 16, 26.
42 Exod. 20, 8.

252. But we note with deep sorrow, and we cannot but reprove the many who, though they perhaps do not deliberately despise this holy law, yet more and more frequently disregard it. Whence it is that our very dear workingmen almost necessarily suffer harm, both as to the salvation of their souls and to the health of their bodies.

253. And so, taking into account the needs of soul and body, we exhort, as it were, with the words of God Himself, all men, whether public officials or representatives of management and labor, that they observe this command of God Himself and of the Catholic Church, and judge in their souls that they have a responsibility to God and society in this regard.

Renewed Dedication

254. From what we have briefly touched upon above, let none of our sons conclude, and especially the laity, that they act prudently if, in regard to the transitory affairs of this life, they become quite remiss in their specific Christian contributions. On the contrary, we reaffirm that they should be daily more zealous in carrying out this role.

255. Indeed, when Christ our Lord made that solemn prayer for the unity of His Church, He asked this from the Father on behalf of His disciples: "I do not pray that Thou take them out of the world, but that Thou keep them from evil." [43] Let no one imagine that there is any opposition between these two things so that they cannot be properly reconciled: namely, the perfection of one's own soul and the business of this life, as if one had no choice but to abandon the activities of this world in order to strive for Christian perfection, or as if one could not attend to these pursuits without endangering his own dignity as a man and as a Christian.

256. However, it is in full accord with the designs of God's providence that men develop and perfect themselves by exercise of their daily tasks, for this is the lot of practically everyone in the affairs of this mortal life. Accordingly, the role of the Church in our day is very difficult: to reconcile this modern respect for progress with the norms of humanity and of the Gospel teaching. Yet, the times call the Church to this role; indeed, we may say, earnestly beseech her, not

[43] John 17, 15.

merely to pursue the higher goals, but also to safeguard her accomplishments without harm to herself. To achieve this, as we have already said, the Church especially asks the cooperation of the laity. For this reason, in their dealings with men, they are bound to exert effort in such a way that while fulfilling their duties to others, they do so in union with God through Christ, for the increase of God's glory. Thus the Apostle Paul asserts: "Whether you eat or drink, or do anything else, do all for the glory of God." [44] And elsewhere: "Whatever you do in word or in work, do all in the name of the Lord Jesus Christ, giving thanks to God the Father through Him." [45]

GREATER EFFECTIVENESS IN TEMPORAL AFFAIRS

257. As often, therefore, as human activity and institutions having to do with the affairs of this life, help toward spiritual perfection and everlasting beatitude, the more they are to be regarded as an efficacious way of obtaining the immediate end to which they are directed by their very nature. Thus, valid for all times is that noteworthy sentence of the divine Master: "Seek first the kingdom of God and His justice, and all these things shall be given you besides." [46] For he who is, as it were a *light in the Lord*,[47] and walks as a *son of light*,[48] perceives more clearly what the requirements of justice are, in the various sectors of human zeal, even in those that involve greater difficulties because of the excessive love which many have for their own interests, or those of their country, or race. It must be added that when one is motivated by Christian charity, he cannot but love others, and regard the needs, sufferings and joys of others as his own. His work, wherever it be, is constant, adaptable, humane, and has concern for the needs of others: For "Charity is patient, is kind; charity does not envy, is not pretentious, is not puffed up, is not ambitious, is not self seeking, is not provoked; thinks no evil, does not rejoice over wickedness, but rejoices with the truth; bears with all things, believes all things, hopes all things, endures all things." [49]

[44] I Cor. 10, 31.
[45] Col. 3, 17.
[46] Matt. 6, 33.
[47] Eph. 5, 8.
[48] Cf. *Ibid.*
[49] I Cor. 13, 4-7.

LIVING MEMBERS OF
THE MYSTICAL BODY OF CHRIST

258. But we do not wish to bring this letter of ours to a close, Venerable Brothers, without recalling to your minds that most fundamental and true element of Catholic teaching, whereby we learn that we are living members of His Mystical Body, which is the Church: "For as the body is one and has many members, and all the members of the body, many as they are, form one body, so also is it with Christ." [50]

259. Wherefore, we urgently exhort all our sons in every part of the world, whether clergy or laity, that they fully understand how great is the nobility and dignity they derive from being joined to Christ, as branches to the vine, as He Himself said: "I am the vine, you are the branches," [51] and that they are sharers of His divine life. Whence it is, that if Christians are also joined in mind and heart with the most Holy Redeemer, when they apply themselves to temporal affairs, their work in a way is a continuation of the labor of Jesus Christ Himself, drawing from it strength and redemptive power: "He who abides in Me, and I in him, he bears much fruit." [52] Human labor of this kind is so exalted and ennobled that it leads men engaged in it to spiritual perfection, and can likewise contribute to the diffusion and propagation of the fruits of the Redemption to others. So also it results in the flow of that Gospel leaven, as it were, through the veins of civil society wherein we live and work.

260. Although it must be admitted that the times in which we live are torn by increasingly serious errors, and are troubled by violent disturbances, yet, it happens that the Church's laborers in this age of ours have access to enormous fields of apostolic endeavor. This inspires us with uncommon hope.

261. Venerable Brothers and beloved sons, beginning with that marvelous letter of Leo, we have thus far considered with you the varied and serious issues which pertain to the social condition of our time. From them we have drawn norms and teachings, upon which we especially exhort you not merely to meditate deeply, but also to do what you can to put them into effect. If each one of you does his best courageously, it will necessarily help in no small measure to estab-

[50] I Cor., 12, 12.
[51] John 15, 5.
[52] *Ibid.*

lish the kingdom of Christ on earth. This is indeed: "A kingdom of truth and of life; a kingdom of holiness and grace; a kingdom of justice, of love and of peace." [53] And this we shall some day leave to go to that heavenly beatitude, for which we were made by God, and which we ask for with most ardent prayers.

262. For it is a question here of the teaching of the Catholic and Apostolic Church, mother and teacher of all nations, whose light illumines, sets on fire, inflames. Her warning voice, filled with heavenly wisdom, reaches out to every age. Her power always provides efficacious and appropriate remedies for the growing needs of men, for the cares and solicitudes of this mortal life. With this voice, the age-old song of the Psalmist is in marvelous accord, to strengthen at all times and to uplift our souls: "I will hear what God proclaims; the Lord—for He proclaims peace to His people, and to His faithful ones, and to those who put in Him their hope. Near indeed is His salvation to those who fear Him, glory dwelling in our land. Kindness and truth shall meet; justice and peace shall kiss. Truth shall spring out of the earth, and justice shall look down from heaven. The Lord Himself will give His benefits; our land shall yield its increase. Justice shall walk before Him, and salvation, along the way of His steps." [54]

263. This is the plea, Venerable Brothers, we make at the close of this Letter, to which we have for a considerable time directed our concern about the Universal Church. We desire that the divine Redeemer of mankind, "who has become for us God-given wisdom, and justice, and sanctification, and redemption" [55] may reign and triumph gloriously in all things and over all things, for centuries on end. We desire that, in a properly organized order of social affairs, all nations will at last enjoy prosperity, and happiness, and peace.

264. As an evidence of these wishes, and a pledge of our paternal good will, we affectionately bestow in the Lord our apostolic blessing upon you, Venerable Brothers, and upon all the faithful committed to your care, and especially upon those who will reply with generosity to our appeals.

265. Given at Rome, at Saint Peter's, the fifteenth day of May, in the year 1961, the third year of our Pontificate.

JOHN XXIII, Pope

[53] *Preface of Jesus Christ the King.*
[54] Ps. 84, 9ff.
[55] I Cor. 1, 30.

PACEM IN TERRIS

Peace on Earth*

April 11, 1963

Introduction

Order in the Universe

Peace on earth, which men of every era have most eagerly yearned for, can be firmly established only if the order laid down by God be dutifully observed. The progress of learning and the inventions of technology clearly show that, both in living things and in the forces of nature, an astonishing order reigns, and they also bear witness to the greatness of man, who can understand that order and create suitable instruments to harness those forces of nature and use them to his benefit.

But the progress of science and the inventions of technology show above all the infinite greatness of God, who created the universe and man himself. . . .

Order in Human Beings

How strongly does the turmoil of individual men and peoples contrast with the perfect order of the universe! It is as if the relationships which bind them together could be controlled only by force. But the creator of the world has imprinted in man's heart an order which his conscience reveals to him and enjoins him to obey: This shows that the obligations of the law are written in their hearts, their conscience utters its own testimony.[1] And how could it be otherwise? For whatever God has made shows forth His infinite wis-

---

* Official translation. The Vatican Polyglot Press.
[1] Romans ii, 15.

dom, and it is manifested more clearly in the things which have greater perfection.[2]

But fickleness of opinion often produces this error, that many think that the relationships between men and states can be governed by the same laws as the forces and irrational elements of the universe, whereas the laws governing them are of quite a different kind and are to be sought elsewhere, namely, where the Father of all things wrote them, that is, in the nature of man. By these laws men are more admirably taught, first of all how they should conduct their mutual dealings among themselves, then how the relationships between the citizens and the public authorities of each state should be regulated, then how states should deal with one another, and finally how, on the one hand, individual men and states, and on the other hand, the community of all peoples, should act towards each other, the establishment of such a world community of peoples being urgently demanded today by the requirements of universal common good.

Part I
Order Between Men

EVERY MAN IS A PERSON WITH RIGHTS AND DUTIES

First of all, it is necessary to speak of the order which should exist between men. Any human society, if it is to be well-ordered and productive, must lay down as a foundation this principle, namely, that every human being is a person, that is, his nature is endowed with intelligence and free will. By virtue of this, he has rights and duties of his own, flowing directly and simultaneously from his very nature, which are therefore universal, inviolable and inalienable.[3]

If we look upon the dignity of the human person in the light of divinely revealed truth, we cannot help but esteem it far more highly. For men are redeemed by the blood of

[2] Cf. Psalms xviii, 8–11.

[3] Cf. Pius XII's radio message on Christmas Eve, 1942, Acta Apostolicae Sedis, Vol. 35, pp. 9–24, and John XXIII's sermon Jan. 4, 1963. Acta Apostolicae Sedis, Vol. 55, pp. 89–91.

Jesus Christ, they are by grace the children and friends of God and heirs of eternal glory.

RIGHTS

THE RIGHT TO LIFE AND A WORTHY STANDARD OF LIVING

Beginning our discussion of the rights of man, we see that every man has the right to life, to bodily integrity and to the means which are necessary and suitable for the proper development of life. These are primarily food, clothing, shelter, rest, medical care and, finally, the necessary social services. Therefore, a human being also has the right to security in cases of sickness, inability to work, widowhood, old age, unemployment, or in any other case in which he is deprived of the means of subsistence through no fault of his own.[4]

RIGHT PERTAINING TO MORAL AND CULTURAL VALUES

By the natural law every human being has the right to respect for his person, to his good reputation, the right to freedom in searching for truth and in expressing and communicating his opinions, and in pursuit of art, within the limits laid down by the moral order and the common good. And he has the right to be informed truthfully about public events.

The natural law also gives man the right to share in the benefits of culture, and therefore the right to a basic education and to technical and professional training in keeping with the stage of educational development in the country to which he belongs. Every effort should be made to insure that persons be enabled, on the basis of merit, to go on to higher studies, so that, as far as possible, they may occupy posts and take on responsibilities in human society in accordance with their natural gifts and the skills they have acquired.[5]

THE RIGHT TO WORSHIP GOD ACCORDING TO ONE'S CONSCIENCE

Every human being has the right to honor God according

4 Cf. Pius XI's encyclical letter "Divini Redemptoris" (Of the Divine Redeemer"), Acta Apostolicae Sedis, Vol. 29, p. 78, and radio message by Pius XII on the Feast of Pentecost. 1941, Acta Apostolicae Sedis, Vol. 33, pp. 195–205.

5 Cf. Pius XII's radio message on Christmas Eve, 1942, op. cit., pp. 9–24.

to the dictates of an upright conscience, and therefore the right to worship God privately and publicly. For, as Lactantius so clearly taught: We were created for the purpose of showing to the God who bore us the submission we owe Him, or recognizing Him alone, and of serving Him. We are obliged and bound by this duty to God. From this religion itself receives its name.[6] And on this point our predecessor of immortal memory, Leo XIII, declared: "This genuine, this honorable freedom of the sons of God, which most nobly protects the dignity of the human person, is greater than any violence or injustice. It has always been sought by the church, and always most dear to her. This was the freedom which the apologists claimed with intrepid constancy, which the apologists defended with their writings, and which the martyrs in such numbers consecrated with their blood."[7]

THE RIGHT TO CHOOSE FREELY ONE'S STATE OF LIFE

Human beings have the right to choose freely the state of life which they prefer, and therefore the right to set up a family, with equal rights and duties for man and woman, and also the right to follow a vocation to the priesthood or the religious life.[8]

The family, grounded on marriage freely contracted, monogamous and indissoluble, is and must be considered the first and essential cell of human society. To it must be given every consideration of an economic, social, cultural and moral nature, which will strengthen its stability and facilitate the fulfilment of its specific mission.

Parents, however, have a prior right in the support and education of their children.[9]

ECONOMIC RIGHTS

Human beings have the natural right to free initiative in the economic field and the right to work.[10]

[6] Divinae Institutiones, Vol. 4, Chap. 28, Subheading 2, editions P. L. 6, 535.

[7] Encyclical letter "Libertas praestantissimum" ("freedom of the most excellent"), Acts of Leo XIII, Vol. 8, pp. 237–38.

[8] Cf. Pius XII radio message on Christmas Eve, 1942, loc. cit.

[9] Cf. Pius XI's encyclical letter "Casti Connubii" ("Of Chaste Marriage") Acta Apostolicae Sedis. Vol. 22, pp. 539–92, and Pius XII's radio message on Christmas Eve, 1942, loc. cit.

[10] Cf. Pius XII's radio message on the Feast of Pentecost, 1941, loc. cit., p. 201.

Indissolubly linked with those rights is the right to working conditions in which physical health is not endangered, morals are safeguarded and young people's normal development is not impaired. Women have the right to working conditions in accordance with their requirements and their duties as wives and mothers.[11]

From the dignity of the human person, there also arises the right to carry on economic activities according to the degree of responsibility of which one is capable.[12] Furthermore —and this must be specially emphasized—there is the right to a working wage, determined according to criterions of justice and sufficient, therefore, in proportion to the available resources, to give the worker and his family a standard of living in keeping with the dignity of the human person. In this regard, our predecessor Pius XII said: "To the personal duty to work imposed by nature, there corresponds and follows the natural right of each individual to make of his work the means to provide for his own life and the lives of his children. So profoundly is the empire of nature ordained for the preservation of man." [13]

The right to private property, even of productive goods, also derives from the nature of man. This right, as we have elsewhere declared, is a suitable means for safeguarding the dignity of the human person and for the exercise of responsibility in all fields; it strengthens and gives serenity to family life, thereby increasing the peace and prosperity of the state.[14]

However, it is opportune to point out that there is a social duty essentially inherent in the right of private property.[15]

THE RIGHT OF MEETING AND ASSOCIATION

From the fact that human beings are by nature social, there arises the right of assembly and association. They have also the right to give the societies of which they are members the form they consider most suitable for the aim they have in view, and to act within such societies on their

---

11 Cf. Leo XIII's encyclical letter "Rerum Novarum" ("Of New Things"), Acts of Leo XIII, Vol. 11, pp. 128–29.

12 Cf. John XXIII's encyclical letter "Mater et Magistra" ("Mother and Teacher"), Acta Apostolicae Sedis, Vol. 53, p. 422.

13 Cf. Pope Pius XII, loc. cit.

14 "Mater et Magistra," p. 428.

15 Cf. ibid., p. 430.

own initiative and on their own responsibility in order to achieve their desired objectives.[16]

We ourselves stated in the encyclical "Mater et Magistra" that, for the achievement of ends which individual human beings cannot attain except by association, it is necessary and indispensable to set up a great variety of such intermediate groups and societies in order to guarantee for the human person a sufficient sphere of freedom and responsibility.[17]

THE RIGHT TO EMIGRATE AND IMMIGRATE

Every human being has the right to freedom of movement and of residence within the confines of his own country and, when there are just reasons for it, the right to emigrate to other countries and take up residence there.[18] The fact that one is a citizen of a particular state does not detract in any way from his membership of the human family as a whole nor from his citizenship of the world community.

POLITICAL RIGHTS

The dignity of the human person involves the right to take an active part in public affairs and to contribute one's part to the common good of the citizenry. For, as our predecessor of happy memory, Pius XII, pointed out: The human individual, far from being an object and, as it were, a merely passive element in the social order, is in fact, must be and must continue to be, its subject, its foundation and its end.[19]

The human person is also entitled to a juridical protection of his rights, a protection that should be efficacious, impartial and inspired by the true norms of justice.

As our predecessor Pius XII teaches: That perpetual privilege proper to man, by which every individual has a claim to the protection of his rights, and by which there is assigned to each a definite and particular sphere of rights, im-

16 Cf. "Rerum Novarum," pp. 134–42; Pius XI's encyclical "Quadragesimo Anno" ("in the fortieth year"), Acta Apostolicae Sedis, Vol. 23, pp. 199–200, and Pius XII's encyclical letter "Sertum Laetitiae" ("A Garland of Joy"), Acta Apostolicae Sedis, Vol. 31, pp. 635–44.

17 Cf. Acta Apostolicae Sedis, Vol. 53, p. 430.

18 Cf. Pius XII's radio message on Christmas Eve, 1942, op. cit., pp. 33–46.

19 Cf. Pius XII's radio message on Christmas Eve, 1944, Acta Apostolicae Sedis, Vol. 37, p. 12.

nune from all arbitrary attacks, is the logical consequence
of the order of justice willed by God.[20]

DUTIES

RIGHTS AND DUTIES NECESSARILY LINKED IN THE ONE PERSON

The natural rights with which we have been dealing are,
however, inseparably connected, in the very person who is
their subject, with just as many respective duties; and rights
as well as duties find their source, their sustenance and their
inviolability in the natural law which grants or enjoins them.

For example, the right of every man to life is correlative
with the duty to preserve it; his right to a decent standard
of living with the duty of living it becomingly; and his right
to investigate the truth freely, with the duty of seeking it
and of possessing it ever more completely and profoundly.

RECIPROCITY OF RIGHTS AND DUTIES BETWEEN PERSONS

Once this is admitted, it is also clear that in human society
to one man's right there corresponds a duty in all other persons: the duty, namely, of acknowledging and respecting the
right in question. For every fundamental human right draws
its indestructible moral force from the natural law, which,
in granting it, imposes a corresponding obligation. Those,
therefore, who claim their own rights, yet altogether forget
or neglect to carry out their respective duties, are people who
build with one hand and destroy with the other. . . .

SOCIAL LIFE IN TRUTH, JUSTICE, CHARITY AND FREEDOM

A political society is to be considered well-ordered, beneficial and in keeping with human dignity if it is grounded on
truth. As the Apostle Paul exhorts us: "Away with falsehood
then; let everyone speak out the truth to his neighbor; membership of the body binds us to one another." [21] This demands that reciprocal rights and duties be sincerely recognized. Furthermore, human society will be such as we have
just described it, if the citizens, guided by justice, apply
themselves seriously to respecting the rights of others and
discharging their own duties; if they are moved by such fer-

---

20 Cf. Pius XII's radio message on Christmas Eve, 1942, op.
cit., p. 21.
21 Ephesians, iv, 25.

vor of charity as to make their own the needs of others and share with others their own goods: If, finally, they work for a progressively closer fellowship in the world of spiritual values. Human society is realized in freedom, that is to say, in ways and means in keeping with the dignity of its citizens, who accept the responsibility of their actions, precisely because they are by nature rational beings.

Human society, venerable brothers and beloved children, ought to be regarded above all as a spiritual reality: in which men communicate knowledge to each other in the light of truth; in which they can enjoy their rights and fulfil their duties, and are inspired to strive for moral good. Society should enable men to share in and enjoy every legitimate expression of beauty, and encourage them constantly to pass on to others all that is best in themselves, while they strive to make their own the spiritual achievements of others. These are the spiritual values which continually give life and basic orientation to cultural expressions, economic and social institutions, political movements and forms, laws, and all other structures by which society is outwardly established and constantly developed.

GOD AND THE MORAL ORDER

The order which prevails in society is by nature moral. Grounded as it is in truth, it must function according to the norms of justice, it should be inspired and perfected by mutual love, and finally it should be brought to an ever more refined and human balance in freedom.

Now an order of this kind, whose principles are universal, absolute and unchangeable, has its ultimate source in the one true God, who is personal and transcends human nature. Inasmuch as God is the first truth and the highest good, He alone is that deepest source from which human society can draw its vitality, if that society is to be well-ordered, beneficial, and in keeping with human dignity.[22] As St. Thomas Aquinas says: "Human reason is the norm of the human will, according to which its goodness is measured, because reason derives from the eternal law which is the divine reason itself. It is evident then that the goodness of

---

[22] Cf. Pius XII's 1942 radio message, op. cit., p. 14.

the human will depends much more on the eternal law than on human reason." [23]

CHARACTERISTICS OF THE PRESENT

Our age has three distinctive characteristics. First of all, the working classes have gradually gained ground in economic and public affairs. They began by claiming their rights in the socio-economic sphere; they extended their action then to claims on the political level; and finally applied themselves to the acquisition of the benefits of a more refined culture. Today, therefore, workers all over the world refuse to be treated as if they were irrational objects without freedom, to be used at the arbitrary disposition of others. They insist that they be always regarded as men with a share in every sector of human society: in the social and economic sphere, in the fields of learning and culture, and in public life.

Secondly, it is obvious to everyone that women are now taking a part in public life. This is happening more rapidly, perhaps, in nations of Christian civilization, and, more slowly but broadly, among peoples who have inherited other traditions or cultures. Since women are becoming ever more conscious of their human dignity, they will not tolerate being treated as mere material instruments, but demand rights befitting a human person both in domestic and in public life.

Finally, the modern world, as compared with the recent past, has taken on an entirely new appearance in the field of social and political life. For since all nations have either achieved or are on the way to achieving independence, there will soon no longer exist a world divided into nations that rule others and nations that are subject to others.

Men all over the world have today—or will soon have— the rank of citizens in independent nations. No one wants to feel subject to political powers located outside his own country or ethnic group. Thus in very many human beings the inferiority complex which endured for hundreds and thousands of years is disappearing, while in others there is an attenuation and gradual fading of the corresponding superiority complex which had its roots in social-economic privileges, sex or political standing.

On the contrary, the conviction that all men are equal by

---

[23] St. Thomas Aquinas, "Summa Theologica," I/A-11/AE, quest. 19, para. 4, cf. para. 9.

reason of their natural dignity has been generally accepted. Hence racial discrimination can no longer be justified, at least doctrinally or in theory. And this is of fundamental importance and significance for the formation of human society according to those principles which we have outlined above. For, if a man becomes conscious of his rights, he must become equally aware of his duties. Thus he who possesses certain rights has likewise the duty to claim those rights as marks of his dignity, while all others have the obligation to acknowledge those rights and respect them.

When the relations of human society are expressed in terms of rights and duties, men become conscious of spiritual values, understand the meaning and significance of truth, justice, charity and freedom, and become deeply aware that they belong to this world of values. Moreover, when moved by such concerns, they are brought to a better knowledge of the true God who is personal and transcendent, and thus they make the ties that bind them to God the solid foundations and supreme criterion of their lives, both of that life which they live interiorly in the depths of their own souls and of that in which they are united to other men in society.

Part II
Relations Between Individuals and the Public Authorities

NECESSITY AND DIVINE ORIGIN OF AUTHORITY

Human society can be neither well-ordered nor prosperous unless it has some people invested with legitimate authority to preserve its institutions and to devote themselves as far as is necessary to work and care for the good of all. These, however, derive their authority from God, as St. Paul teaches in the words, "Authority comes from God alone." [24] These words of St. Paul are explained thus by St. John Chrysostom: What are you saying? Is every ruler appointed by God? I do not say that, he replies, for I am not dealing now with individual rulers, but with authority itself. What I say is, that it is the divine wisdom and not mere chance that

[24] St. Paul's Epistle to the Romans, xiii, 1-6.

has ordained that there should be government, that some should command and others obey.[25] Moreover, since God made men social by nature, and since no society can hold together unless some one be over all, directing all to strive earnestly for the common good, every civilized community must have a ruling authority, and this authority, no less than society itself, has its source in nature, and has, consequently, God for its authority.[26]

But authority is not to be thought of as a force lacking all control. Indeed, since it is the power to command according to right reason, authority must derive its obligatory force from the moral order, which in turn has God for its first source and final end. Wherefore our predecessor of happy memory, Pius XII, said: "That same absolute order of beings and their ends which presents man as an autonomous person, that is, as the subject of inviolable duties and rights, and as at once the basis of society and the purpose for which it exists, also includes the state as necessary society invested with the authority without which it could not come into being or live. . . . And since this absolute order, as we learn from sound reason, especially from the Christian faith, can have no origin save in a personal God who is our Creator, it follows that the dignity of the state's authority is due to its sharing to some extent in the authority of God himself.[27]

Where the civil authority uses as its only or its chief means either threats and fear of punishment or promises of rewards, it cannot effectively move men to promote the common good of all. Even if it did so move them, this would be altogether opposed to their dignity as men, endowed with reason and free will. As authority is chiefly concerned with moral force, it follows that civil authority must appeal primarily to the conscience of individual citizens, that is, to each one's duty to collaborate readily for the common good of all. Since by nature all men are equal in human dignity, it follows that no one may be coerced to perform interior acts. That is in the power of God alone, who sees and judges the hidden designs of men's hearts. Those therefore who have authority in the state may oblige men in conscience

25 Op. cit., xiii, 1-2; Homily 23, Edition P. G. 60, 615.
26 Leo XIII's encyclical letter "Immortale Dei" ("Of Immortal God"), Acts of Leo XIII, Vol. 5, p. 120.
27 Cf. Pius XII's 1944 radio message, op. cit., p. 15.

only if their authority is intrinsically related with the authority of God and shares in it.[28]

By this principle the dignity of the citizens is protected. When, in fact, men obey their rulers, it is not all as men that they obey them, but through their obedience it is God, the provident Creator of all things, whom they reverence, since he has decreed that men's dealings with one another should be regulated by an order which he himself has established. Moreover, in showing this due reverence to God, men not only do not debase themselves but rather perfect and ennoble themselves. For to serve God is to rule.[29]

Since the right to command is required by the moral order and has its source in God, it follows that, if civil authorities legislate for or allow anything that is contrary to that order and therefore contrary to the will of God, neither the laws made nor the authorizations granted can be binding on the consciences of the citizens, since God has more right to be obeyed than men.[30] Otherwise, authority breaks down completely and results in shameful abuse. As St. Thomas Aquinas teaches: Human law has the true nature of law only insofar as it corresponds to right reason, and therefore is derived from the eternal law. Insofar as it falls short of right reason, a law is said to be a wicked law. And so, lacking the true nature of law, it is rather a kind of violence. [31]

It must not be concluded, however, because authority comes from God, that therefore men have no right to choose those who are to rule the state, to decide the form of government and to determine both the way in which authority is to be exercised and its limits. It is thus clear that the doctrine which we have set forth is fully consonant with any truly democratic regime.[32]

28 Cf. Encyclical Letter "Diuturnum Illud" ("That Longlived"), Acts of Leo XIII, Vol. 2, p. 274.
29 Cf. Ibid, p. 278, and encyclical "Immortale Dei," op. cit., p. 130.
30 Acts of the Apostles, v, 29.
31 St. Thomas Aquinas, op. cit., quest., 93, para. 3; Cf. Pius XII's 1944 radio message, op. cit., pp. 5–23.
32 Cf. "Diuturnum Illud," op. cit., pp. 271–72; and Pius XII's 1944 radio message, op. cit., pp. 9–23.

ATTAINMENT OF THE COMMON GOOD

PURPOSES OF THE PUBLIC AUTHORITY

Individual citizens and intermediate groups are obliged to make their specific contributions to the common welfare. One of the chief consequences of this is that they must bring their own interests into harmony with the needs of the community, and must dispose of their goods and their services as civil authorities have prescribed, in accord with the norms of justice, in due form and within the limits of their competence. This they must do by means of formally perfect actions, the content of which must be morally good, or at least capable of being directed towards good.

Indeed, since the whole reason for the existence of civil authorities is the realization of the common good, it is clearly necessary that, in pursuing this objective, they should respect its essential elements, and at the same time conform their laws to the needs of a given historical situation.[33]

Assuredly, the ethnic characteristics of the various human groups are to be respected as constituent elements of the common good,[34] but these values and characteristics by no means exhaust the content of the common good. For the common good is intimately bound up with human nature. It can never exist fully and completely unless, its intimate nature and realization being what they are, the human person is taken into account.[35]

In the second place, the very nature of the common good requires that all members of the political community be entitled to share in it, although in different ways according to each one's tasks, merits and circumstances. For this reason, every civil authority must take pains to promote the common good of all, without preference for any single citizen or civil group. As our predecessor of immortal memory, Leo XIII, has said: The civil power must not serve the advantage of any one individual or of some few persons, inasmuch as it

[33] Cf. Pius XII's 1942 radio message, op. cit., p. 13, and Leo XIII's "Immortale Dei," op. cit., p. 120.

[34] Cf. Pius XII's encyclical letter "Summi Pontificatus" ("Of the Supreme Pontificate"). Acta Apostolicae Sedis, Vol. 31, pp. 412–53.

[35] Cf. Pius XI's encyclical letter "Mit Brennender Sorge" ("For With Burning Sorrow"), Acta Apostolicae Sedis, Vol. 29, p. 159, and encyclical letter "Divini Redemptoris." Acta Apostolica Sedis, Vol. 29, p. 159, and encyclical letter "Divini Redemptoris," Acta Apostolica Sedis, Vol. 29, pp. 65–106.

was established for the common good of all.[36] Considerations of justice and equity, however, can at times demand
that those involved in civil government give more attention
to the less fortunate members of the community, since they
are less able to defend their rights and to assert their
legitimate claims.[37]

In this context, we judge that attention should be called
to the fact that the common good touches the whole man,
the needs both of his body and of his soul. Hence it follows
that the civil authorities must undertake to effect the common good by ways and means that are proper to them. That
is, while respecting the hierarchy of values, they should
promote simultaneously both the material and the spiritual
welfare of the citizens.[38]

These principles are clearly contained in the doctrine
stated in our encyclical, "Mater et Magistra," where we
emphasized that the common good of all embraces the sum
total of those conditions of social living whereby men are
enabled to achieve their own integral perfection more fully
and more easily.[39]

Men, however, composed as they are of bodies and immortal souls, can never in this mortal life succeed in satisfying all their needs or in attaining perfect happiness. Therefore, all efforts made to promote the common good, far from
endangering the eternal salvation of men, ought rather to
serve to promote it.[40]

RESPONSIBILITIES OF THE PUBLIC AUTHORITY, AND RIGHTS AND DUTIES OF INDIVIDUALS

It is agreed that in our time the common good is chiefly
guaranteed when personal rights and duties are maintained.
The chief concern of civil authorities must therefore be to
insure that these rights are acknowledged, respected, coordi-
nated with other rights, defended and promoted, so that in
this way each one may more easily carry out his duties.
For to safeguard the inviolable rights of the human person,

---

36 "Immortale Dei," op. cit., p. 121.
37 Cf. "Rerum Novarum," op. cit., pp. 133–34.
38 Cf. "Summi Pontificatus," op. cit., p. 433.
39 Acta Apostolicae Sedis, Vol. 53, p. 19.
40 Cf. "Quadragesimo Anno," Vol. 23, p. 215.

and to facilitate the fulfilment of its duties, should be the essential office of every public authority.[41]

This means that, if any government does not acknowledge the rights of man or violates them, it not only fails its duty, but its orders completely lack juridical force.[42]

RECONCILIATION AND PROTECTION OF RIGHTS AND DUTIES OF INDIVIDUALS

One of the fundamental duties of civil authorities, therefore, is to coordinate social relations in such fashion that the exercise of one man's rights does not threaten others in the exercise of their own rights nor hinder them in the fulfilment of their duties. Finally, the rights of all should be effectively safeguarded and, if they have been violated, completely restored.[43]

DUTY OF PROMOTING THE RIGHTS OF INDIVIDUALS

It is also demanded by the common good that civil authorities should make earnest efforts to bring about a situation in which individual citizens can easily exercise their rights and fulfil their duties as well. For experience has taught us that, unless these authorities take suitable action with regard to economic, political and cultural matters, inequalities between the citizens tend to become more and more widespread, especially in the modern world, and as a result human rights are rendered totally ineffective, and the fulfillment of duties is compromised.

It is therefore necessary that the Administration give wholehearted and careful attention to the social as well as to the economic progress of the citizens, and to the development, in keeping with the development of the productive system, of such essential services as the building of roads, transportation, communications, water supply, housing, public health, education, facilitation of the practice of religion and recreational facilities. It is necessary also that governments make efforts to see that insurance systems are made available to the citizens, so that, in case of misfortune or

---

[41] Cf. Pius XII's 1941 Feast of Pentecost radio message, op. cit., p. 200.

[42] Cf. "Mit Brennender Sorge," op. cit., p. 159; "Divini Redemptoris," op. cit., p. 79 and Pius XII's 1942 radio message; op. cit., pp. 9–24.

[43] Cf. "Divini Redemptoris," op. cit., p. 81, and 1942 radio message, loc. cit.

increased family responsibilities, no person will be without the necessary means to maintain a decent standard of living. The government should make similarly effective efforts to see that those who are able to work can find employment in keeping with their aptitudes, and that each worker receives a wage in keeping with the laws of justice and equity. It should be equally the concern of civil authorities to insure that workers be allowed their proper responsibility in the work undertaken in industrial organization, and to facilitate the establishment of intermediate groups which will make social life richer and more effective. Finally, it should be possible for all the citizens to share as far as they are able in their country's cultural advantages.

HARMONIOUS RELATION BETWEEN PUBLIC AUTHORITY'S TWO FORMS OF INTERVENTION

The common good requires that civil authorities maintain a careful balance between coordinating and protecting the rights of the citizens, on the one hand, and promoting them, on the other. It should not happen that certain individuals or social groups derive special advantage from the fact that their rights have received preferential protection. Nor should it happen that governments, in seeking to protect these rights, become obstacles to their full expression and free use. For this principle must always be retained: that state activity in the economic field, no matter what its breadth or depth may be, ought not to be exercised in such a way as to curtail an individual's freedom of personal initiative. Rather it should work to expand that freedom as much as possible by the effective protection of the essential personal rights of each and every individual.[44]

The same principle should inspire the various steps which governments take in order to make it possible for the citizens more easily to exercise their rights and fulfill their duties in every sector of social life.

STRUCTURE AND OPERATION OF PUBLIC AUTHORITY

It is impossible to determine, once and for all, what is the most suitable form of government, or how civil authorities can most effectively fulfill their respective functions, i.e., the legislative, judicial and executive functions of the

44 "Mater et Magistra," op. cit., p. 415.

state. In determining the structure and operation of government which a state is to have, great weight has to be given to the historical background and circumstances of given political communities, circumstances which will vary at different times and in different places. We consider, however, that it is in keeping with the innate demands of human nature that the state should take a form which embodies the three-fold division of powers corresponding to the three principal functions of public authority. In that type of state, not only the official functions of government but also the mutual relations between citizens and public officials are set down according to law, which in itself affords protection to the citizens both in the enjoyment of their rights and in the fulfillment of their duties.

If, however this political and juridical structure is to produce the advantages which may be expected of it, public officials must strive to meet the problems which arise in a way that conforms both to the complexities of the situation and the proper exercise of their function. This requires that, in constantly changing conditions, legislators never forget the norms of morality, or constitutional provisions, or the objective requirements of the common good. Moreover, executive authorities must coordinate the activities of society with discretion, with a full knowledge of the law and after a careful consideration of circumstances, and the courts must administer justice impartially and without being influenced by favoritism or pressure. The good order of society also demands that individual citizens and intermediate organizations should be effectively protected by law whenever they have rights to be exercised or obligations to be fulfilled. This protection should be granted to citizens both in their dealings with each other and in their relations with government agencies.[45]

LAW AND CONSCIENCE

It is unquestionable that a legal structure in conformity with the moral order and corresponding to the level of development of the political community is of great advantage to achievement of the common good.

And yet, social life in the modern world is so varied, complex and dynamic that even a juridical structure which has

[45] Cf. Pius XII's 1942 radio message, op. cit., p. 21.

been prudently and thoughtfully established is always inadequate for the needs of society.

It is also true that the relations of the citizens with each other, of citizens and intermediate groups with public authorities, and finally of the public authorities with one another are often so complex and so sensitive that they cannot be regulated by inflexible legal provisions. Such a situation therefore demands that the civil authorities have clear ideas about the nature and extent of their official duties if they wish to maintain the existing juridical structure in its basic elements and principles, and at the same time meet the exigencies of social life, adapting their legislation to the changing social scene and solving new problems. They must be men of great equilibrium and integrity, competent and courageous enough to see at once what the situation requires and to take necessary action quickly and effectively.[46] . . .

Part III
Relations Between States

SUBJECTS OF RIGHTS AND DUTIES

Our predecessors have constantly maintained, and we join them in reasserting, that political communities are reciprocally subjects of rights and duties. This means that their relationships also must be harmonized in truth, in justice, in a working solidarity, in liberty. The same moral law which governs relations between individual human beings serves also to regulate the relations of political communities with one another. This will be readily understood when one reflects that the individual representatives of political communities cannot put aside their personal dignity while they are acting in the name and interest of their countries. And that they cannot therefore violate the very law of their being, which is the moral law.

It would be absurd, moreover, even to imagine that men could surrender their own human attributes, or be compelled to do so, by the very fact of their appointment to

[46] Op. cit., pp. 15–16.

public office, whereas they have been given that noble assignment precisely because the wealth of their human endowments has earned them their reputation as outstanding members of the body politic. Furthermore, authority is a necessary requirement of the moral order in human society. It may not therefore be used against that order. And the very instant such an attempt were made, it would cease to be authority. . . .

Lastly, it is to be borne in mind that also in the regulating of relations between political communities, authority is to be exercised for the achievement of the common good, which constitutes the reason for its existence.

But a fundamental factor of the common good is acknowledgment of the moral order and respect for its prescriptions. Order between the political communities must be built upon the unshakable and unchangeable rock of the moral law, made manifest in the order of nature by the Creator himself and by Him engraved on the hearts of men with letters that may never be effaced. . . .

IN TRUTH

First among the rules governing the relations between states is that of truth. This calls, above all, for the elimination of every trace of racism, and the consequent recognition of the principle that all states are by nature equal in dignity. Each of them, accordingly, is vested with the right to existence, to self-development, to the means fitting to its attainment and to be the one primarily responsible for this self-development. Add to that the right of each to its good name, and to the respect which is its due. Very often, experience has taught us, individuals will be found to differ considerably, in knowledge, virtue, talent and wealth. Yet these inequalities must never be held to excuse any man's attempt to lord it over his neighbors unjustly. They constitute rather a source of greater responsibility in the contribution which each and everyone must make towards mutual improvement.

Similarly, political communities may have reached different levels of culture, civilization or economic development. Neither is that a sufficient reason for some to take unjust advantage of their superiority over others. Rather should they see in it an added motive for more serious commitment to the common cause of social progress.

It is not true that some human beings are by nature superior and others inferior. All men are equal in their natural dignity. Consequently, there are no political communities which are superior by nature and none which are inferior by nature. All political communities are of equal natural dignity, since they are bodies whose membership is made up of these same human beings. Nor must it be forgotten, in this connection, that peoples can be highly sensitive, and with good reason, in matters touching their dignity and honor.

Truth further demands that the various media of social communications made available by modern progress, which enable the nations to know each other better, be used with serene objectivity. That need not, of course, rule out any legitimate emphasis on the positive aspects of their way of life. But methods of information which fall short of the truth, and by the same token impair the reputation of this people or that, must be discarded.[47]

IN JUSTICE

Relations between political communities are to be further regulated by justice. This implies, over and above recognition of their mutual rights, the fulfillment of their respective duties.

Political communities have the right to existence, to self-development and to the means necessary for this. They have the right to play the leading part in the process of their own development and the right to their good name and due honors. From which it follows as a simultaneous consequence that they have also the corresponding duty of respecting these rights in others and of avoiding any act of violation. Just as an individual man may not pursue his own interests to the detriment of other men, so, on the international level, one state may not develop itself by restricting or oppressing other states. St. Augustine rightly says, "What are kingdoms without justice but bands of robbers?"[48] . . .

THE TREATMENT OF MINORITIES

From the 19th century there has been a rather wide-

47 Cf. Pius XII's radio message on Christmas Eve, 1940, Acta Apostolicae Sedis, Vol. 33, pp. 5–14.
48 St. Augustine's "De Civitate Dei," book IV, chapt. 4, edition P. L. 41, p. 115; cf. Pius XII's radio message on Christmas Eve, 1939, Acta Apostolicae Sedis, Vol. 32, pp. 5–13.

spread tendency in historical evolution that political communities equate themselves to national communities. However, for various reasons, it has not always been possible to make geographical boundaries coincide with ethnic ones. This gives rise to the phenomenon of minorities and to the relative complex problems.

In the first place, it must be made clear that justice is seriously violated by whatever is done to limit the strength and numerical increase of these lesser peoples. The injustice is even more serious if such sinful projects are aimed at the very extinction of these groups.

On the other hand, the demands of justice are admirably observed by those civil authorities who promote the natural betterment of those citizens belonging to a smaller ethnic group, particularly when that betterment concerns their language, the development of their natural gifts, their ancestral customs, and their accomplishments and endeavors in the economic order.[49]

It should be noted, however, that these minority groups, either because of a reaction to their present situation or because of their historical difficulties are often inclined to exalt beyond due measure anything proper to their own people, so as to place them even above human values, as if that which is proper to humanity were to be at the service of that which is proper to the nation. Reason rather demands that these very people recognize also the advantages that accrue to them from their peculiar circumstances. For instance, no small contribution is made towards the development of their particular talents and spirit by their daily dealings with people who have grown up in a different culture. This, however, will be true only if they will know how to act as a bridge, which facilitates the circulation of life in its various expressions among different traditions or civilizations, and not a zone of discord which can cause great damage and choke natural development.

ACTIVE SOLIDARITY

Certainly relations between states must be regulated by the norms of truth and justice, but they also derive great benefits from active solidarity, through mutual cooperation on various levels, such as, in our own times, has already taken place with laudable results in the economic, social,

[49] Cf. Pius XII's 1941 radio message, op. cit., pp, 10–21.

political, educational, health and sport spheres. We must remember that, of its very nature, civil authority exists, not to confine its people within the boundaries of their nation, but rather to protect, above all else, the common good of that particular civil society, which certainly cannot be divorced from the common good of the entire human family.

This entails not only that civil societies should pursue their particular interests without hurting others, but also that they should join forces and plans whenever the efforts of an individual government cannot achieve its desired goals. But in the execution of such common efforts, great care must be taken lest what helps some nations should injure others.

Furthermore, the universal common good requires that in every nation friendly relations be fostered in all fields between the citizens and their intermediate societies.

There are groupings of people of more or less different racial backgrounds. However, the elements which characterize an ethnic group must not be transformed into a watertight compartment in which human beings are prevented from communicating with their fellowmen belonging to different ethnic groups. That would contrast with our contemporary situation, in which the distances separating peoples have been almost wiped out. Nor can one overlook the fact that, even though human beings differ from one another by virtue of their ethnic peculiarities, they all possess certain essential common elements, and are inclined by nature to meet each other in the world of spiritual values, whose progressive assimilation opens to them the possibility of perfection without limits. They have the right and duty therefore to live in communion with one another.

PROPER BALANCES BETWEEN POPULATION, LAND AND CAPITAL

As everybody knows, there are countries with an abundance of arable land and a scarcity of manpower, while in other countries there is no proportion between natural resources and the capital available. This demands that peoples should set up relationships of mutual collaboration, facilitating the circulation from one to the other of capital, goods and manpower.[50]

Here we deem it opportune to remark that, whenever

---

[50] Cf. "Mater et Magistra," op. cit., p. 439.

possible, the work to be done should be taken to the workers, not vice versa.

In this way a possibility of a better future is offered to many persons without being forced to leave their own environment in order to seek residence elsewhere, which almost always entails the heartache of separation and difficult periods of adjustment and social integration.

THE PROBLEM OF POLITICAL REFUGEES

The sentiment of universal fatherhood which the Lord has placed in our heart makes us feel profound sadness in considering the phenomenon of political refugees: a phenomenon which has assumed large proportions and which always hides numberless and acute sufferings.

Such expatriations show that there are some political regimes which do not guarantee for individual citizens a sufficient sphere of freedom within which their souls are allowed to breathe humanly. In fact, under those regimes even the lawful existence of such a sphere of freedom is either called into question or denied. This undoubtedly is a radical inversion of the order of human society, because the reason for the existence of public authority is to promote the common good, a fundamental element of which is the recognition of that sphere of freedom and the safeguarding of it.

At this point it will not be superfluous to recall that such exiles are persons, and that all their rights as persons must be recognized, since they do not lose those rights on losing the citizenship of lands of which they are former members.

Now among the rights of a human person there must be included that by which a man may enter a political community where he hopes he can more fittingly provide a future for himself and his dependents. Wherefore, as far as the common good rightly understood permits, it is the duty of that state to accept such immigrants and to help to integrate them into itself as new members.

Wherefore, on this occasion, we publicly approve and commend every undertaking, founded on the principles of human solidarity and Christian charity, which aims at making migration of persons from one country to another less painful.

And we will be permitted to signal for the attention and gratitude of all right-minded persons the manifold work which specialized international agencies are carrying out in this very delicate field.

DISARMAMENT

On the other hand, it is with deep sorrow that we note the enormous stocks of armaments that have been and still are being made in more economically developed countries, with a vast outlay of intellectual and economic resources. And so it happens that, while the people of these countries are loaded with heavy burdens, other countries as a result are deprived of the collaboration they need in order to make economic and social progress.

The production of arms is allegedly justified on the grounds that in present-day conditions peace cannot be preserved without an equal balance of armaments. And so, if one country increases its armaments, others feel the need to do the same; and if one country is equipped with nuclear weapons, other countries must produce their own, equally destructive.

Consequently, people live in constant fear lest the storm that every moment threatens should break upon them with dreadful violence. And with good reason, for the arms of war are ready at hand. Even though it is difficult to believe that anyone would deliberately take the responsibility for the appalling destruction and sorrow that war would bring in its train, it cannot be denied that the conflagration may be set off by some uncontrollable and unexpected chance. And one must bear in mind that, even though the monstrous power of modern weapons acts as a deterrent, it is to be feared that the mere continuance of nuclear tests, undertaken with war in mind, will have fatal consequences for life on the earth.

Justice, then, right reason and humanity urgently demand that the arms race should cease. That the stockpiles which exist in various countries should be reduced equally and simultaneously by the parties concerned. That nuclear weapons should be banned. And that a general agreement should eventually be reached about progressive disarmament and an effective method of control. In the words of Pius XII, our predecessor of happy memory: "The calamity of a world war, with the economic and social ruin and the moral excesses and dissolution that accompany it, must not be permitted to envelop the human race for a third time." [51]

All must realize that there is no hope of putting an end to
the building up of armaments, nor of reducing the present
stocks, nor, still less, of abolishing them altogether, unless
the process is complete and thorough and unless it proceeds
from inner convictions: unless, that is, everyone sincerely co-
operates to banish the fear and anxious expectation of war
with which men are oppressed. If this is to come about, the
fundamental principle on which our present peace depends
must be replaced by another, which declares that the true and
solid peace of nations consists not in equality of arms, but
in mutual trust alone. We believe that this can be brought to
pass, and we consider that it is something which reason requires, that it is eminently desirable in itself and that it will
prove to be the source of many benefits.

In the first place, it is an objective demanded by reason.
There can be, or at least there should be, no doubt that relations between states, as between individuals, should be regulated not by the force of arms, but by the light of reason,
by the rule, that is, of truth, of justice and of active and
sincere cooperation.

Secondly, we say that it is an objective earnestly to be desired in itself. Is there anyone who does not ardently yearn
to see war banished, to see peace preserved and daily more
firmly established?

And finally, it is an objective which will be a fruitful
source of many benefits, for its advantages will be felt
everywhere, by individuals, by families, by nations, by the
whole human family. The warning of Pius XII still rings
in our ears: "Nothing is lost by peace. Everything may be
lost by war." [52]

Since this is so, we, the vicar on earth of Jesus Christ, Saviour of the world and author of peace, and as interpreter of
the very profound longing of the entire human family, following the impulse of our heart, seized by anxiety for the
good of all, we feel it our duty to beseech men, especially
those who have the responsibility of public affairs, to spare
no labor in order to insure that the world events follow a
reasonable and human course.

In the highest and most authoritative assemblies, let men

[51] Cf. Pius XII's 1941 radio message, op. cit., p. 17, and Benedict
XV's exhortation Aug. 1, 1917, Acta Apostolicae Sedis, Vol. 9, p. 418.

[52] Cf. Pius XII's radio message on Aug. 24, 1939, Acta Apostolicae
Sedis, Vol. 31, p. 334.

give serious thought to the problem of a peaceful adjustment
of relations between political communities on a world level:
an adjustment founded on mutual trust, on sincerity in negotiations, on faithful fulfillment of obligations assumed. Let
them study the problem until they find that point of agreement from which it will be possible to commence to go forward towards accords that will be sincere, lasting and fruitful.

We, for our part, will not cease to pray God to bless these
labors so that they may lead to fruitful results.

IN LIBERTY

It has also to be borne in mind that relations between states
should be based on freedom, that is to say, that no country
may unjustly oppress others or unduly meddle in their
affairs. On the contrary, all should help to develop in others
a sense of responsibility, a spirit of enterprise and an earnest
desire to be the first to promote their own advancement in
every field.

THE EVOLUTION OF ECONOMICALLY
UNDERDEVELOPED COUNTRIES

Because all men are joined together by reason of their
common origin, their redemption by Christ and their
supernatural destiny, and are called to form one single family, we appealed in the encyclical "Mater et Magistra" to
economically developed nations to come to the aid of those
which were in the process of development.[53]

We are greatly consoled to see how widely that appeal
has been favorably received. And we are confident that even
more so in the future it will contribute to the end that the
poorer countries, in as short a time as possible, will arrive at
that degree of economic development which will enable every
citizen to live in conditions in keeping with his human dignity.

But it is never sufficiently repeated that the cooperation, to
which reference has been made, should be effected with the
greatest respect for the liberty of the countries being developed, for these must realize that they are primarily responsible, and that they are the principal artisans in the promotion of their own economic development and social progress.

[53] Cf. Acta Apostolicae Sedis, Vol. 53, pp. 440–41.

Our predecessor Pius XII already proclaimed that in the field of a new order founded on moral principles, there is no room for violation of freedom, integrity and security of other nations, no matter what may be their territorial extension or their capacity for defense. It is inevitable that the powerful states, by reason of their greater potential and their power, should pave the way in the establishment of economic groups comprising not only themselves but also smaller and weaker states as well. It is nevertheless indispensable that in the interests of the common good they, as all others, should respect the rights of those smaller states to political freedom, to economic development and to the adequate protection, in the case of conflicts between nations, of that neutrality which is theirs according to the natural, as well as international, law. In this way, and in this way only, will they be able to obtain a fitting share of the common good, and assure the material and spiritual welfare of their people.[54]

It is vitally important, therefore, that the wealthier states, in providing varied forms of assistance to the poorer, should respect the moral values and ethnic characteristics peculiar to each, and also that they should avoid any intention of political domination. If this is done, a precious contribution will be made towards the formation of a world community, a community in which each member, whilst conscious of its own individual right and duties, will work in a relationship of equality towards the attainment of the universal common good.[55]

SIGNS OF THE TIMES

Men are becoming more and more convinced that disputes which arise between states should not be resolved by recourse to arms, but rather by negotiation.

It is true that on historical grounds this conviction is based chiefly on the terrible destructive force of modern arms. And it is nourished by the horror aroused in the mind by the very thought of the cruel destruction and the immense suffering which the use of those armaments would bring to the human family. And for this reason it is hardly possible to imagine that in the atomic era war could be used as an instrument of justice.

[54] Cf. Pius XII's 1941 radio message, op. cit., pp. 16–17.
[55] "Mater et Magistra," op. cit., p. 443.

Nevertheless, unfortunately, the law of fear still reigns among peoples, and it forces them to spend fabulous sums for armaments: not for aggression, they affirm—and there is no reason for not believing them—but to dissuade others from aggression.

There is reason to hope, however, that by meeting and negotiating, men may come to discover better the bonds that unite them together, deriving from the human nature which they have in common. And that they may also come to discover that one of the most profound requirements of their common nature is this: that between them and their respective peoples it is not fear which should reign but love, a love which tends to express itself in a collaboration that is loyal, manifold in form and productive of many benefits.

Part IV
Relationship of Men and of Political Communities with the World Community

INTERDEPENDENCE BETWEEN POLITICAL COMMUNITIES

Recent progress of science and technology has profoundly affected human beings and influenced men to work together and live as one family. There has been a great increase in the circulation of ideas, of persons and of goods from one country to another, so that relations have become closer between individuals, families and intermediate associations belonging to different political communities, and between the public authorities of those communities. At the same time the interdependence of national economies has grown deeper, one becoming progressively more closely related to the other, so that they become, as it were, integral parts of the one world economy. Likewise the social progress, order, security and peace of each country are necessarily connected with the social progress, order, security and peace of all other countries.

At the present day no political community is able to pursue its own interests and develop itself in isolation, because the degree of its prosperity and development is a reflection

and a component part of the degree of prosperity and development of all the other political communities.

INSUFFICIENCY OF MODERN STATES TO ENSURE THE UNIVERSAL COMMON GOOD

The unity of the human family has always existed, because its members were human beings all equal by virtue of
their natural dignity. Hence there will always exist the objective need to promote, in sufficient measure, the universal
common good, that is, the common good of the entire human
family.

In times past, one would be justified in feeling that the
public authorities of the different political communities might
be in a position to provide for the universal common good,
either through normal diplomatic channels or through top-
level meetings, by making use of juridical instruments such
as conventions and treaties, for example: juridical instruments suggested by the natural law and regulated by the law
of nations and international law.

As a result of the far-reaching changes which have taken
place in the relations between the human family, the universal common good gives rise to problems which are complex, very grave and extremely urgent, especially as regards
security and world peace.

On the other hand, the public authorities of the individual
political communities—placed as they are on a footing of
equality one with the other—no matter how much they multiply their meetings or sharpen their wits in efforts to draw
up new juridical instruments, they are no longer capable of
facing the task of finding an adequate solution to the problems mentioned above. And this is not due to a lack of good
will or of a spirit of enterprise, but because of a structural defect which hinders them.

It can be said, therefore, that at this historical moment
the present system of organization and the way its principle
of authority operates on a world basis no longer correspond
to the objective requirements of the universal common good.

There exists an intrinsic connection between the common
good on the one hand and the structure and function of public authority on the other. The moral order, which needs
public authority in order to promote the common good in
human society, requires also that the authority be effective
in attaining that end. This demands that the organs through
which the authority is formed, becomes operative and pur-

sues its ends, must be composed and act in such a manner as
to be capable of bringing to realization the new meaning
which the common good is taking on in the historical evolution of the human family.

Today the universal common good poses problems of
worldwide dimensions, which cannot be adequately tackled
or solved except by the efforts of public authorities endowed
with a wideness of powers, structure and means of the same
proportions: that is, of public authorities which are in a position to operate in an effective manner on a worldwide basis.
The moral order itself, therefore, demands that such a form
of public authority be established.

PUBLIC AUTHORITY INSTITUTED BY COMMON CONSENT AND NOT IMPOSED BY FORCE

A public authority, having worldwide power and endowed with the proper means for the efficacious pursuit of its
objective, which is the universal common good in concrete
form, must be set up by common accord and not imposed by
force. The reason is that such an authority must be in a position to operate effectively yet, at the same time, its action
must be inspired by sincere and real impartiality: in other
words, it must be an action aimed at satisfying the objective
requirements of the universal common good. The difficulty is
that there would be reason to fear that a supernational or
worldwide public authority, imposed by force by the more
powerful political communities, might be or might become
an instrument of one-sided interests and even should this not
happen, it would be difficult for it to avoid all suspicion of
partiality in its actions, and this would take from the effica-
ciousness of its activity.

Even though there may be pronounced differences between
political communities as regards the degree of their economic
development and their military power, they are all very sensitive as regards their juridical equality and their moral dignity. For that reason, they are right in not easily yielding
in obedience to an authority imposed by force, or to an authority in whose creation they had no part, or to which they
themselves did not decide to submit by conscious and free
choice.

THE UNIVERSAL COMMON GOOD AND PERSONAL RIGHTS

Like the common good of individual political communities, so too the universal common good cannot be determined

except by having regard to the human person. Therefore, the public authority of the world community, too, must have as its fundamental objective the recognition, respect, safeguarding and promotion of the rights of the human person, this can be done by direct action when required, or by creating on a world scale an environment in which the public authorities of the individual political communities can more easily carry out their specific functions.

THE PRINCIPLE OF SUBSIDIARITY

Just as within each political community the relations between individuals are governed by the principle of subsidiarity, so too the relations between the public authority of each political community and the public authority of the world community must be regulated by the light of the same principle. This means that the public authority of the world community must tackle and solve problems of an economic, social, political and cultural character which are posed by the universal common good. For, because of the vastness, complexity and urgency of those problems, the public authorities of the individual states are not in a position to tackle them with any hope of a positive solution.

The public authority of the world community is not intended to limit the sphere of action of the public authority of the individual political community, much less to take its place. On the contrary, its purpose is to create, on a world basis, an environment in which the public authorities of each political community, its citizens and intermediate associations, can carry out their tasks, fulfil their duties and exercise their rights with greater security.[56]

MODERN DEVELOPMENTS

As is known, the United Nations Organization (U.N.O.) was established on June 26, 1945, and to it there were subsequently added intergovernmental agencies with extensive international tasks in the economic, social, cultural, educational and health fields. The United Nations Organization had as its essential purpose the maintenance and consolidation of peace between peoples, fostering between them friendly relations, based on the principles of equality, mutual re-

[56] Cf. Pius XII's allocution on Sept. 19, 1948, Acta Apostolicae Sedis, Vol. 40, p. 412.

spect, and varied forms of cooperation in every sector of hu
man society.

An act of the highest importance performed by the Unite
Nations Organization was the Universal Declaration o
Human Rights, approved in the General Assembly of Decem
ber 10, 1948. In the preamble of that declaration, the recog
nition and respect of those rights and respective liberties i
proclaimed as an ideal to be pursued by all peoples and al
countries.

Some objections and reservations were raised regardin;
certain points in the declaration. There is no doubt, how
ever, that the document represents an important step on the
path towards the juridical-political organization of the
world community. For in it, in most solemn form, the dig
nity of a person is acknowledged to all human beings. And a a
a consequence there is proclaimed as a fundamental right
the right of free movement in the search for truth and in the
attainment of moral good and justice, and also the right to a
dignified life, while other rights connected with those men
tioned are likewise proclaimed.

It is our earnest wish that the United Nations Organizatior
—in its structure and in its means—may become ever more
equal to the magnitude and nobility of its tasks, and that the
day may come when every human being will find therein
an effective safeguard for the rights which derive directly
from his dignity as a person, and which are therefore uni
versal, inviolable and inalienable rights. This is all the more
to be hoped for since all human beings, as they take an
ever more active part in the public life of their own politica;
communities, are showing an increasing interest in the affairs
of all peoples, and are becoming more consciously aware that
they are living members of a world community.

Part V
Pastoral Exhortations

Duty of Taking Part in Public Life

Once again we deem it opportune to remind our children
of their duty to take an active part in public life, and to con
tribute toward the attainment of the common good of the en-

tire human family as well as to that of their own political community. They should endeavor, therefore, in the light of the faith and with the strength of love, to insure that the various institutions—whether economic, social, cultural or political in purpose—should be such as not to create obstacles, but rather to facilitate or render less arduous man's perfections of himself both in the natural order as well as in the supernatural.

SCIENTIFIC COMPETENCE, TECHNICAL CAPACITY AND PROFESSIONAL EXPERIENCE

Nevertheless, in order to imbue civilization with sound principles and enliven it with the spirit of the gospel, it is not enough to be illumined with the gift of faith and enkindled with the desire of forwarding a good cause. For this end it is necessary to take an active part in the various organizations and influence them from within. And since our present age is one of outstanding scientific and technical progress and excellence, one will not be able to enter these organizations and work effectively from within unless he is scientifically competent, technically capable and skilled in the practice of his own profession. . . .

RELATIONS BETWEEN CATHOLICS AND NON-CATHOLICS IN SOCIAL AND ECONOMIC AFFAIRS

The doctrinal principles outlined in this document derive from or are suggested by requirements inherent in human nature itself, and are, for the most part, dictates of the natural law. They provide Catholics, therefore, with a vast field in which they can meet and come to an understanding both with Christians separated from this Apostolic See, and also with human beings who are not enlightened by faith in Jesus Christ, but who are endowed with the light of reason and with a natural and operative honesty. In such relations let the faithful be careful to be always consistent in their actions, so that they may never come to any compromise in matters of religion and morals.

At the same time, however, let them be, and show themselves to be, animated by a spirit of understanding and detachment, and disposed to work loyally in the pursuit of objectives which are of their nature good, or conducive to good.[57]

57 Ibid, p. 456.

However, one must never confuse error and the person who errs, not even when there is question of error or inadequate knowledge of truth in the moral or religious field The person who errs is always and above all a human being, and he retains in every case his dignity as a human person, and he must be always regarded and treated in accordance with that lofty dignity. Besides, in every human being, there is a need that is congenital to his nature and never becomes extinguished, compelling him to break through the web of error and open his mind to the knowledge of truth. And God will never fail to act on his interior being, with the result that a person, who at a given moment of his life lacks the clarity of faith or even adheres to erroneous doctrines, can at a future date be enlightened and believe the truth. Meetings and agreements, in the various sectors of daily life, between believers and those who do not believe or believe insufficiently because they adhere to error, can be occasions for discovering truth and paying homage to it.

It must be borne in mind, furthermore, that neither can false philosophical teachings regarding the nature, origin and destiny of the universe and of man, be identified with historical movements that have economic, social, cultural or political ends, not even when these movements have originated from those teachings and have drawn and still draw inspiration therefrom. Because the teachings, once they are drawn up and defined, remain always the same, while the movements, working on historical situations in constant evolution, cannot but be influenced by these latter and cannot avoid, therefore, being subject to changes, even of a profound nature. Besides, who can deny that those movements, in so far as they conform to the dictates of right reason and are interpreters of the lawful aspirations of the human person, contain elements that are positive and deserving of approval?

It can happen, then, that a drawing nearer together or a meeting for the attainment of some practical end, which was formerly deemed inopportune or unproductive, might now or in the future be considered opportune and useful. But to decide whether this moment has arrived, and also to lay down the ways and degrees in which work in common might be possible for the achievement of economic, social, cultural and political ends which are honorable and useful: these are the problems which can only be solved with the virtue of prudence, which is the guiding light of the virtues that regulate the moral life, both individual and social. Therefore, as far as Catholics are concerned, this decision rests primarily with those who live and work in the specific sectors of human society in which those problems arise, always, however, in accordance with the principles of the natural law, with the social doctrine of the church, and with the directives of ecclesiastical authority. For it must not be forgotten that the church has the right and the duty not only to safeguard the principles of ethics and religion, but also to intervene authoritatively with her children in the temporal sphere, when there is a question of judging about the application of those principles to concrete cases.[58]

LITTLE BY LITTLE

There are some souls, particularly endowed with generosity, who, on finding situations where the requirements of justice are not satisfied or not satisfied in full, feel enkindled with the desire to change the state of things, as if they wished to have recourse to something like a revolution.

It must be borne in mind that to proceed gradually is the law of life in all its expressions, therefore in human institutions, too, it is not possible to renovate for the better except by working from within them, gradually. Pius XII proclaimed: Salvation and justice are not to be found in revolution, but in evolution through concord. Violence has always achieved only destruction, not construction, the kindling of passions, not their pacification, the accumulation of hate and ruin, not the reconciliation of the contending parties. And it has reduced men and parties to the difficult task of rebuilding, after sad experience, on the ruins of discord . . .[59]

[58] Ibid; cf. "Immortale Dei Actas," op. cit., p. 100; Pius XI's encyclical "Ubi Arcano" ("Where in the Inscrutable Design"), Acta Apostolicae Sedis, Vol. 14, p. 698, and Pius XII's allocution on Sept. 11, 1947, Acta Apostolicae Sedis, Vol. 39, p. 486.

[59] Cf. Pius XII's allocution on June 13, 1943, Acta Apostolicae Sedis, Vol. 35, p. 175.

Index